THE ONLINE DESKBOOK

ONLINE MAGAZINE'S ESSENTIAL DESK REFERENCE

FOR ONLINE AND INTERNET SEARCHERS

THE ONLINE DESKBOOK
ONLINE Magazine's Essential Desk Reference
For Online And Internet Searchers

Mary Ellen Bates

Edited and with a Foreword by Reva Basch

Wilton, CT
1996

 Printed on recycled paper.

To Dave, with thanks for all his patience, love and understanding,
and to Lucy, who kept me company

Table of Content

Table of Contents

KEY INFORMATION ON ONLINE RESOURCES
PROFESSIONAL ONLINE SERVICES

GENERAL ONLINE SERVICES

Foreword

There was a time, in the not too distant past, when those of us who thought about such things at all had no problem defining what "online" meant. It was a cozy, finite world, populated almost exclusively by librarians and independent information specialists, along with a few so-called "end-users"—primarily chemists and sci-tech-medical researchers, plus a sprinkling of attorneys, journalists, and corporate marketing and planning types. There were perhaps a half-dozen major online "hosts" (such a quaint, friendly-sounding term), some of whom focused on business, others on science and technology. DIALOG was the epitome of the "supermarket" search services, offering databases in everything from accounting to zoology, with frequent stops along the continuum. Boutique services, specializing in broadcast transcripts, human resources information, and investment tips, were starting to emerge. The databases themselves were highly structured and heavily indexed collections of document summaries and citations; not until the mid-80s did the complete text of articles begin to appear online in any significant way. An online search, whether you performed it yourself or had one done to your specifications, was just the first phase of the research process. References in hand, the next step was your library periodical collection, for shelf-scanning and photocopying, or submitting an interlibrary loan request and waiting, often weeks, for hardcopy "backup" from an outside institution.

This was online research, as recently as five years ago. The players and the products were clear-cut and easily identifiable. Searching was universally expensive—generally charged by the minute, with additional fees for each item you printed or looked at online. The economic factor, combined with the esoteric incantations necessary to pull relevant material from the databases, kept online well within the province of the information profession. Librarians were firmly entrenched as intermediaries in the research process. Although most of us rejected the label, we were viewed as gatekeepers, holders of the keys to the vault of knowledge. When it came to online searching, the prevailing attitude was "don't try this at home"—or, for that matter, back at your own workstation.

Then, in the early 1990s, the world began to change. Many of the traditional online services and database providers merged or were acquired. Products were repositioned, rebranded; identities began to blur as the information industry responded to new competitive pressures. Databases were sliced and diced, the subfiles repackaged and marketed to new audiences. Menus and graphical interfaces were slapped onto existing search systems in an often misguided attempt to make them user-friendly (a buzzword we haven't heard much lately). At the same time, many companies were investing in new technology to replace or supplement their 1960s-era mainframe computers and text-retrieval software. So-called natural language or plain-English search modes, boosted by relevance-ranking, arose as an alternative to Boolean ANDs and ORs. The online information industry had been trying for years to attract end-users—who represented a much bigger market for them than librarians and professional searchers—but now, they were starting to put their capital expenditure and development money where their marketing mouths had been. By the mid-1990s, it was possible to get acceptable search results on several major online services without having heard of Boolean logic.

These internal shifts were enormous, though largely invisible to the outside world. Online was still the province of information specialists, academics, and scientific researchers. Those of us who searched databases for a living had developed our own snappy, shorthand occupational descriptions for parties and casual conversations: "I'm an electronic librarian" worked for me, accompanied by an assessment of whether this person was really interested in what I did for a living, or if the dreaded and familiar MEGO syndrome (My Eyes Glaze Over) had already begun to set in.

But then the Internet hit, and nothing was the same. Suddenly, literate individuals knew, or thought they knew, what "online" meant. Librarians found themselves labeled "infosurfers," and now had to differentiate the kind of database searching they did from what it was—and was not—possible to do on the Net. The immediate and tremendous success of the World Wide Web fueled the growth of general online utilities like CompuServe, Prodigy, and America Online. These services had been around for years, populated by hobbyists, recreational conversationalists, and occasional information-seekers. Now, they were benefiting from the overall rise in online-consciousness, and it didn't take long until they repositioned themselves as easy access points to the World Wide Web.

Today, as Pogo said, we are surrounded by insurmountable opportunity. The three main segments of the online universe—professional research services, general information services, and the Internet—are enriching and enhancing each other. The professional services are becoming more intuitive; costs, while still significant, are gradually becoming easier to predict and control. The general-interest services have begun to offer much more value to the serious information seeker, both locally and through gateways to the World Wide Web. The Net itself, once a homely, cantankerous entity whose inner beauty was apparent only to UNIX-geeks, has undergone not just cosmetic surgery, but a personality transplant as well. Everybody is intrigued by the Net, captivated by the charms of the Web. We can't get enough of online.

With all this transformation and cross-fertilization, it's become even harder to sift substance from style. What are the pros and cons of using one of the professional, heavy-duty online services, and which are best for particular applications? When does it make sense to open an account with a general-interest service like CompuServe or AOL? What is the Internet really good for?

Mary Ellen Bates is one of those rare individuals, rooted in traditional library and information science, who has followed the online industry through all its recent metamorphoses. She can look critically at the new graphical interfaces and evaluate them knowledgeably in terms of both useability and underlying content. If you sacrifice power when moving from the bare command line to a point-and-click environment, she suggests ways to compensate for that tradeoff. She explains why the cheapest or the easiest route isn't always the best, and underscores when it is. She does a masterful job of outlining each major service, its basic functionality, its strengths, and its weaknesses.

This book can be used in several different ways, depending on your needs, regardless of your level of online expertise. Whether you're a neophyte or a seasoned searcher, an information professional or an information consumer, *The Online Deskbook* gives you all the input you need to select a "home" service, or one or more supplementary ones. The clear, succinct command summaries provide an invaluable quick reference tool and a handy comparison of cross-system capabilities. Even if you've mastered a particular online service, the detailed search tips and techniques in each section reveal—or remind you about—some hidden features and capabilities. Trust me on this; I learned from this book.

The poet Robert Hunter said:

You can't overlook the lack, Jack
of any other highway to ride
It's got no signs or dividing lines
and very few rules to guide.

For everyone embarked on an exploration of the online realm, or thinking about starting such a journey, Mary Ellen has provided us with a topographic map of the territory. Onward!

Reva Basch
Berkeley, California
April 9, 1996

Acknowledgments

I remember when I received the telephone call from Jeff Pemberton, describing a special writing project that had been in the back of his mind for a while. Would I be interested in writing an online deskbook? He already had some ideas on what to include and he just knew I'd enjoy writing it, so how about it? Well, it's been an experience...and I am grateful to Jeff Pemberton for envisioning the book and giving me the opportunity to turn his ideas into print. I also want to thank John Bryans, who has been unfailingly enthusiastic and encouraging as this book took form, and Paula Hane and Nancy Garman, who got me started writing for the online industry and who are delightful people to work with.

Reva Basch served as editor and co-pilot of *The Online Deskbook*, and I can't imagine a better editor. We may disagree on the abbreviation of "electronic mail" but her advice and suggestions have always been helpful. Reva's encouragement, thoughtfulness, and friendship I value, and her writing ability, I envy. Reva also introduced me to The WELL, a truly incredible online group of people. My life hasn't been the same since.

Many thanks to the customer service departments of all the online services covered in this deskbook. They provided user documentation and new subscriber kits as well as helpful insight into the quirks and features of their systems. At the pace at which online services are growing and improving, describing any of these systems has been a challenge. I appreciate the help of each service's customer support department in keeping me updated on system changes. All errors or omissions are, of course, mine. I particularly would like to thank Maria Pastino, NewsNet Senior Customer Support Representative, and Lisa Glandon, LEXIS-NEXIS Senior Market Specialist, two of the most responsive, knowledgeable, and friendly user support people I have ever met.

I want to acknowledge the ongoing support and enthusiasm of John Makulowich, world-wide Internet trainer extraordinaire. His comments and suggestions on the Internet chapter were invaluable. His home page never ceases to amaze me with its collection of the best and the brightest of the Net—http://www.cais.com/makulow/verbwork.html.

John Levis provided valuable pointers on medical information sources, not to mention a cheery voice on the phone as we work on AIIP projects. And many thanks to Pamela Owen, who read some of the initial chapters and offered constant encouragement during the writing of this book.

I want to thank my sister, Sarah Bates Van de Wetering, for all her support in this adventure. An accomplished writer herself, her perspectives and suggestions on preparing to write this book were especially appreciated.

And thanks to the "music that played the band..." You accompanied this book and kept me going. Fare you well.

Mary Ellen Bates
Washington, DC
April 5, 1996

Introduction

Although online databases have been around, at least in some form, for over 20 years, they have gained a much higher profile since the popularity of the Internet. So, what is an "online database" anyway? The term has been used to describe huge databases of newspaper and magazine articles such as LEXIS-NEXIS or DIALOG, and it has been used to describe electronic conferencing systems such as CompuServe or America Online. And while "surfing the Internet" usually refers to browsing through the World Wide Web, electronic discussions, and shared files, it can also mean using the Internet as a research tool to access government bulletin boards, newswires, and companies' home pages.

Generally, an online database is defined as an organized collection of electronic information available to subscribers or the public either for a fee or without charge. It is usually updated regularly; it may or may not contain older material. In addition to the actual data, online databases include some way to search through and retrieve specific items—a way to turn *data* into *information*. The "search engine" may be fairly primitive, only allowing the user to browse through titles, or very sophisticated, allowing users to search by multiple criteria and combine search sets, to rank the retrieved documents by relevancy, and to review the material in a number of electronic or print formats.

Online databases can consist of:

- the full text of magazine, newswire, and newspaper articles
- summaries or extracts of articles, conference proceedings, government reports, books, and technical documents
- directories of companies, associations, people, products, or places
- numeric data such as company financial information, demographic statistics, or import/export data
- specialized information such as trademark images, airline schedules, or chemical structures

Usually, the online service offers a number of options for viewing or printing specific information. Typically, you can review titles and/or the subject terms assigned to each document, your search term(s) as they appear in the document (also known as KWIC or Keyword-in-Context), a brief listing of each document (e.g., title, author, date and source), or the full text of the record. Usually, the records are displayed on the screen and captured to your computer using the "session record," "capture," or "file save" function of your communications software, or printed directly to your local printer. Often the information can be sent to an electronic mail account, a fax machine, or printed and mailed to you.

Also included in the concept of online resources are electronic bulletin boards—conversations among experts, novices, and other interested people in a given topic. The subjects of these electronic conferences range from public relations professionals discussing average fees, to medical researchers describing current research on AIDS, to fans of Phish discussing the next concert tour.

EXAMPLE OF ONLINE RESEARCH

To give an example of the types of information available, following is a description of a hypothetical search for information on the Smith Widget Company.

First, I look up basic information on the Smith Widget Company in one of the company directory databases. I find that Smith Widget was founded in 1968, had sales last year of $5 million, employs 400 people, is headquartered in San Mateo, California, and has subsidiaries in Oregon and Colorado. I get the names of the top executives and, because Smith Widget's stock is traded publicly, I also find background information on the executives and their current salaries. I look at the company's sales for each division over the past five years and see that it has grown 25 percent since 1993.

Next, I search a database of biographical information and get in-depth biographies on some of the Smith Widget executives. I find that the vice president for marketing graduated from the same college I did, so I make a note to mention that when I contact her.

I log on to several of the databases containing the full text of newspaper and magazine articles and search for articles in the past year focusing on Smith Widget. I find material from local newspapers, a business journal, several newsletters that focus on the widget industry, and an interview in the *Wall Street Journal* with the CEO discussing the challenges faced by the widget industry and by Smith Widget Company.

After that, I connect to a worldwide database of patents and look at the patents held by Smith Widget on innovative new methods of manufacturing widget flanges. I look up some export statistics to see trends and to find out which countries are buying U.S. widgets.

Finally, I scan Smith Widget's press releases to find out about recent contracts it has been awarded, an announcement of its quarterly earnings released last week, and background on its recent corporate reorganization.

Granted, this may be more information than you need, but this illustrates the variety and depth of information available through online databases. A search such as the one just described might cost between $300 and $800 depending on the online system(s) being searched and the extent of the information retrieved.

This book breaks out the online world into three main categories—professional online services (sometimes called research online services), general online services (sometimes called consumer online services), and the Internet. A number of sources are available in more than one of these categories, and I try to make this clear in each section.

In addition to providing access to databases of information, general online services also support electronic discussion groups (called forums, conferences, or bulletin board systems), live online conversations (called chat services or online conferences), and electronic mail services. A thorough review of all of these features goes beyond the scope of this book. I mention discussion groups and online conversations when they are particularly useful, but I am not reviewing the online services' email systems.

PROFESSIONAL ONLINE SERVICES

These services are usually available to subscribers for a fee—either a flat monthly fee or, more commonly, a per-transaction fee based on some combination of connect time, number of records viewed, and number of searches run. Professional online services can be fairly expensive, with an average search costing anywhere from a few dollars to several hundred dollars. These services provide powerful and flexible search engines, have well-organized and extensive databases, and provide users with training, regular updates on new services, and marketing or sales representatives to call for help.

Typically, users of professional online services have high expectations and want clear, thorough, updated documentation. There are usually extensive display options, customizable reports, and options to deliver the information via electronic mail, fax, or print copy in addition to viewing the data on the screen. These services are most frequently used by professional searchers—librarians, researchers and other professionals with extensive information needs. Professional online services covered in this book include DataStar, DataTimes, DIALOG, Dow Jones News/Retrieval, LEXIS-NEXIS, and NewsNet.

GENERAL ONLINE SERVICES

These services are geared more to the casual searcher and generally include information for both home and business uses. The cost for a general online service is usually considerably lower than professional online services—often a monthly fee of $10 or $20 and connect-time charges of less than $10/hour. The search engines are usually simpler to use and less powerful than professional online services, and the databases are sometimes truncated versions of the files available on the professional services. Usually, there are limited options for customizing the display of retrieved information, and delivery options are often limited to online viewing and capturing the data to a disk.

There is usually no formal user training, and the system documentation tends to be geared to the novice rather than to an experienced searcher. These systems are usually very easy to navigate through, with menus or graphics (for Windows or Macintosh) to guide the user.

As these general services expand and their subscriber bases grow, they have begun providing access to more and more business-oriented databases, often at a very low price. Finding stock quotes, recent information on a company, or some background articles on an industry is now possible on services that catered primarily to the "recreational" online user a few years ago.

General online services covered in this book include America Online, CompuServe, Microsoft Network, and Prodigy.

INTERNET

The Internet has grown from the domain of computer hackers who know UNIX operating system commands to a resource where computer novices and experts alike can have electronic discussions, read position papers, download product information and place orders with vendors, and monitor the goings-on of the U.S. Congress.

Although there are significant costs involved in *maintaining* information on the Internet, the cost to users is very low. Most Internet service providers (including the four general online services mentioned earlier) cost a searcher at most a few dollars an hour.

The strengths of the Internet—its depth and variety of information—are also its weaknesses. The Internet has been described as the Library of Congress without a card catalog, and although there are a number of search and navigation tools available, finding reliable information can be a challenge.

The changes in access and browsing tools and indexing software, and the growing presence of commercial organizations, mean that searching the Internet will be a much different, and probably better, experience in the year 2000 than it is today.

EQUIPMENT

Online searching doesn't require sophisticated equipment, although if you expect to spend a significant amount of time online you may want more powerful tools than the minimum required to get online.

For most purposes, the following are the basic requirements for accessing online resources:
• a personal computer
• a modem (2400bps or higher; 14400bps for heavy-duty searching, when using a GUI or point-and-click communications software package, or for using one of the Internet "browsers")
• communications software (many online services provide their own dedicated software package)
• a telephone line

Virtually any personal computer meets the minimum requirements. A frequent searcher probably wants a 9600bps or higher modem. (The modem speed refers to the speed in bits per second at which data is transferred between your computer and the host computer, so a telephone connection at 9600bps is capable of transferring data four times as fast as a connection set at 2400bps.)

You can use almost any telephone line to connect to online services. If you intend to be online for more than an hour or so a day, it makes sense to have a second telephone line installed for your modem. If you have call waiting on your telephone line, you must remember to disable it before connecting to an online service. The "click-click" of a waiting call is enough to cause the online service to disconnect you. Check with your local telephone company on how to disable call waiting on a per-call basis. Often, you can disable call waiting by dialing *70 before placing the call.

There are a number of communications software packages available in addition to the online services' proprietary packages, ranging from shareware software to packages with plenty of bells and whistles. As long as it allows you to do some minimal configuration, any communications software package should be sufficient. A frequent searcher should use a package that has a good-sized buffer, enabling him to scroll back through previous screens of text to view again retrieved material.

The following table indicates which online services reviewed in this book provide specialized communications software and whether the proprietary package is required to access the system or is simply an alternative to a standard communications package:

Online Service	Proprietary Communications Software Package
America Online	required
CompuServe	optional
DataStar	optional
DataTimes	optional but highly recommended
DIALOG	optional
Dow Jones News/Retrieval	optional
Internet	optional (a browser such as Mosaic or Netscape highly recommended)
LEXIS-NEXIS	optional but highly recommended
Microsoft Network	required
NewsNet	optional
Prodigy	required

The final requirement for online searching is a spirit of adventure and the thrill of the chase. Online searching is as much an art as a science, and it takes practice and an open mind to tease out the information you want. See the section "Where to Get More Information" for some recommended reading.

BASIC SEARCHING COMMANDS

Each online system has its own search language; to find the term "snake oil" in the headline of an article you might enter s snake()oil/ti in one system; headline(snake oil) in a second; and snake.hl. adj oil.hl. in a third. However, the basic conventions used to identify a phrase, to limit a search to headlines, or to search for a word with any of its possible endings are similar.

Boolean logic is the basis for most online searching. The three "connectors," or terms used to combine or exclude search concepts, are AND, OR and NOT. X AND Y means that both X and Y *must* occur in the same record. X OR Y means that either X *or* Y *or both* must occur in the record. X NOT Y means that X *must* appear in the record and Y *cannot* appear in the record.

You can also search for a phrase such as "heart attack" or for words appearing near each other—"*recycling* in the same sentence as *plastics.*" This "adjacency" searching allows you to specify how close the two words must be to each other. You can require that they occur next to each other (**heart adj attack**), within three words of each other (**drug near3 abuse**), or within the same paragraph (**Clinton same Court**). The connector term you use (adj, same, near) varies from system to system, but all professional online services offer some version of adjacency searching.

You can also include word variations in your search. A search for plastics recycling should include "plastic" as well as "plastics" and the various forms of the word "recycle"—recycling, recycled, recycles, recycler, recycle, and so on. Rather than type out all the variants, you can indicate that you want any word that begins RECYCL. The symbol for truncation is usually a question mark, an exclamation point, or an asterisk.

The "Key Information on Online Resources" section includes tables for the basic commands, connector terms, and truncation symbols for each of the online services reviewed.

BENEFITS AND PITFALLS OF ONLINE SEARCHING

Not a week goes by without another breathless newspaper or magazine article extolling the virtues of online searching as the ideal mechanism for finding any information on any topic, at virtually no cost. Unfortunately, the ugly truth is that some searches don't lend themselves to online research. Of course, hindsight is 20/20 and sometimes it's only after the fact that you realize that the information you need just isn't available online.

It takes experience (often painful and/or expensive experience) to recognize when an online search is not appropriate. One way to avoid learning the hard way is to log off if you aren't finding something reasonably close to what you want after the first few tries. Call the customer service department of the online vendor. Get their suggestions on how to proceed; ask them if they think your proposed search is likely to find anything.

In addition, keep in mind that some information simply hasn't been digitized. Reasons for this range from budget limitations of government agencies preventing them from maintaining an Internet site, to the absence of a viable market for scanning in the full text of articles from more than 20 years ago, to the lack of anything being written on a very narrowly-defined topic.

Some examples of information not usually found online include:
- documents filed with government agencies
- some government-generated information
- narrowly-focused industry information ("What's the market for fountain pens in Arizona?")
- information proving the *absence* of something ("Show me that apple orchards aren't subject to blight")
- articles published before the late 1970s
- topics too broad to categorize ("What's new in the computer industry?")
- charts and graphs included within articles

One of the best ways to decide where to go for information is to think of who would be interested enough to collect it in the first place. If the topic being researched focuses on a specific industry, think about what trade groups include members in the industry. What magazines cover the industry? Is it regulated by any government agencies, either local or national? How are new developments usually announced—in academic journals, the popular press, press releases, or at trade shows or professional conferences? Answers to these questions may guide you to the most appropriate sources, which may or may not provide information online.

Another factor to keep in mind is that some material available in both electronic and print sources may be obtained through traditional paper-based research faster and more cheaply than through an online search. Say you needed a list of trade associations of soft drink manufacturers. If you had convenient access to a library, it would be less expensive to look up the information in the *Encyclopedia of Associations* than it would be to run an online search of the equivalent database. Since this kind of search is straightforward, it can easily be done using the printed index. You may not need to use any of the sophisticated search power of an online system, but you would have to pay a premium to retrieve each record online. If you cannot conveniently get to a library and you do not own a copy of the *Encyclopedia of Associations*, then the online alternative makes sense.

If, on the other hand, you need to look for trade associations with more than 15,000 members located in California that focus on any aspect of manufacturing, an online search would be much more sensible than a manual one. The time you would spend scanning through a printed list of manufacturing associations to find the ones that meet your criteria is far more costly than the fee for performing an online search for the same information.

Some information is only available online. Press releases, for example, cannot easily be obtained through any print sources, short of calling the public relations department of the organization issuing the press release and hoping they can get their hands on a copy to send to you. An online search of press releases allows you to scan for recent developments in a certain field, or by a certain company, or mentioning a certain event. Attempting to find press releases meeting these criteria by searching through print resources would be very time-consuming and possibly fruitless.

When deciding how and where to find information, remember to factor in your time, convenience, the kind of information you need, how quickly you need it, the scope of what is available electronically, the online costs, and your familiarity with the online system to be searched. Only then can you decide which information sources are best-suited for each project.

KEY INFORMATION ON ONLINE RESOURCES

PROFESSIONAL
ONLINE SERVICES

DataStar Information Retrieval Service

CONTACT INFORMATION

NAME   Knight-Ridder Information, Inc.

ADDRESS   2440 El Camino Real
                            Mountain View, CA 94040

TELEPHONE   800/334-2564; 415/254-8800

CUSTOMER   Monday through Friday 8:00am - 8:00pm Eastern time
SERVICE HOURS

EMAIL   through Internet: customer@corp.dialog.com

WEB HOME PAGE   http://www.dialog.com

SERVICE   1:00am - 11:30 pm Eastern time
AVAILABILITY   (except Sunday between 1:00am - 4:00am)

DESCRIPTION OF INFORMATION AVAILABLE

DataStar, a professional online service originally based in Switzerland, is best known for its collection of information sources on the pharmaceutical, biomedical, and healthcare industries. DataStar is also a good source for European business and news sources—newspapers, wire stories, and company information. It also offers gateway access to TradStat, a unique database of import and export data. DataStar is the only online service to carry the electronic version of *Fulltext Sources Online (FSO)*, essential in any online searcher's toolkit; *FSO* lists the online services that carry the full text of individual magazines, newspapers, and other periodicals.

A fair number of DataStar's databases, particularly the full-text European newspapers and newswires, are in languages other than English. Fortunately for English-speaking searchers, many of these databases include English subject terms so a rudimentary search, at least, can be done.

DataStar has always supported plain ASCII dial-up using any standard communications software package, referred to here as command mode searching. In 1995, DataStar introduced KR ProBase, a proprietary communications software package that offers searchers point-and-click access to its online system.

ROADMAP OF RESOURCES

DataStar offers a good variety of finding aids to assist searchers in selecting the most appropriate database. The primary tools are its printed *Database Catalogue*, the *DataStar Datasheets*, which give more in-depth information on each database, and BASE, the online guide to each database.

The printed *Database Catalogue* is sent to all subscribers once a year and includes a brief description of each database. The *Catalogue* also sorts the databases by broad subject group—particularly helpful when selecting among several databases that all provide financial information on European companies, for example.

The printed *Datasheets* are two or four pages of information on each DataStar file. The *Datasheets* include a detailed description of what the file covers, a sample document, a list of the "paragraphs" (fields) and an example of how to search each, and additional notes on how to best search the database. *Datasheets* for newly-added files and updates of superseded *Datasheets* are mailed automatically to all subscribers; the original set of *Datasheets* must be purchased by new users. These *Datasheets* are quite helpful and all are written in English, even if the database itself is in another language.

BASE is the online guide to databases—essentially a searchable electronic version of the *Datasheets*. You can use it to identify a source for German-language newspapers, or a database of biotech articles that includes patent numbers, or directory databases that let you search by Standard Industrial Classification codes.

Another tool for selecting the most appropriate database is CROS, an online directory index to the databases on DataStar. You can run a search in CROS to determine which databases have records matching your search criteria. You cannot display the actual records; this database is a guide to help you choose databases in which to run your search.

CROS is menu-driven, so when you first enter CROS you are prompted to select a broad subject category in which to search. You can select *all* DataStar databases, but the search is completed much faster if you narrow down your selection to the most likely ones. The CROS categories are arranged hierarchically, so for example, if you select the category Drug Information, you are prompted to select which subcategory you want to search. See Figure 1 for an example of a CROS search in command mode. You can also create your own database grouping to search by selecting option 10 at the first CROS menu.

I find it particularly helpful that, in command mode, CROS displays the total number of documents in each database along with the number of hits for the search terms specified; it's significant to know that out of a database of 80,000 records 50 fit your criteria, as opposed to finding 150 documents out of a database of 1,000,000. Unfortunately, a CROS search in KR ProBase does not include a list of the total number of documents in each file.

DataStar maintains a home page on the Internet at http://www.dialog.com. In addition to general information on Knight-Ridder, it has a short description of DataStar and a searchable index of all the DataStar databases, extracted from the BASE database.

KR ProBase, DataStar's proprietary search software, can also be considered a finding aid. The information in the BASE database is also stored on your computer and is accessible (offline) through KR ProBase. You can browse through a listing of available databases, arranged by subject, and you can display sample documents and review

FIGURE 1
CROS Search in Command Mode

```
TYPE DATABASE NAME_: cros

*SIGN-ON  02.27.05          01.12.95

D-S/CROS/                 SESSION   5
COPYRIGHT BY Knight-Ridder Information, Bern, Switzerland
 1 All Databases
 2 Business & Market Research
 3 Companies
 4 News
 5 Biomedical Sciences
 6 Drug Information
 7 Science & Technology
 8 Social Sciences & General Reference
 9 Trial Files
10 Your Choice
Please enter choice or HELP and choice
_: 6


60 All Drug Information
61 New Drugs
62 Drug Directories
63 Drug Legislation
64 Literature on Drugs
65 Pharmaceutical Industry News
66 Pharmaceutical Company Directories
67 Pharmaceutical Events
Please enter choice or HELP and choice
_: 61


610 All New Drugs
611 Drugs in Development
612 New Drug Products
613 Drug Patents
Please enter choice or HELP and choice
_: 612


D-S - SEARCH MODE - ENTER SEARCH TERMS
 CROS   1_: amgen


 CROS   1_: AMGEN
```

IPLL	IMSWORLD NEW PRODUCT LAUNCHES '82-	4	OF	80970
IPOP	IMSWORLD PRODUCT MONOGRAPHS	5	OF	361367
IPPP	IMSWORLD PRODUCT MONOGS & PRICES	5	OF	361367
PHLP F	PHARMAPROJECTS:LAUNCHED PRODUCTS	1	OF	1105

the searchable fields and date coverage. This information is also available when you are composing a search—a "Search In" box displays the fields in which you can limit the search terms and shows the field codes used, e.g., CO for company name, IR for industry terms, and CN for country. I find it very helpful to have this information displayed on the screen as I'm composing my search; it reminds me of fields I might not have thought of and helps me remember which fields have unusual formats. See Figure 2 for the KR ProBase search screen.

FIGURE 2
KR ProBase Search Screen

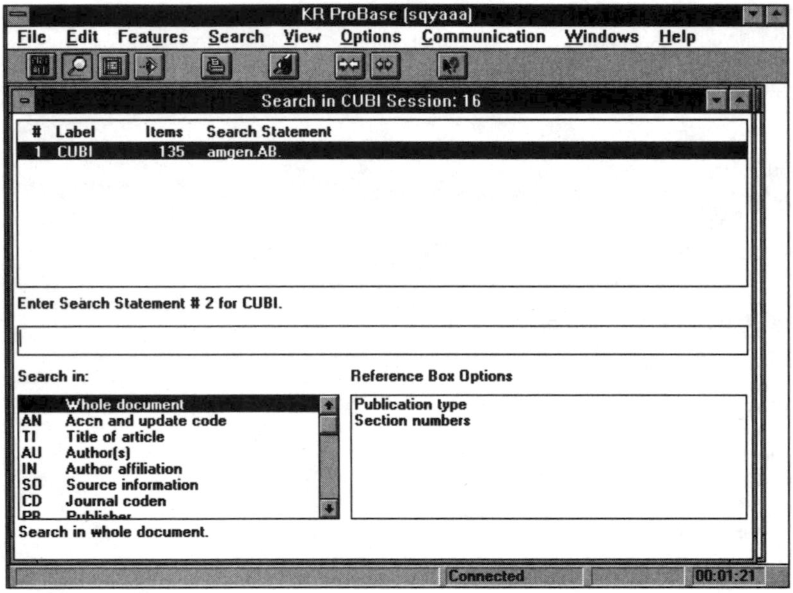

TIPS FOR USING DATASTAR'S FINDING AIDS

Compose a fairly broad search when using CROS. Rather than including every aspect of your search in a search statement ([A or B or C] and [D or E] and F), limit the search to a few key ideas. The purpose of a CROS search is to identify the databases most likely to have the material you want, not to hone down the search to the specific records you need.

Once you have the results of your CROS search, you can have the list of databases sorted by number of documents listed, you can repeat the search in a new set of databases, or you can begin the search for real in any of the databases listed. On KR ProBase, you simply click on the listing(s) you want and the search is re-executed in those databases.

You may be confused at first when you try to compose a search in CROS using KR ProBase. This software does not recognize CROS as a regular database and does not let you select it as you would any other database. You must click on the [CROS] icon along the tool bar or pull down the [Features] menu and select [CROS].

BASE, the database that contains descriptions of all the DataStar files, is searchable both online and from within KR ProBase (by selecting [Description of Database(s)] from the Databases menu). See Figure 3 for information on the KOSM database, displayed from the KR ProBase Description of Databases. As with CROS, use fairly broad terms to search BASE since there is no single set of subject or indexing terms among databases. To find databases that offer, say, full-text articles on drug

FIGURE 3
KR ProBase Database Description

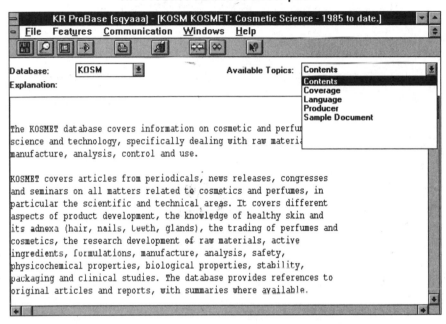

research, remember to try alternate terms such as pharmaceuticals, pharmacology, biochemistry, and medicine.

Knight-Ridder has a fax-on-demand service through which you can request updates or documentation on DataStar (as well as DIALOG) services. You can call the ASAF (As Soon As Faxable) service at 800/496-4470 or 415/496-4470 (using a touch-tone phone) and request document 4000 for a listing of DataStar search tools. The index is sent to your fax machine almost immediately and lists the documentation available and each item's ASAF order number. The guides available include a comparison chart of DIALOG and DataStar commands, tips on finding financial information on European companies, and cost-saving techniques for searching full-text sources on DataStar. There is no charge for this service. ASAF is particularly useful if you need help during weekends or evenings when the Customer Service offices are closed.

Commonly-Used Commands

DataStar allows command mode (plain ASCII) searching and access via its proprietary GUI software, KR ProBase.

Begin a search

Command mode:
..C [file name]
KR ProBase:
click on **[Databases]** icon

Search terms:
x AND y
x OR y
x BUT NOT y
x NEXT TO y
x WITHIN n WORDS OF y
x SAME SENTENCE y
x SAME PARAGRAPH y
x SAME FIELD y

x **AND** y
x **OR** y
x **NOT** y
x **ADJ** y (x must precede y)
not available
x **WITH** y
x **SAME** y
x **SAME** y.**TI.** (both words in title)
x **SAME** y.**DE,AB.** (both words in descriptor or abstract field)

Date Searching

Varies by database. Usually:
YY.**YR.**
YR=YY
YYMMDD.**DT.**
DT=YYMMDD
..L 1 **YR>94** (limit set 1 to Year greater than 1994)
..START YYMMDD (specifies the earliest database update to be searched for all future search sets)

Field Searching

word.**TI.** (restricts search to title)

Truncation

word**$** (for unlimited number of letters)
word**$3** (for 3 or fewer letters)

Display results

Command mode:
..p free 1-5 (print documents 1 through 5 from the last search set in the free format)

..p ti,so,ab 1 (print the title, source, abstract of document 1)
..p m,short 2 (print document 2 in short format, with Management formatting, i.e., removing paragraph labels)
..p 2 all 3 5 (print all paragraphs of documents 3 and 5 from search set 2)
KR ProBase:
Click on [**Titles**] icon to browse titles. Choose a format, then double-click on [Title], or click on [**Document**] icon to change the format in which the document is to be displayed.

Help

No system-wide help available in command mode.
..[Command] HELP is available for some commands such as PRINT, SET, and RANK
KR ProBase:
click on [**Help**] icon

Cost:
for session charges
up to this point

Command mode:
..COST
KR ProBase:
pull down [**Features**] menu, click on [**Cost**]

for database rates

Command mode:
..PRICE [file name]
KR ProBase:
From Databases screen, highlight database name, pull down [**Databases**] menu, click on [**Price**]

for total cost when logging off

Displayed automatically when logging off.

Log off

Command mode:
..off
..off cont (disconnects, but retains search until you log on again during the same day)
KR ProBase:
Click on the [**Disconnect**] icon

GETTING CONNECTED

Until mid-1995, your only option for searching DataStar was to use a standard communications package and search in plain ASCII command mode. Knight-Ridder, DataStar's and DIALOG's parent company, is developing several point-and-click proprietary software packages to assist users in searching DataStar and DIALOG. KR ProBase was specifically designed to help experienced online searchers use a system with which they might not be familiar. The intent of KR ProBase is to retain all the functionality and power of command mode searching while freeing searchers from having to remember DataStar system commands.

Logging on to DataStar:
via Tymnet: Please log in: **rserve**
via Sprintnet: **@ c rserve**
via Internet: **telnet rserve.rs.ch**
DataStar is also available through the HomeBase menu on DIALOG or by typing **BEGIN DataStar** at DIALOG's "?" prompt.

DataStar supports speeds from 300bps through 14400bps. Modem settings should be:
TTY emulation
FULL duplex
1 stop bit, 8 data bits, no parity

Access via the Internet is less expensive than through Sprintnet or Tymnet ($3/hour as opposed to $11/hour), but there are tradeoffs to consider. Since DataStar uses the X.25 packet network protocol and the Internet uses the TCP/IP protocol, you lose some functionality, primarily the loss of a break key and the remapping of the backspace key. (Try <ctrl><H>, <shift><backspace> or <ctrl><backspace>.)

System requirements for KR ProBase:
486 PC with Windows 3.1 or higher
8MB RAM
23MB disk space
9600bps modem or higher
(also supports TCP/IP Internet connection and Novell LAN servers)

POWER TOOLS

DataStar has developed a number of online power tools, enabling you to search smarter and more cost-effectively. Most of these commands are available in both command mode and when using KR ProBase.

..**LIMIT** (or click on [Limit] from the [Search] pull-down menu) lets you limit the results of a previous set by date, language, and other criteria, depending on the database. Type ..L HELP in command mode to see a list of the fields by which you can limit in the current database. (In KR ProBase, the limit fields are displayed automatically.) In databases of magazine articles, for example, you can often limit by year (..LIMIT 2 YR>94); in online directories, you can often limit by sales (..LIMIT 1 SA>500000); in pharmaceutical research databases, you can often limit by the date a drug was approved (..LIMIT 3 DA<950701).

..**ROOT** (or click on [Root] from the [Search] pull-down menu) displays all the words in the current database(s) that begin with whatever word-stem you specify. This command is helpful in determining how the database lists author names (Is it ABBEY-E or Abbey, Edward or Abbey E.J.?), or for seeing what subject terms are used in a database. For example, to see a list of MEDLINE subject terms beginning with "Gene," a command mode ..ROOT display would be:

D-S - SEARCH MODE - ENTER SEARCH TERMS
MEDL 1_: **..root gene.de.**

	MEDWORD	ROOT GENE$.DE.	
R1	58630	DOCS	GENE
R2	2252	DOCS	GENE-AMPLIFICATION
R3	33	DOCS	GENE-AMPLIFICATION-DE
R4	207	DOCS	GENE-AMPLIFICATION-GE
R5	145	DOCS	GENE-AMPLIFICATION-MT
R6	490	DOCS	GENE-AMPLIFICATION-NS
R7	13	DOCS	GENE-AMPLIFICATION-PH
R8	5	DOCS	GENE-AMPLIFICATION-RE
R9	286	DOCS	GENE-CONVERSION
R10	6	DOCS	GENE-CONVERSION-DE
R11	15	DOCS	GENE-CONVERSION-GE
R1	97	DOCS	GENE-CONVERSION-NS
R13	7	DOCS	GENE-CONVERSION-PH
R14	2	DOCS	GENE-CONVERSION-RE
R15	2193	DOCS	GENE-DELETION
R16	756	DOCS	GENE-DELETION-NS
R17	166	DOCS	GENE-DOSAGE
R18	18	DOCS	GENE-DOSAGE-NS

ENTER '*' TO CONTINUE ROOT

D-S - SEARCH MODE - ENTER SEARCH TERMS
MEDL 1_: *

	MEDWORD	ROOT GENE$.DE.	(CONTIN.)
R1	18	DOCS	GENE-DOSAGE-NS
R2	19479	DOCS	GENE-EXPRESSION
R3	2897	DOCS	GENE-EXPRESSION-DE
R4	836	DOCS	GENE-EXPRESSION-GE
R5	61	DOCS	GENE-EXPRESSION-IM
R6	3467	DOCS	GENE-EXPRESSION-NS
R7	695	DOCS	GENE-EXPRESSION-PH
R8	102	DOCS	GENE-EXPRESSION-RE
R9	10955	DOCS	GENE-EXPRESSION-REGULATION
R10	2760	DOCS	GENE-EXPRESSION-REGULATION-BACTERIA+
R1	309	DOCS	GENE-EXPRESSION-REGULATION-BACTERIA+
R12	216	DOCS	GENE-EXPRESSION-REGULATION-BACTERIA+
R13	1193	DOCS	GENE-EXPRESSION-REGULATION-BACTERIA+
R14	159	DOCS	GENE-EXPRESSION-REGULATION-BACTERIA+
R15	20	DOCS	GENE-EXPRESSION-REGULATION-BACTERIA+
R16	2594	DOCS	GENE-EXPRESSION-REGULATION-DE
R17	1209	DOCS	GENE-EXPRESSION-REGULATION-DEVELOPM+
R18	78	DOCS	GENE-EXPRESSION-REGULATION-DEVELOPM+

ENTER '*' TO CONTINUE ROOT

D-S - SEARCH MODE - ENTER SEARCH TERMS
MEDL 1_:

Unfortunately, unlike the EXPAND command on DIALOG, ..ROOT only displays words that begin with the letters you specify. If you want to see alternate spellings for Belorus, you need to issue a ..ROOT command for Belaru, Belorus, and Belurus. On the other hand, many of the databases have "rotated" index terms. For example, if you wanted to see all the companies in the DBUS database with "Squibb" in the company name, you can use the ..ROOT command on the word Squibb in the company name field and see the following list of "Squibb" companies:

```
D-S/DBUS/D&B US DUNS MARKET IDENTIFIERS SESSION 73
COPYRIGHT BY Dun & Bradstreet, High Wycombe, UK

D-S - SEARCH MODE - ENTER SEARCH TERMS
DBUS    1_: ..root squibb.co.

            ROOT SQUIBB$.CO.
R1    108  DOCS                    SQUIBB
R2      1  DOC               SQUIBB-ALVAH-M-COMPANY-INC
R3     85  DOCS   BRISTOL-MYERS-SQUIBB-COMPANY-INC
R4      1  DOC               SQUIBB-CORPORATION
R5      1  DOC      BRISTOL-MYERS-SQUIBB-CO
R6      1  DOC               SQUIBB-DALZELL-MANSUETTO-CO
R7      6  DOCS              SQUIBB-E-R-SONS-INC
R8      1  DOC               SQUIBB-LAND-CO-INC
R9      1  DOC               SQUIBB-MACHINE-TOOL-INC
R10     2  DOCS              SQUIBB-MANUFACTURING-INC
R11     1  DOC       WESTWOOD- SQUIBB-PHARMACEUTICALS-INC
R12     1  DOC           U-S- SQUIBB-PHARMACEUTICAL-DIV
R13     1  DOC    BRISTL-MYERS- SQUIBB-PHRM-GROUP
R14     1  DOC               SQUIBB-PROPERTIES-INC
R15     2  DOCS  BRISTOL-MYERS-SQUIBB-PUERTO-RICO-INC
R16     1  DOC       E-R-SQUIBB-SONS-INTER-AMERICAN-+
R17     3  DOCS              SQUIBB-TAYLOR-INC
R18     1  DOC    BRISTOL-MYRS-SQUIBB-US-PHARM
ENTER '*' TO CONTINUE ROOT
```

Note that this display includes company names that don't begin with Squibb—a handy way to make sure you catch all the permutations of the name.

..DB (no directly equivalent KR ProBase command) gives you quick information on the database you are currently searching or any other database for which you need information. You can truncate the file label to get listings of all files beginning with the letters you specify.

For example, to get information on the Textline files in command mode:

```
D-S - SEARCH MODE - ENTER SEARCH TERMS
BASE    1_: ..db tx*
    1   TXCO   REUTER   TEXTLINE   COMPANY LOOK-UP
    2   TXLD   REUTER   TEXTLINE   - TODAY
    3   TXLN   REUTER   TEXTLINE   '92-
    4   TXYY   REUTER   TEXTLINE   '89-'91
    5   TX88   REUTER   TEXTLINE   '80-'88

Enter choice(s) to receive important information
_: 3
```

DATABASE INFORMATION FOR 'TXLN'

REUTER TEXTLINE '92-
COPYRIGHT BY Reuters Ltd, London, UK

The following functions are available:

STARTDATE   PRINTOFF   ALERT
KWIC   RANK/MAP

This is a FULL Text Database.

This Database is updated DAILY. The last update is 951202.

Total Documents in this Database: 6917071

Prices for this database:

USD	60.00	PER HOUR	
	0.00	ONLINE DOCUMENT	FREE/BIBL/SHORT
	1.22		MEDIUM/LONG/MAXIMUM
	1.22	OFFLINE DOCUMENT	ALL FORMATS
	1.22	ALERT DOCUMENT	ALL FORMATS
	1.31	ALERT QUERIES	DAILY/WEEKLY/
			BI-WEEKLY/MONTHLY

For more information refer to the BASE database - search as BASE-TXLN.

DataStar allows you to set or change a number of system defaults using the ..SET command in command mode. The equivalent KR ProBase ..SET commands are hidden in a number of pull-down menus, usually under an icon called either Options or Features, and not all ..SET options have been implemented in KR ProBase. Following are a few of the more helpful ..SET commands.

..SET PLURALS ON (or click on [Plurals] from the [Options] pull-down menu) automatically searches both the singular and plural versions of English-language words. With ..SET PLURALS ON, a search for women retrieves woman as well.

..SET MEDWORD (or click on [Medword] from the [Options] pull-down menu) retrieves both the British and American spellings of words. Unfortunately, it only works in the biomedical databases, but this is a handy tool for the words that we English-speaking people forget can be spelled in different ways. How many American searchers remember to search for aluminium as well as aluminum?

Two helpful settings for managing your online costs are ..SET NOTICE [NN] and ..SET BUDGET [NN] (available on KR ProBase by selecting [Notice] or [Budget] from the [Features] pull-down menu). If, for example, you set the [Notice] feature to 15, then you are notified whenever you issue a print or display command that incurs print charges of $15 or more. The [Set Budget] feature keeps track of your total charges (both print charges and online charges) and it carries over the cost from one search session to the next. If you have a total online budget for the month of $3000, you can type **..SET BUDGET 3000** and DataStar continues to add up your charges until your charges come to $3000. With every print command after you have incurred $3000, you are asked whether you want to continue and you then see the cumulated charges. You can add additional dollars to the setting (**..SET BUDGET +200**) or clear the budget value by turning off the budget setting (**..SET BUDGET OFF**). DataStar calculates the charges in either U.S. dollars or Swiss francs, depending on your account.

..SAVE TS [search name] and **..SAVE PS [search name]** (or click on [Save As] from the [File] pull-down menu on KR ProBase) save your search strategy for later use. The default is to save the search as a temporary save (TS) deleted at the end of the day. A Permanent Save (PS) is saved until you delete it. **..STARSAVE TS [search name]** and **..STARSAVE PS [search name]** save not only your ..SEARCH and ..LIMIT statements, but also note the database(s) you selected and repeat the search in those same files. To re-execute a saved search, you use the following command:

FOR	USE
..SAVE TS [search name]	..EXEC TS [search name] repeats the search in the currently selected database(s)
..SAVE PS [search name]	..EXEC PS [search name] repeats the search in the currently selected database(s)
..STARSAVE TS [search name]	..EXEC TSS [search name] repeats the search in the originally selected database(s)
..STARSAVE PS [search name]	..EXEC PSS [search name] repeats the search in the originally selected database(s)

This is a great command if you repeatedly search the same files to monitor news. Unfortunately, the print documentation scarcely mentions this feature. The only way you would find out about it is to type **..save help** in command mode.

Currently, you can search up to 60 databases simultaneously on DataStar in command mode and 15 on KR ProBase ver. 1.x, by using its **StarSearch** feature. Version 2 of KR ProBase supports searching up to 60 simultaneous databases. You begin a search in one database. To add an additional database, type **..ADD [database name]** (or click on the [Databases] tool bar icon on KR ProBase). You can either type in a new search strategy to be run on the new database or you can use the **..REPEAT** command (or click on [Repeat] from the [Search] pull-down menu on KR ProBase) to have the same search run on the new database. NOTE: results from the two searches are not automatically combined; they remain separate search sets. To combine the results of separate

FIGURE 4
StarSearch in Command Mode

TYPE DATABASE NAME_: **medl**

*SIGN-ON 04.25.41   27.12.95

D-S/MEDL/MEDLINE 1992-DEC 4/95(-ED 951019) SESSION   67
COPYRIGHT BY National Library of Medicine, Bethesda MD, USA

D-S - SEARCH MODE - ENTER SEARCH TERMS
MEDL   1_: **start jan 94**

   RESULT   488489

COMMAND ACCEPTED.
STARTDATE ACTIVATED FOR MEDL.
NEXT UPDATE AFTER JAN 94 HAS BEEN LOADED ON 940101.

D-S - SEARCH MODE - ENTER SEARCH TERMS
MEDL   1_: **carpal-tunnel-syndrome**

   RESULT   398

MEDL   2_: **..repeat emed**

PROCESSING OF DATABASES BEING PREPARED, PLEASE WAIT.
STARTDATE ACTIVATED FOR EMED.
NEXT UPDATE AFTER 940101 HAS BEEN LOADED ON 940104.

D-S/EMED/EMBASE '88- 9550   SESSION   69
COPYRIGHT BY Elsevier Science BV, Amsterdam, Netherlands
D-S SEARCH MODE
EMED   2_: CARPAL-TUNNEL-SYNDROME
         RESULT   426

D-S - SEARCH MODE - ENTER SEARCH TERMS
EMED   3_: **..add biol**

STARTDATE ACTIVATED FOR BIOL.
NEXT UPDATE AFTER 940101 HAS BEEN LOADED ON 940104.

D-S/BIOL/BIOSIS PREVIEWS '85- V98/I50   SESSION   69
COPYRIGHT BY Biological Abstracts Inc, Philadelphia PA, USA

D-S - SEARCH MODE - ENTER SEARCH TERMS
BIOL   3_: **carpal adj tunnel adj syndrome**

   RESULT   210

BIOL   4_: **3.ti,kw.**

   RESULT   193

BIOL   5_: **..combine 1,2,4**

   RESULT   1017

FIGURE 4 (continued)

```
D-S - SEARCH MODE - ENTER SEARCH TERMS
BIOL    6_: ..dedup


6:      291 DOCUMENTS DROPPED AS DUPLICATES
7:      726 DOCUMENTS KEPT


D-S - SEARCH MODE - ENTER SEARCH TERMS
BIOL    8_: ..d all
```

QN DATABASE	DOCS	SEARCH TERMS	
1 MEDL	398	CARPAL-TUNNEL-SYNDROME	
2 EMED	426	CARPAL-TUNNEL-SYNDROME	
3 BIOL	210	CARPAL ADJ TUNNEL ADJ SYNDROME	
4 BIOL	193	3.TI,KW.	
5	1017	..COMBINE 1,2,4	
6	291	DUPLICATES	FROM STATEMENT 5
7	726	KEPT	FROM STATEMENT 5

END OF DISPLAY

searches into a single set, use **..COMBINE [search set numbers-1,2,5]**. Then you can remove any duplicate records from the combined set with **..DEDUP [search set]**. (The ..COMBINE and ..DEDUP commands are combined in a single command in KR ProBase—click on [Remove Duplicates] from the [Search] pull-down menu). The DEDUP command creates two resulting sets, the first containing the *duplicate* records and the second containing only the *unique* records. See Figure 4 for an example of StarSearch in command mode.

..MAP (no equivalent command in KR ProBase) extracts data from specified fields of retrieved records, creates a temporary stored search, and executes the search in another database. This lets you, for example, extract all the drug names from the retrieved records of a search set and then search another database for those drug names, without having to type in each name. You can also use ..MAP to take patent numbers, company names, or DUNS numbers (the unique identifying number for each company in the Dun & Bradstreet databases) from retrieved documents in one search set and search for those patents or companies in another database.

Unfortunately, ..MAP is not adequately explained in any of the printed documentation for DataStar; there is one short description of the command in the DataStar Quick Guide, but no mention of it in the DataStar Guide. **..MAP HELP** in command mode yields only a list of the fields on which a ..MAP command can be run. There is a small data card that describes ..MAP, sent to subscribers in 1994. However, anyone subscribing to DataStar since then would completely miss any mention of this very useful tool.

The syntax for ..MAP is non-intuitive and the help message is equally puzzling:

..MAP [set number]/[paragraph label]/[document number(s)]/[TYPE=]/[STEPS=]/[destination database paragraph label]

Fortunately, if you just type ..MAP, you are prompted for each element of the command. Needless to say, if you want to make use of this command, call Customer Service and ask them to walk you through the steps.

..SORT (or click on [Sort] from the [View] pull-down screen on KR ProBase) lets you rearrange the records in a search set. Type ..SORT HELP for a list of the SORTable fields in the current database. For bibliographic files, you can usually sort the results by title, date, document length, subject or industry codes, or source (i.e., the magazine or journal in which the article appeared). For company directory files, you can usually sort by total sales, number of employees, current ratio, and so on.

..RANK (not available on KR ProBase) is a useful command for determining the relative frequency of a term within a group of retrieved records. For example, to find the most commonly-used subject term for a concept, run a search for the concept in, say, the title and abstract fields. ..RANK the resulting set by DEscriptors; this displays a list of the indexing terms, indicating how many times each term appears in your search set. Another use for ..RANK is to identify companies involved in a new technology—search for articles on the technology and ..RANK the resulting set by company name to see what names show up most frequently. A version of ..RANK is available on KR ProBase when searching the CROS database only. In this case, ..RANK sorts the databases by number of hits in each file. Unfortunately, this powerful command is virtually undocumented. There is a brief mention in the *User Guide* of its use in the CROS database, and the online help (..RANK HELP) is cryptic and unhelpful.

..PARK and ..GO (or click on [Park/Pause] and [Go] from the [Features] pull-down menu on KR ProBase) let you pause your search for a short time to think through a strategy, check a *DataSheet*, or review your notes. ..PARK suspends the database charge for up to seven minutes; you can resume your online session and the database charges resume when you type ..GO.

Veteran DIALOG searchers need to be careful of using the KEEP command in DataStar. ..KEEP (available when logging off from KR ProBase) is a different creature than the KEEP command on DIALOG. You can use ..KEEP to save a search strategy or selected documents, but you cannot directly print those documents later. Actually, the accession numbers of the selected documents are stored in a separate database called ..KEEP. You can access the ..KEEP database and submit the documents to a document delivery vendor for ordering the full text of the documents. The other use for the ..KEEP database is to re-retrieve items from a prior search. For example, if you ran a search on a topic, you could use ..KEEP to save the relevant documents and then print a bibliography of those documents. Later, you could go back to the ..KEEP database, re-execute the search (by typing ..C KEEP, then RE-SEARCH), and print the full text of any of the documents you need.

PRICING

DataStar charges are based on connect time and per-document fees. The connect-time costs vary from database to database but (with the exception of the Derwent patent databases) are in one of the following per-hour price "tiers": $15, $30, $60, $90 or $120. Per-document charges also vary from database to database and range from $0.18 to $5 or more for the full text of a record. There is no charge for the BASE and NEWS databases.

Historically, North American subscribers have enjoyed a $20/hour discount for searching between 1:00pm and 1:00am Eastern time—the off-peak hours for this Swiss-based vendor. Since DataStar's acquisition by Knight-Ridder, DIALOG and DataStar have been moving to more homogeneous pricing structures and this $20/hour discount may be discontinued soon.

There are no annual or start-up fees, although Knight-Ridder does charge $99 for the KR ProBase software. Also, unfortunately, there is a charge for both the *DataStar Guide* and the initial set of *Datasheets*. KR ProBase users have an electronic version of the *Datasheets* on their computer; it comes with the KR ProBase software and is automatically updated when you log on to DataStar. KR ProBase also comes with its own user guide which I found to be poorly indexed and difficult to use. The KR ProBase guide provided no help for command mode searching, so if you intend to do any searching in command mode you would benefit from purchasing the *DataStar Guide* and probably the *Datasheets* as well. Although the *Guide* is outdated, at least it has information on the basic search and display commands as well as descriptions of all the search tools available through 1992.

OTHER FEATURES

DataStar provides good customer support to its subscribers in the U.S. and Europe. There are training sessions in major U.S. and European cities and self-guided training materials are available. DataStar also offers teletraining, a 20- to 30-minute session consisting of either a system overview or a review of system enhancements at no charge and a one-hour session on basic searching, new system features, TradStat, or DataMail for $50. Knight-Ridder Information publishes a monthly newsletter that describes new databases and system features and the month's free time offer (usually 30 minutes free usage on a particular database) and Happy Hour (one hour free connect time on a database; documents are charged). The newsletter also includes new and updated *Datasheets*. For more current news, see the Announcements option when you first connect to DataStar (in command mode) or click on [Announcements] from the [Features] pull-down menu on KR ProBase. And finally, the NEWS database contains additional information on all DataStar databases, new system features, and upcoming training seminars.

Online help leaves a bit to be desired (and it usually appears IN ALL CAPS, which makes it difficult to read). The KR ProBase software contains additional help information; the printed guides for command searching and KR ProBase are adequate, if poorly indexed.

In addition to displaying search results on the screen, you can have your search results redirected and printed at DataStar's computer center in Switzerland and mailed, or you can have the results sent to an electronic mail account on DataStar's DataMail system, to an Internet account, or to a fax machine. KR ProBase also allows you to download documents in a Microsoft Word 6.0-compatible format called KR ProBase Document File (.PB) format in which the field names are set apart and highlighted and the document looks more presentable. KR ProBase also lets you export tabular material such as financial data from annual reports into spreadsheet files.

..SET SUBACCOUNT allows you to track your search sessions by whatever accounting code you need. (In KR ProBase, select [Subaccount] from the [Options] menu in the Database screen.) This command causes DataStar to prompt you for a subaccount code whenever you change databases. All charges incurred during that search appear under the specified code on your invoice. If you use **..SET SUBACCOUNT ON**, DataStar prompts you for the subaccount code in all future search sessions. If you use **..SET SUBACCOUNT [code]**, DataStar applies the subaccount code to that search and prompts for a subaccount code the next time you log on to DataStar.

One of the nicest features of DataStar is its "free format" option. Rather than having to remember what fields or formats incur a charge in each database you search, you can have the records displayed in that database's free format by typing **..P [set number] FREE [record numbers]** (or click on [Free] in the list of formats available in the Titles screen on KR ProBase). This displays all the fields which do not incur a charge. This option is particularly useful in those databases that charge for the display of titles and other fields that are usually free.

..SET HIGHLIGHT helps you quickly find your search terms in retrieved records. You can have the search terms enclosed in <brackets> or *asterisks* or displayed in bold type on the screen. This feature is helpful when you are browsing records on the screen, but can be confusing when the records are downloaded and printed. Before you download your search results, remember to turn the highlight feature off by typing **..SET HIGHLIGHT OFF**. There is no equivalent command for ..SET HIGHLIGHT on KR ProBase. The search terms are automatically highlighted in reverse video when you view the retrieved records on KR ProBase; the highlighting does not appear in the downloaded or printed records.

Your current **session costs** are displayed automatically whenever you change files and when you log off. NOTE: The total given for each database search session is *not* a cumulative total of your costs. The total search costs are displayed only when you log off. If you need to keep track of your cumulative costs, remember to **..SET BUDGET [amount]**. When a budget has been set, DataStar displays the cumulative total each time you change files or type **..COST**. It's too bad that this cumulative information isn't displayed routinely.

The cost is expressed in either Swiss francs or U.S. dollars, depending on your account. You can also get estimates of your session costs at any time by typing **..COST** (or clicking on [Cost] from the [Features] pull-down menu on KR ProBase). You can turn the session cost display off by typing **..SET COST OFF**.

..ALERT is DataStar's electronic clipping service. You run the search once in the database you would like monitored on a regular basis. Then you type ..ALERT to set up the clipping service. The syntax is somewhat confusing—the full ..ALERT command is ..ALERT ST=nbr/P=pn/ID=descr/SORT=/NP=/MB=/COP=/FREQ=/DAY=/EXP=. Fortunately, you are prompted for each part of the command if you simply type ..ALERT. The retrieved documents can be delivered to an email account on DataStar's DataMail system, to an Internet email address, to a fax machine, or can be printed and mailed.

EVALUATION OF DATASTAR

DataStar is one of those professional online systems, like DIALOG, that you either love or hate. Its commands are not intuitive, but it offers a lot of search power and provides excellent coverage of business and medical information. If you need international business information, biotechnology sources, or pharmaceutical news, DataStar offers you the best selection of information resources.

What do I like most about DataStar?
• I like the collection of power tools DataStar provides. ..ROOT, ..STARSAVE, ..MAP, ..ADD, ..DEDUP, ..MEDWORD, and ..SET PLURALS are all useful commands that make searching easier and more cost-effective.

• I like the cost-control features, particularly the ..SET BUDGET command and the free format that lets me view all the fields in a record for which there is no display charge.

• I like the flexibility of downloading documents in a number of formats, particularly the management format (..P M,[format]), which eliminates field codes and the need for extensive post-processing of the search results.

What do I like least about DataStar?
• I don't like KR ProBase. It is intended for experienced searchers who aren't familiar with DataStar, but it takes as much time to figure out how KR ProBase works as it would take an experienced searcher to learn the regular system commands for a command mode search. The software (at least the 1995 version 1.0x) is not intuitive. The tool bar changes from screen to screen and it is difficult to find the command you want. And to add insult to injury, DataStar charges $99 for KR ProBase; all other major online services give their proprietary software away. Knight-Ridder is working on version 2.0 of KR ProBase and hopes to fix some of the troublesome aspects of the software's user interface.

• The documentation is inadequate and out-of-date. Neither the *DataStar Guide* (for command mode searchers) nor the *KR ProBase User's Guide* has an adequate index, making it difficult for users to find the information they need. The *DataStar Guide* sent to me in late 1995 was from 1991-1992; it included no documentation on STARSAVE, MAP, or RANK, nor did it have the new name for DataStar's electronic clipping service. DataStar charges subscribers for the *Guide*; $70 for an outdated manual seems unreasonable.

CONTACT INFORMATION

NAME   DataTimes Corp.

ADDRESS   14000 Quail Springs Parkway
                      Suite 450
                      Oklahoma City, OK 73134

TELEPHONE   800/642-2525; 405/751-6400

CUSTOMER   Monday through Friday 8:00am - 10:00pm Eastern time
SERVICE HOURS

EMAIL   through EyeQ software: click on the [Customer Service] icon
                      through Internet: datatime@datatimes.com

WEB HOME PAGE   http://www.enews.com/clusters/datatimes/

SERVICE   5:00am - 2:00am Eastern time, 7 days a week. System is
AVAILABILITY   often available earlier than 5:00am.

DESCRIPTION OF INFORMATION AVAILABLE

DataTimes began its life as the electronic morgue for individual newspapers, and the core of its service offering has traditionally been its collection of local newspapers. In addition to 120 U.S. newspapers, DataTimes now provides access to transcripts of television broadcasts, the PROMT and Trade and Industry Database files, TRW Business Credit reports, and data from Disclosure, Investext, Standard & Poors, American Business Information, and other financial information sources.

DataTimes originally targeted professional online searchers such as librarians as its primary market. With the introduction of a new pricing structure, a revamp of its user interface, and the development of proprietary software with a much more user-friendly feel, DataTimes is marketing its service to business people who are not presently searching online databases. The tradeoff has been the addition of an easy-to-use search engine but the loss of some of the power tools that frequent online searchers have come to expect from a professional online service, such as the ability to view an index of search terms, display the number of articles available for each word in the search statement, or save a search for reuse later.

DataTimes encourages subscribers to use its proprietary EyeQ search software. Users who are not running Windows or who use Apple computers can dial up to DataTimes through any communications software package. Both see the same general information on the screen; the EyeQ screen is much easier to use and offers point-and-click navigation.

DataTimes offers two search "modes"—Command Searching and Natural Language Searching. Both cover the same sources. Command Searching requires a greater familiarity with Boolean commands, but offers a greater degree of search refinement. Natural Language offers simpler search screens and a somewhat limited range of search options, but is much easier for less-experienced online searchers.

Using EyeQ, the main screen guides users through a selection of the information sources available. See Figure 5. You can select [Search] (and then search using either Natural Language or Boolean search terms), [Today's News] (which searches all the news sources, limiting the search to today's date), [Business Analyst] (which currently has stock quotes and portfolio management and will have company financials, directories, and company and industry profiles late in 1996), [Executive Reports] (10- to 20-page profiles on companies and industries), [Private Eye] (electronic clipping service), and [Customer Service] (billing history, account profile information, and electronic mail to customer service).

Command Search

The Command Search function is reasonably intuitive. You type in your search using Boolean connectors and clicking on the [Fields], [Dates], or [Categories] boxes if you need help in narrowing down the search. See Figure 6.

FIGURE 5
Main EyeQ Screen

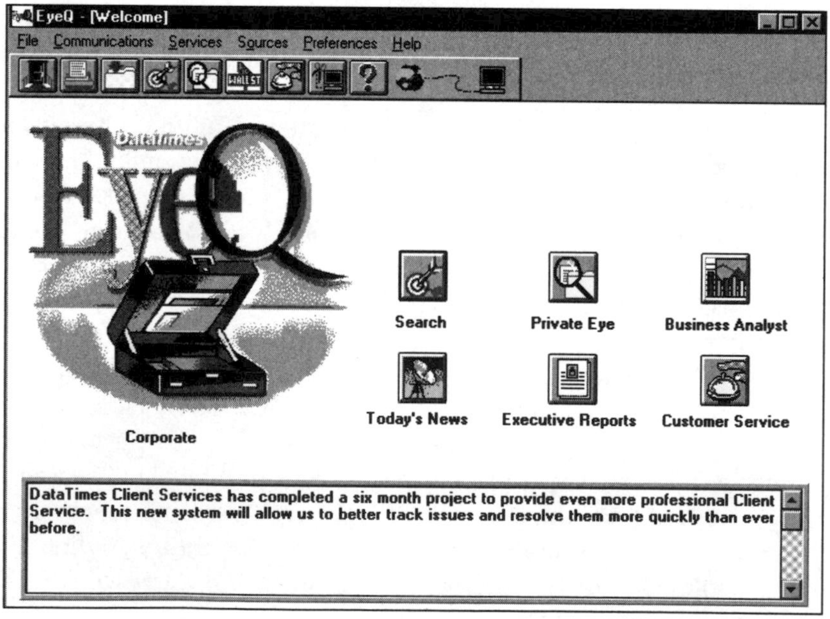

Once the search is completed, the results are sorted in reverse chronological order. The user scans the brief citation format (date, source code, first 20 or 30 characters of the title, and number of pages) and selects the items to be displayed in bibliographic citation, lead paragraph, KWIC, or full-text format. Records can be downloaded either as plain ASCII text or in rich-text format, a nice feature. (Rich-text format retains the formatting of the original article, including fonts, columns, and graphics.) Results can also be sent via first class mail, fax, or overnight delivery for an additional fee.

Users should be careful at the search results screen; it is deceptively easy to click on likely-looking records and forget to select one of the less expensive display formats rather than the default FULL format. If you're too late, you may find that you have inadvertently ordered and been billed for the full text of a number of marginally-relevant articles.

The Command Search mode allows users to revise a search, combine sets, limit the search by field, limit to sources in a specific geographic area, or narrow the date restriction. The context-sensitive help screens are well-written and useful.

Natural Language Searching

The search screen template for the Natural Language search mode has a simplified format, prompting the user for Who, What, When, and Where. See Figure 7. (Actually, Who and What search the same fields—a search for Summer Olympics in the Who box retrieves exactly the same records as a search for Summer Olympics in the What box.) The When box (that

FIGURE 6
Command Search Screen

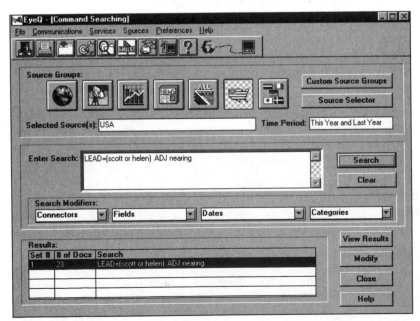

FIGURE 7
Natural Language Search Screen

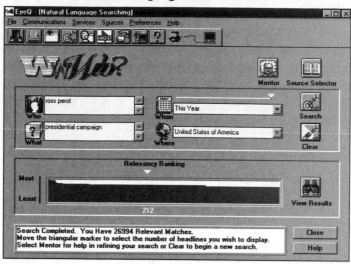

is, the date restrictor) defaults to "This year and last year," a reasonable assumption. You can also search by specific date range, current year, all years, and so on. The Where box indicates which sources to search. The search screen assumes that two words next to each other are to be searched as a phrase—Summer Olympics is searched as Summer within 2 words of Olympics, in this order. The system combines Who and What entries with an OR connector, ranking higher in relevance those retrieved documents that contain both Who and What terms.

Once the search is completed, the results are ranked according to relevancy and they are displayed in a brief title format. See Figure 8. The relevancy ranking is determined by the density of search terms in the first few paragraphs of each document, although with some articles this may not be the most reliable indicator of relevance. Be sure to scan at least the top 25 percent or 50 percent of the headlines; otherwise, you may miss relevant but misranked items.

ROADMAP OF RESOURCES

Source Selector/Source Groups

Determining what information sources are available and selecting among them can be done by either using the "Source Selector" (in which you select subsets of newspapers, magazines, and other online material, sorted by industry, by geographic region, by type of information resource, and so on) or by "Custom Source Groups" (in which you can pre-select subsets of material, e.g., all newspapers and magazines from the Southwest). Users who are not familiar with the wide variety of online sources available find this helpful; more experienced searchers may find that the Source Selector's preformatted categories get in the way more than they assist in search formulation.

From within either the Natural Language or Command search screens, you can click on the [Source Selector] icon to identify the specific news sources you wish to search. The sources are sliced and diced several ways, and the Source Selector allows you to select sources by group or by individual title.

Note that the following categories are also labeled as "Source Groups" and appear as a row of icons across the top of the search screen (for Command Searching) or under the [Where] button (for Natural Language Searching). Confused yet? See Figure 9 for an example of the Source Selector for the News Groups.

FIGURE 8
Natural Language Search Results Screen

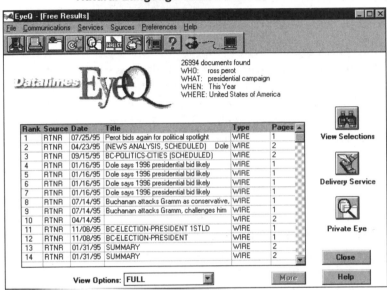

FIGURE 9
EyeQ Source Selector

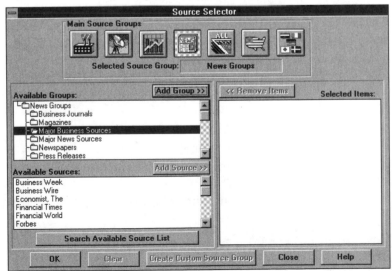

The Source Groups are broken down into the following classifications:

- Industry—subsorted by specific industry such as Building Construction, or Software & Data Processing. Although it is tempting to select a single industry group, it is possible to be overly specific and eliminate sources that, though not strictly focused on the industry in question, also include discussions of your research topic. For example, DataTimes lists the following subcategories under the broad industry group Health & Drugs:

  HEALTH & DRUGS
      HEALTH
          INSTITUTIONAL SERVICES

  Unfortunately, there are only three sources included in the Institutional Services category, although it is likely that relevant articles could be found in other sources than the three listed. Rather than selecting the narrowest Source Group, select a broader group that encompasses your topic as well as related concepts. This avoids the problem of losing valuable information that appeared in magazines or newsletters that cover a related field to the one you are researching.

- Today's News—newswires and daily newspapers that offer same-day online availability. The search is automatically limited to today's date.

- Finance—subsorted by category such as Business Credit, Fund Management, and Investment Analyst Reports. The same caution applies here as to the Industry subcategories—be careful of selecting too narrow a subcategory and eliminating valuable information sources. Another factor to keep in mind is that the Finance category includes not only articles, but financial reports from Disclosure, Investext, Standard & Poors, and so on. These reports incur charges of up to $25 for the full records. The following notice appears on the search results screen when you select items for display:

The following special fees apply to selected document(s):

	FULL	KWIC	LEAD	CITE
Disclosure	$25.00	$5.00	$5.00	$0.50
S&P	$10.00	$1.00	$1.00	$0.50
TRW	$7.50	$5.00	$1.00	$0.50
Investext	$6.50*	$1.00	$1.00	$0.50

*price per page

However, it is not clear to which documents those fees apply, and the source code in the preliminary display of retrieved records do not indicate which are subject to special fees.

For example, the result of a search of Finance sources might include the following:

Source	Date	Headline	Type	Pages
IVMKG	6/13/95	Gradco System - Company.	FINSRC	7
IVMER	5/30/95	Eaton Corp - Company ...	FINSRC	6
IVSBH	5/24/95	Scitex Corp - Company...	FINSRC	2

A user would not necessarily know that source code IVSBH stands for Investext—Smith Barney Shearson and subject to a $6.50 charge for each page of the report. The report on Gradco System listed in the preceding example would incur a charge of $45.50. Since there is no printed index of sources alphabetically by source code, you have no easy way of checking the source code before ordering the document.

- News Groups—subsorted by type of publication. This category divides the online sources into Business Journals (e.g., *Nashville Business & Lifestyles*), Business Magazines (e.g., *Mercer Business*), Major Business Sources (e.g., *The Economist*), Transcripts, and so on. The last category in this section is "Other Groups by Provider," i.e., all sources sorted by publisher. The same source may appear in several categories; *CBS Morning News* transcripts are included in Transcripts, Major News Sources, and Other Groups by Provider (under the subgroup Burrelle's Broadcast Transcripts).

- All Text—all sources from published periodicals and broadcast transcripts, sorted alphabetically. This category excludes financial information sources such as Disclosure or investment analyst reports.

- United States Only—all U.S. articles from periodicals and broadcast transcripts. If you select the upper-most sort, "United States of America," you see an alphabetical list of all sources published in the U.S. You can select one of the subcategories (Central United States, Eastern United States, or Western United States) or you can narrow it down to a metropolitan area. To select sources from the San Francisco Bay area, you would select:
United States
   Western United States
      Pacific Region United States
         California
            San Francisco Bay Area

- International—all articles from periodicals published outside the U.S., sorted by the region (e.g., Pacific Rim, Europe) and by the country in which the periodical is published. There is also a subcategory for World Wide which includes periodicals that focus on the international market generally (such as *Fish Farming International*). Curiously, though, some periodicals that provide excellent worldwide coverage, such as *The Economist* or *Computergram International*, do not appear in this section but are listed under the country in which they are published. Use this Source Selector category with caution.

Business Analyst

The Business Analyst icon promises to offer one-stop shopping for financial data, combining information from sources such as Disclosure, Investext, Standard & Poors, and Tradeline. Unfortunately, at press time, this feature was not fully operational. Current stock quotes are available, as is the "portfolio manager," which tracks stock performance. The other services under this icon are expected to be available some time in 1996.

Executive Reports

This section of DataTimes provides pre-packaged reports on companies and industries, compiled by Avenue Technologies. The reports are broken out into three sections: U.S. Companies, International Companies, and Industry Scorecard. Both public companies and major private companies are covered.

Be careful when searching, particularly when looking for industry reports. You cannot browse a listing of titles or subject terms and may miss a useful report if the industry term used for the report is not the one you expect. For example, there is no report for "Banks" or "Banking Industry," but there are reports for "Pacific States Banks" and "Mountain States Banks." There is no report for "Steel Industry," but there is one for "Iron-Steel-Mills." Try several alternate terms if you don't turn up anything useful with the first search term.

Company reports have a brief table of contents available for viewing prior to ordering the reports. Be sure to look over the table of contents to make sure the report covers the area(s) you need. Unfortunately, industry reports do not offer a table of contents or indication of exactly which SIC codes or companies are included in the report.

TIPS FOR USING DATATIMES' FINDING AIDS

DataTimes' primary search aid is its [Mentor] feature. Used with Natural Language Searching and intended to help users refine an overly-broad search, it is at least a first stab at adding an intelligent agent to the searcher's arsenal. According to DataTimes executives, it works best when a search yields at least 500 or 1,000 records and the searcher is looking for a few pertinent articles rather than a comprehensive list of articles.

At the Natural Language Searching screen, you first enter the terms you want searched, the time period to include, and the Source Group to search. DataTimes ranks the resulting set of documents by expected relevance, based on the frequency of the search terms in the first few paragraphs of each document. You can either view the records, sorted in relevance order, or you can click on the [Mentor] icon. If you ask [Mentor] for help, the system analyzes the retrieved documents and suggests additional industry terms, company names, likely sources, and keywords to search. I have not found the suggested terms to be particularly helpful; the [Mentor] function creates an illusion of intelligence that just isn't there yet.

An example: I searched for articles on Windows 95 and retrieved thousands of documents. I asked [Mentor] for help. The industry terms it suggested were, first, Technology, then Business Data Processing, then Software & Data. I would have expected Software to be the most useful term to narrow down the search set. Other industry terms included in the [Mentor] list were, among others, Advertising, Publishing, and Media. In the list of companies it suggested, it had Microsoft listed five times, Apple Computer three times, and Windows 95 as a "company." The other suggestions were equally puzzling. Rather than rely on [Mentor], a searcher is better served by using the Command Searching screen and refining the search by using field limitation (LEAD=Microsoft, for example).

In general, be as specific as you can in your searching, particularly when using Natural Language Searching. Rather than selecting [United States of America] as a Source Group (which includes Investext company reports as well as articles), select [All text], [Newspapers], or [Finance]. Use several related terms; this helps the relevancy ranking engine sort the retrieved items more reliably.

Commonly-Used Commands

DataTimes' EyeQ software eliminates the need for typed commands for some of the following actions, using point-and-click selections instead. DataTimes Online (plain ASCII log-on) presents a similar screen-by-screen interface; most of the navigation commands are made by selection from a menu of options.

The use of search terms varies with the type of search interface you select. The first column lists the search terms for Command Searching; the second column lists the search terms for Natural Language Searching. Both columns apply specifically to the EyeQ software. For DataTimes Online, the search terms are the same; navigational commands are menu-driven.

	Command Searching	**Natural Language Searching**
Begin a search	click on the [Search], [Business Analyst], [Executive Reports], or [Today's News] icon	click on the [Search], [Business Analyst], [Executive Reports], or [Today's News] icon
Search terms:		
x AND y	x **AND** y	x **AND** y
x OR y	x **OR** y	x, y
x BUT NOT y	x **NOT** y	x **NOT** y
x NEXT TO y	x **ADJ** y *	x y
x WITHIN n WORDS OF y	x **NEARn** y	x **NEARn** y
x SAME SENTENCE y	x **NEAR15** y	x **NEAR15** y
x SAME PARAGRAPH y	x **SAME** y	x **SAME** y
x SAME FIELD y	not available	not available
Date Searching	Use the [Dates] pull-down menu	Use the [When] search box
Field Searching	**HEAD=**x	**HEAD=**x
Truncation	word*	word*

Commonly-Used Commands [continued]

	Command Searching	Natural Language Searching
Display results	click [**View Results**] icon	click [**View Results**]
Help	click [**Help**] icon	click [**Help**] icon
Cost:		
for session charges up to this point	click [**Customer Service**] icon "Billing History"	click [**Customer Service**] icon "Billing History"
for database rates	click [**Help**] icon	click [**Help**] icon
for total cost when logging off	displayed when logging off	displayed when logging off
Log off	<Alt> <F4> or click [**Disconnect**] icon	<Alt> <F4> or click [**Disconnect**] icon

* ADJ actually searches for x within 2 words of y. You cannot strictly limit the search to x next to y

GETTING CONNECTED

DataTimes strongly encourages users to access DataTimes through its proprietary Windows-based software, EyeQ, which automatically logs them on to DataTimes.

Access is also available in "native mode" through DataTimes Online. This is a plain ASCII version; most of the EyeQ functions are available through DataTimes Online but without the point-and-click functionality of GUI software. Mac users must use DataTimes Online; if you have an IBM-compatible computer that can support EyeQ, that is the more desirable method of searching DataTimes.

EyeQ automatically logs the user into DataTimes via the closest Tymnet or Sprintnet node.

DataTimes Online access:
via Tymnet: Please log in: **datatimes**; [no carriage return]
via Sprintnet: **@c datatimes**
DataTimes supports speeds from 1200bps through 19200bps, although use of the EyeQ software at less than 9600bps is not recommended.

Modem settings should be:
VT100 emulation
FULL duplex
1 stop bit, 7 data bits, even parity
The EyeQ software is automatically configured with the proper settings.

System requirements for the EyeQ software are:
IBM-compatible PC with 386 processor or better (Macintosh software not yet available)
4MB RAM
Windows 3.1 or higher
10MB available on hard disk
modem with a speed of at least 2400bps (9600bps or faster recommended)

POWER TOOLS

DataTimes redesigned its software to make the system easier to use, particularly for users who are not professional online searchers. The trade-off has been the removal of some of the power tools available on other professional online services. To get the most out of DataTimes, take control of the searching by using Command Searching rather than Natural Language Searching. Use field and descriptor searching and the capability of combining search statements. With Natural Language Searching, you lose the ability to do either a comprehensive or a pinpoint search.

Take advantage of the Source Selector and Custom Source Groups. If you usually search for information on a single industry, take the time to create a Custom Source Group with the most useful trade and industry publications. If you regularly search for regional news, create a Source Group that pulls together the daily newspapers, regional business journals, and local magazines into a single group you can use for each search.

Use the Private Eye electronic clipping service for any topic in which you have a continuing interest. If you plan on traveling and won't have access to online searching but still need to monitor a particular topic, you can change the settings of your Private Eye folder so that the updates are faxed automatically to wherever you are staying.

PRICING

DataTimes' pricing was recently restructured to encourage browsing and remove the pressure of connect-time charging. DataTimes charges a $39 monthly fee, plus a $12/hour connect charge.

Within the Search and Today's News icons, there is no charge for the initial display, which includes date, Source Code, the first 30 to 40 words of the title, and the page count. Full-text articles cost $3 each; a bibliographic citation is $0.50; the lead paragraph or Keyword-in-Context (KWIC) formats cost $1. Investext documents incur an additional surcharge of $6.50 per page.

Other company, industry, and financial reports cost between $0.10 and $34.95, depending on the format and source. The Private Eye electronic clipping service incurs a fee of $15 per folder per month, plus the standard per-document fees when documents are viewed.

In addition, some Business Analyst reports cannot be viewed on the screen, but must be delivered via fax or print; delivery fees run from $1 per page for fax to $15 for overnight delivery.

OTHER FEATURES

Training is available at seminars held in major U.S. cities. If a subscriber is not near a city in which a seminar is held, the subscriber's account representative can provide telephone training instead.

DataTimes' **Customer Service** icon offers more "service" than many of DataTimes' competitors. Click on the [Customer Service] icon at the main screen and you are given three options: Billing History, Customer Information, and Customer Service Messages. The Billing History icon lists the current and prior months' total invoices and detailed information on every transaction. This display is particularly helpful if you need to pass the online charges on to another department, a client, or an expense code. Each line of the detailed listing includes the date, user ID and client code, number of records displayed, from which files and in which format, and the total charge. The Customer Information icon enables subscribers to update their billing information and user profile. The third icon, Customer Service Messages, puts you into DataTimes' electronic mail system. You can send queries to Customer Service and track both your messages and the responses from DataTimes. Messages are usually responded to within 24 hours; if you can wait a day to get your question answered, this is a more reliable way to get technical issues resolved than calling the Customer Service telephone number.

EVALUATION OF DATATIMES

One of DataTimes' strengths has always been its coverage of local newspapers and broadcast transcripts. If you need local coverage of an issue, DataTimes is often the place to start.

DataTimes has moved much of the intelligence back onto its users' machines. That means that you can prepare parts of your search ahead of time, such as designing a customized list of sources to search and changing the client tracking code. It also means that much of the online help is actually available to you when you are offline as well. You can set system defaults and do other housekeeping chores offline. The downside of this feature is that the EyeQ software takes up a good bit of real estate on your hard drive (10MB and 4MB RAM), so a user with an older PC may notice a much slower response time for functions that require disk reads.

DataTimes has made a strategic decision to go after the huge market of business people who don't currently do their own online searching, under the assumption that this group would use online databases if given the opportunity, easy-to-use search software, and a pricing structure that doesn't penalize users for taking extra time to formulate their searches and view the results.

That means that searchers who like to roll their sleeves up and get under the hood may feel somewhat frustrated and the searchers who don't care how it's done, but just want some information, may be pleased. (Keep in mind that the newspapers, but not other exclusive DataTimes sources, are also available through Dow Jones News/Retrieval, should you want to use DJN/R's search software instead of the Command or Natural Language Searching of DataTimes.)

What do I like most about DataTimes?
• EyeQ is one of the most intuitive front-end software packages of the professional online services. The welcome screen clearly displays the system options and the underlying search screens are clear and relatively self-evident.

- I like DataTimes' pricing structure, in which most of the expense of a search is incurred when you actually display information. The low telecommunications charge of $12/hour (along with a monthly fee of $39) means that I can think through my search as I go along, take time browsing through the retrieved documents, and consult the online help screens as I need to without worrying about the meter running. Three dollars for the full text of an article is competitive, and no document costs more than $34.95 (with the exception of Investext documents, which are priced at $6.50/page). This makes estimating the cost of a search a relatively simple process.

- I appreciate the ability to construct my own Custom Source Groups for those frequent searches in a select group of magazines. My Custom Source Group of "usual suspects," for example, includes *Business Week, Forbes, Fortune, The Economist*, and a few of the major newspapers. This simplifies those searches for some recent news about a certain company or industry by enabling me to limit my search to the general business sources most likely to give a decent overview on the subject.

- DataTimes is an easy system to learn and use, and offers a wide variety of online resources to searchers who are put off by the arcane search language or confusing initial menus of other online systems.

What do I like least about DataTimes?
- While trying to accommodate the needs of less-proficient searchers, DataTimes has removed many of the tools on which more experienced online searchers have come to depend. The first thing I missed when I fired up EyeQ was documentation with the experienced searcher in mind. There is no description of how to do Boolean searching: Does SAME mean same paragraph or same sentence? Is truncation done with a question mark, an exclamation mark, or an asterisk? I learned by accident that field searching is permitted within Natural Language Searching; nowhere in the documentation is this mentioned.

- Within some of the search screens, particularly with the parts of Business Analyst that were working at press time, the documentation's description did not match what I saw on the screen. I wound up looking at a set of options with which I was not familiar, such as stock price analytics, and I found that neither the printed nor the online documentation gave me much guidance.

- One of the tools many experienced searchers rely on is the [Browse the Index] feature. Say I am looking for articles on Wenckebach, a heart condition. I can try to guess all the ways that word may be misspelled (Wenckeback, Wencheback, Wenkebach, etc.), but I would rather be able to browse the index of searchable terms and simply select the correct and misspelled terms as they appear. This problem is particularly thorny when searching newspapers (one of DataTimes' strong points); how do I even begin to guess all the ways Muammar Qaddafi's name may be spelled without the ability to browse the index?

- I have found that searches on DataTimes often seem to take more time than a comparable search on another professional online service; unfortunately, the

<break> key does not work reliably and I must wait several minutes while the unwanted search is run.

- As noted in the "Finding Aids" section, I found the [Mentor] function to be misleading and unhelpful. Users would be better served with more extensive documentation and explanation of how best to formulate and modify a search rather than with an intelligent agent that does not add much intelligence to the search process.

- Although the pricing structure is simple and the per-article charge quite reasonable, I found it distressingly easy to incur full-format charges by either selecting items from sources for which there is a surcharge (such as Disclosure and Investext), or by inadvertently displaying selected records in the default FULL format rather than KWIC or LEAD.

CONTACT INFORMATION

NAME	Knight-Ridder Information, Inc.
ADDRESS	2440 El Camino Real Mountain View, CA 94040
TELEPHONE	800/334-2564; 415/254-8800
CUSTOMER SERVICE HOURS	Monday through Friday 8:00am - 8:00pm Eastern time
EMAIL	through Internet: customer@corp.dialog.com
WEB HOME PAGE	http://www.dialog.com/dialog/dialog1.html
SYSTEM AVAILABILITY	24 hours/day; 7 days a week except Sunday between 5:00am and 1:00pm Eastern time

DESCRIPTION OF INFORMATION AVAILABLE

DIALOG is one of the oldest online information services, and now consists of over 450 databases. It provides extensive coverage of business journals, newsletters, newspapers, financial profiles and other company information, and patents and trademarks from worldwide sources. It also offers databases of medical literature, chemical substances, the social sciences, and science and technology.

DIALOG has been a leader in developing powerful search and retrieval tools to enable searchers to find information efficiently. As a result, it is not an easy system for the first-time searcher to use. The basic service is command-driven, and the search language is not always intuitive. DIALOG is a system that takes some time to learn, but is well worth the effort for the frequent searcher.

ROADMAP OF RESOURCES

DIALOG offers a number of **online finding tools** at reduced cost or at no charge. With the number of databases available, it is easy for a searcher to rely on a few familiar sources and ignore other possible resources. It is often worth the time to check for alternative sources in order to avoid missing valuable but infrequently used databases.

DIALINDEX—File 411, a database of indexes to almost all DIALOG databases. This database enables you to try a preliminary search in a number of databases to determine which is most useful.

DIALOG Bluesheets—online on File 415 and in abbreviated format in print. Bluesheets are two- to eight-page documentation on each database (printed on blue paper), including a description of the database records and sources, a sample record, information on all searchable indexes, and search tips. An online search enables you to scan individual file descriptions to identify files with appropriate subject coverage.

Chronolog—monthly newsletter, available both online on File 410 and in print. Use the Chronolog to find announcements of new files, for search tips and techniques, and help with searching unfamiliar databases.

Database Catalogue—printed annually. The *Catalogue* includes an alphabetical listing of each file with one-paragraph descriptions, an index by broad subject category, and a listing by database number.

DIALOG WWW home page on the Internet—http://www.dialog.com/dialog/dialog1.html. Provides access for both subscribers and nonsubscribers to system documentation, file descriptions, and search guides.

TIPS FOR USING DIALOG'S FINDING AIDS

DIALINDEX (File 411) is a collection of the file indexes for most DIALOG databases. Essentially, you can run a preliminary search through any or all DIALOG databases to determine the most useful files. DIALINDEX can be searched by predetermined categories (e.g., patents, agriculture, energy, all full-text databases), or you can specify the files you wish to include in your search. The cost for searching DIALINDEX is $30/hour, making this a cost-effective way to try out a search prior to incurring connect charges in the regular files. Remember, you are only searching indexes. You cannot display the results of a search in DIALINDEX.

Searches in DIALINDEX work best if they are fairly broad. Unless you know that all the files being searched include the same field names, do not limit your search by field. For example, if I ran a search in the International Business News category (INTLNEWS) for SIC code 3942 (SC=3942), I would retrieve no records in ABI/INFORM, which has no field for SIC codes. A better search that would include all the possible ways to identify articles that cover the SIC code 3942 (the code for dolls) might be s sc=3942 or doll? ?/ti,de,id. This would retrieve any record with "doll" or "dolls" in the SIC code field, the title, the descriptor field, or the identifier field.

Use DIALINDEX as a way of identifying files you might not have expected to contain the information you need. Using a broad initial search enables you to search across disciplinary fields and locate sources that approach your topic from an unexpected angle. For example, a business searcher looking for articles on genetic engineering might only look in PROMT, ABI/INFORM, and the Newsletter Database. An engineering searcher might limit the search to BIOSIS Previews, Derwent Biotechnology Abstracts, and CAB Abstracts databases. If either searcher

FIGURE 10
DIALINDEX Search

File 411:DIALINDEX(R)

DIALINDEX(R)
   (c) 1995 Knight-Ridder Info

*** DIALINDEX search results display in an abbreviated ***
*** format unless you enter the SET DETAIL ON command. ***
? **sf biotech, multiind**
   You have 56 files in your file list.
   (To see banners, use SHOW FILES command)
? **s genetic?(3n)engineer?(25n)strawberr?**
Your SELECT statement is:
   s genetic?(3n)engineer?(25n)strawberr?

Items	File	
6	5:	BIOSIS PREVIEWS(R)_1969-1995/Dec W2
4	50:	CAB Abstracts_1972-1995/Nov
1	76:	Life Sciences Collection_1978-1995/Oct
3	129:	PHIND(Archival)_1980-1995/Dec W5
1	144:	Pascal_1973-1995/Dec
10	149:	IAC(SM) Health & Wellness DB(SM)_76-95/Dec W3
11	285:	BioBusiness(R)_1985-1995/Nov W2
7	286:	Biocommerce Abs.& Dir._1981-1995/Dec 18
4	357.	Derwent Biotechnology Abs_1982-1990/Dec DE
2	434:	SciSearch(R)_1974-1995/Dec W1
4	636:	IAC Newsletter DB(TM)_1987-1995/Dec 29
20	6:	IAC PROMT(R)_1972-1995/Dec 29
1	18:	IAC F&S INDEX(R)_1980-1995/DecW4
1	30:	AsiaPacific_1985-1995/Nov B2
10	148:	IAC Trade & Industry Database_1976-1995/Dec 29
7	545:	Investext(R)_1982-1995/Dec 20
1	563:	ICC Int.Bus.Res_1986-1995/Dec W2
1	583:	IAC Globalbase(TM)_1986-1995/Dec W2
1	622:	Financial Times Fulltext_1986-1995/Dec 23
4	624:	McGraw-Hill Publications Onl._1985-1995/Dec 27
2	637:	Journal of Commerce_1986-1995/Dec 28
2	765:	Frost & Sullivan_Jan 1992-1995/Aug
1	766:	FIND(R)/SVP Market Research_1993-1995/Aug
1	799:	Textline Curr.Glob.News_1994-1995/Dec 29
6	772:	Textline Global News_1990-1993
6	771:	Textline Global News_1980-1989

26 files have one or more items; file list includes 56 files.

had searched DIALINDEX first, the possibilities for a cross-disciplinary search would have become apparent. See Figure 10 for a DIALINDEX search of the biotech and multi-industry files for information on genetically-engineered strawberries.

DIALOG Bluesheets are invaluable in preparing for searches in unfamiliar databases. Each database description includes subject coverage, sources, inclusive dates, a sample record, field names and descriptions, LIMIT options, and available output formats. The online version of the Bluesheets, File 415, can be used to identify files that include a specific field (ticker symbol, for example) and files that provide full-text records.

DIALOG HOMEBASE provides menu-driven access to DIALOG files. Use HOMEBASE as an alternative to DIALINDEX or the *Bluesheets*. If you are not certain which files to select, you can use the HOMEBASE menus to choose among the preset DIALINDEX categories for a search.

Knight-Ridder Information also maintains an Internet home page containing information about the system. This site provides access to back issues of the *Chronolog* newsletter, *Bluesheets*, the Database Catalogue, how-to guides, and other documentation. You can log in and scan through the database descriptions to identify the most relevant files to search; you can request that documentation be faxed to you; and you can telnet directly to DIALOG through this home page. The same information can be obtained through the free files on DIALOG (*Chronolog*, *Bluesheets*, and DIALOG Publications); this home page enables users to search the documentation without incurring any Tymnet or Sprintnet charges.

DIALOG's ASAF service (As Soon as Faxable) provides fax delivery of a wide variety of system documentation pages, how-to reference cards, service descriptions, and product guides. If you need a quick description of how DIALOG's ERA pricing works, or some pointers on how to find financial information on a company, or if you need help configuring your telecommunications software, you can request the relevant information and receive it on your fax machine within minutes. To order an ASAF document or to receive an index of available documents, dial 800/496-4470 or 415/254-8246 from a touch-tone telephone. There is no charge for this service.

Commonly-Used Commands

Begin a search	B <file number>
Search terms:	
x AND y	S x AND y
x OR y	S x OR y
x BUT NOT y	S x NOT y
x NEXT TO y	S x(W)y (x must precede y)
	S x(N)y (x next to y, in any order)
x WITHIN n WORDS OF y	S x(nW)y (x must be n words before y)
	S x(nN)y (x and y must be within n words of each other, in any order)
x SAME SENTENCE y	not specifically available—use S x(15N)y

x SAME PARAGRAPH y	not specifically available—use **S x(40N)y**
x SAME FIELD y	**S x(F)y**
Date Searching	varies with the file
	often **S PD=YYMMDD**
	LIMIT Sn/YYYY (to restrict a set to records with a certain date)
Field Searching	**S word/TI** or **S (x or y)/DE,AB**
Truncation	word**?** (for any number of characters)
	word**??** (for one or two additional characters)
	w**?**rd (to retrieve w**o**rd, w**a**rd)
Display results	for continuous online display, use TYPE: **T <set number>/<format>/<item numbers>** e.g., **T 4/9/1,3-5** or **T 4/TI/ALL**. For screen-by-screen online display, use DISPLAY: **D<set number>/<format>/<item numbers>** e.g, **D 4/9/1,3-5** or **D 4/TI/ALL**. For offline printing or email delivery, use PRINT: **P <set number>/<format>/<item numbers> <via dialmail>** e.g., **P 4/9/1,3-5 VIA DIALMAIL**
Help	**H <command or file number>** or **?<command or file number>** e.g., **H RANK** or **? RATES 545**
Cost:	
for session charges up to this point	**COST**
for database rates	**HELP RATES <file number>**
for total cost when logging off	session cost automatically displayed when logging off
Log off	**LOGOFF** or **BYE** or **QUIT** or **STOP**

GETTING CONNECTED

via Tymnet:	Please log in: **dialog**
via Sprintnet:	**@c dialog**
via Internet:	**telnet dialog.com**

DIALOG is also available through gateways on DataStar (also produced by Knight-Ridder Information), WESTLAW, EasyNet, and other networks. To access DIALOG from DataStar, type **..c dialog**.

DIALOG supports speeds from 300bps through 9600bps. Modem settings should be:
TTY emulation
ASCII protocol
full duplex
1 stop bit, 7 data bits, even parity OR 1 stop bit, 8 data bits, no parity

No special software is required; any communications software package that supports the settings listed previously can be used. DIALOG offers a front end software package called DIALOGLink, specifically designed for DIALOG searching. Versions are available for DOS, Windows, and Macintosh computers. DIALOGLink offers a type-ahead buffer, the ability to scroll back through previous screens of text, and a feature that tracks search costs and enables simplified bill-back of expenses. The only way to download images (available in the TRADEMARKSCAN Federal, Chapman & Hill Chemical Database, and Derwent World Patent Index databases) is with DIALOGLink. Images cannot be downloaded or transferred through other communications software or through the Internet. DIALOGLink is particularly useful for slow typists who can take advantage of the type-ahead buffer and type in their search strategies while offline. The type-ahead buffer is also valuable when a searcher needs to enter long strings of text such as chemical structures or patent numbers, or when issuing TYPE commands by record accession number.

Access via the Internet is less expensive than through a commercial public data network ($6/hour as opposed to $12/hour and up for the commercial networks). However, there are trade-offs to be considered before using the Internet as an access point. DIALOG uses a different communications protocol than the Internet. As a result, certain functions either do not work or fail to work reliably. The problems commonly encountered include:

- <backspace> key does not work properly
- <break> key does not work

Users who do not have local access to a node of a commercial public data network may find that the cost differential between Internet access and a long-distance telephone call makes the Internet an attractive alternative. If so, be mindful of the fact that you are not be able to use the <break> key. To avoid problems with the <backspace> key, DIALOG recommends that users type LINEMODE at the telnet prompt prior to connecting to DIALOG.

POWER TOOLS

Duplicate Detection

Command: **RD <set number>** (to remove the duplicates from the set) or **ID <set number>** (to group together records with identical titles).

Duplicate detection searches the records in a set and identifies duplicate citations. It can be used when searching a single file or multiple files. Since it looks for exact title matches only, if one database enhances the title with additional words, both citations are retained. Duplicate detection is supported in about two-thirds of the DIALOG files. If the RD command is applied to a set that includes records from files that do not support duplicate detection, you may see a system message notifying you of this fact. Records from those files are retained in the resulting set and the system scans the remaining records for duplicates.

If two identical citations are detected in a multiple file search, the record from the first file selected is retained. In other words, if you start a search in Files 154 and 72 by typing B 154, 72 and issued the RD command on a retrieved set, the duplicate record from File 154 is retained in the resulting set and the identical record in File 72 is removed from the resulting set. If you are searching a combination of full-text and abstract- or bibliographic citation-only databases, remember to list them in a BEGIN command with the full-text databases first. Otherwise, an RD command could result in a record with only the bibliographic citation being retained instead of the full-text version of the article from another database.

"Finder" Files

DIALOG has developed several files specifically designed to assist searchers in identifying the best files to search. In essence, they are combined indexes of specific fields—the product name fields (PN= , PC=, and SC=) in File 413, the Company Name (CO=) field in File 416 and the Journal Name (JN=) field in File 414. Keep in mind that these finder files are updated monthly and may not include information on recently-added records discussing new companies or products.

When using any of these finder files, be sure to use the EXPAND command, as there is no guarantee of uniformity among files. The EXPAND command gives you a behind-the-scenes look at the database by letting you look at the words in the database that are alphabetically similar to the word you want. For example, if you EXPAND on the company name "Esprit," you see all the different ways in which "Esprit" is listed.

```
? e co=esprit
```

Ref	Items	Index-term
E1	1	CO=ESPRI CONCEPT
E2	1	CO=ESPRI TRAVEL INC
E3	0	*CO=ESPRIT
E4	1	CO=ESPRIT ASIA HOLDINGS
E5	1	CO=ESPRIT COMMUNICATIONS
E6	1	CO=ESPRIT DE CORP GMBH
E7	302	CO=ESPRIT DE CORP.
E8	1	CO=ESPRIT DE CORP. ESPRIT COLLECTION
E9	2	CO=ESPRIT DE CORP. ESPRIT KIDS
E10	1	CO=ESPRIT DE CORPS KIDS
E11	2	CO=ESPRIT ELECTRONICS
E12	1	CO=ESPRIT EUROPE
E13	1	CO=ESPRIT FAR EAST LTD.
E14	2	CO=ESPRIT INC.
E15	5	CO=ESPRIT INTERNATIONAL DIV.
E16	2	CO=ESPRIT KIDS

...

DIALOG Product Name Finder (File 413): This file provides pointers to which DIALOG files have "product name" fields in which a certain product name appears. These include Product Name (PN=), Product Code (PC=), and Standard Industrial Classification Code (SC=). You can search for a specific trade name such as "Alpo" or for a generic product such as "dog food." As with the other finder files, keep in mind that this file only includes databases with product name indexes. Some files such as PR Newswire and Newsletter Database do not assign product name fields, so they are not included in this finder file.

Use the preformatted [Report Product] (report s1/product) for a tabular display of results. Following is the result of a search for dog food listings (s dog()food). Note the mix of entries for both specific trade names and for the generic subject "dog food."

DIALOG(R)File   413:DIALOG Product Name Finder(TM)
              (c) 1995 Knight-Ridder Info All rts. reserv.

191 Products Available

	Product	File Number	Type	Record Count
1	ALPO CANNED DOG FOOD	570	BIBLIOGRAPHIC	1
2	ALPO CANNED DOG FOOD - CHUNKY BEEF & CHICKEN	570	BIBLIOGRAPHIC	1
3	ALPO CANNED DOG FOOD - CHUNKY CHICKEN DINNER	570	BIBLIOGRAPHIC	1
4	ALPO DOG FOOD	570	BIBLIOGRAPHIC	1
5	ALPO DRY DOG FOOD	570	BIBLIOGRAPHIC	1
6	ALPO DRY DOG FOOD - SENIOR	570	BIBLIOGRAPHIC	1
...				
23	CANNED DOG FOOD	18	BIBLIOGRAPHIC	33
24	CANNED DOG FOOD	148	BIBLIOGRAPHIC	2
25	CANNED DOG FOOD	570	BIBLIOGRAPHIC	1
26	CANNED DOG FOOD	211	BIBLIOGRAPHIC	1
27	CANNED DOG FOOD	16	FULLTEXT	112
28	CANNED DOG FOOD	648	FULLTEXT	2
29	CANNED DOG FOOD	621	FULLTEXT	1
30	CANNED DOG FOOD	83	NUMERIC	2
31	CANNED DOG FOOD	81	NUMERIC	2
32	CAT AND DOG FOOD CANNING AND DOSING MACHINE	592	DIRECTORY	1
33	CHAPPI PARTNERS DOG FOOD - LEICHTER	570	BIBLIOGRAPHIC	1
...				

DIALOG Company Name Finder (File 416): This file contains the entries for all company name indexes in DIALOG files that include a company name field. This file enables searchers to identify quickly which files contain information on a specific company without incurring connect charges in a number of different files. There is no attempt at standardization among files, so be sure to scan for abbreviations and alternate spellings that might be used in different databases. For example, John Brown Company might be listed as CO=JOHN BROWN CO in one file, CO=BROWN, JOHN CO in a second, and CO=J BROWN in a third file. Remember, too, that this file only includes indexes to files that contain a company name field. The company may also be covered in other files, including PAPERS, Newsletter Database, and wire services, that do not have a CO= field.

Take advantage of File 416's preformatted [Company Report] option (report s1/company) to display the retrieved material in tabular format and to automatically begin the search in the selected files. The [Company Report] format lists company name, file in which the record appears, format of the file (directory, full-text articles, financial record, patent, and so on), and the number of records in the file that contain that company name.

DIALOG Journal Name Finder (File 414): This file consists of information on which journals, magazines, and newspapers are included in which DIALOG databases. Use this file when you need to search a specific source, or to confirm whether the record format in a specific file is full-text or limited to bibliographic citations. DIALOG has a preformatted [Report] available for a very readable display of search results. After searching for a journal title (e.g., s jn=newsweek), display the results with the command report s1/journal. The resulting table lists the files that have a journal name field with the value "NEWSWEEK," indicates whether the file is full-text or only bibliographic cites, and lists the current number of records from *Newsweek* in each file.

```
File 414:      DIALOG Journal Name Finder(TM) 1995/Dec
               (c) 1995 Knight-Ridder Info

        Set       Items     Description
        -------------------------------------
? s jn=newsweek
        S1        40        .IN=NEWSWEEK
? report s1/journal
        S2        40        Sort 1/ALL/JN,TY,D,RC,D
        DIALOG(R)File 414:DIALOG Journal Name Finder(TM)
        (c) 1995 Knight-Ridder Info All rts. reserv.
```

40 Journals Available

	Journal	File Number	Type	Record Count
1	NEWSWEEK	47	FULLTEXT	39554
2	NEWSWEEK	149	FULLTEXT	1684
3	NEWSWEEK	16	FULLTEXT	1329
4	NEWSWEEK	148	FULLTEXT	761
5	NEWSWEEK	485	FULLTEXT	360
6	NEWSWEEK	15	FULLTEXT	76
7	NEWSWEEK	88	BIBLIOGRAPHIC	39498
8	NEWSWEEK	484	BIBLIOGRAPHIC	15473
9	NEWSWEEK	262	BIBLIOGRAPHIC	13994
10	NEWSWEEK	137	BIBLIOGRAPHIC	6324
11	NEWSWEEK	18	BIBLIOGRAPHIC	1808
12	NEWSWEEK	151	BIBLIOGRAPHIC	294

...

ADDITIONAL POWER SEARCH TOOLS

ADD

Command: **add [file number, file number]**

When searching multiple files (see ONESEARCH, which follows), you can add additional files to the OneSearch session. This command is helpful if you begin a search in a new file, then realize after a few searches that you need to bring in additional sources. ADD allows you to retain the search sets and any "kept" records from the original search, while including new files in the remainder of the OneSearch. Use REPEAT (see the following) to rerun the previously created search statements on the full set of files.

MAP

Command: **map [field name] [temp] [set number]**

This command creates a temporary or permanent saved search consisting of the terms in the specified field in the specified set. It is most often used to extract terms from records and then search on those extracted terms. Uses for the MAP command include selecting companies by name in a Dun & Bradstreet directory file, saving the DUNS number with MAP, and then executing the resulting set in a database of articles that also uses the DUNS number as a searchable field, or to search for a specific patent and then retrieve all the referenced patents listed in the original patent. This is one of the few DIALOG commands that is not particularly intuitive—I recommend you review your MAP search strategy with DIALOG's customer service department if you are not familiar with MAPping.

ONESEARCH

Command: **b nn,nn,nn** (where nn is the file number)

OneSearch is the ability to search multiple DIALOG files simultaneously. Combined with the RD (remove duplicates) command, this enables searchers to search more efficiently and cost-effectively than searching each file individually. Searching multiple files means that the search needs to be typed in only once and the retrieved documents can be reviewed together. You are charged for the connect time actually spent in each file. Be sure that you are combining similar types of files—a OneSearch search in a bibliographic file and a company directory file results in misleading results, for example. Also, be cautious of using controlled vocabulary terms in OneSearch. A search for the subject term "AIDS" may result in many records in one database, but no hits in a second file that uses the subject term "Acquired Immune Deficiency Syndrome."

RANK

Command: **rank [set number]/[all][item numbers]/[field name(s)]**

RANK provides a statistical analysis of search results by tabulating the frequency of occurrence of terms. For example, you might run a quick search of articles with a key phrase in the title (s adult()literacy/ti) and then have the subject terms RANKed to identify what subject terms are most commonly used in the retrieved records. This provides you with a good idea of what subject terms are likely to retrieve other relevant articles on adult literacy. This command can also be used to obtain a count of the number of companies headquartered in each state, for example, or the number of patents on a specific type of product held by competitors.

```
? s adult()literacy/ti
          10469     ADULT/TI
           6392     LITERACY/TI (ABILITY TO READ AND WRITE — ALSO,
                    COMMUNICA...)
     S1     679     ADULT()LITERACY/TI
? rank s1/1-100/de
Completed Ranking 100 records
DIALOG RANK Results
-------------------
RANK: S1//1-100 Field: /DE File(s): 1
(Rank fields found in 100 records -- 323 unique terms)

RANK      No.Items
No.        Ranked     Term
---------------
1             92      ADULT LITERACY
2             49      ADULT BASIC EDUCATION
3             42      LITERACY EDUCATION
4             32      FOREIGN COUNTRIES
5             20      ADULT EDUCATION
6             13      ADULT READING PROGRAMS
7             13      TEACHING METHODS
8             11      FUNCTIONAL LITERACY
...
```

REPEAT

Command: repeat

Use this command in conjunction with ADD when using OneSearch. For example, you can start a search in three regional newspapers for information on a local company. You realize that the company has been very active in a new technology; perhaps some of the industry publications have covered this new development. You ADD three more files of trade and industry publications. Now you want to rerun the search statements already executed on the full set of files. REPEAT re-executes the search sets, beginning the numbering from Set 1. See Figure 11.

REPORT

Command: report [set number]/[field(s)]/[item numbers]

Report produces a compact tabular display of information from a search set, extracting only the specific fields you need. This command works in databases with set-length fields such as directory files. DIALOG also has preformatted Reports available for specific files. For example, report sn/titles generates a nicely formatted display of titles, dates, and report numbers in the market research files (Files 545, 761 through 766). Check the *Bluesheet* documentation to determine the availability of the REPORT command and for a list of the REPORTable fields in the file you are using.

FIGURE 11
ADD and REPEAT Commands

```
?b papersca current2
SYSTEM:OS  - DIALOG OneSearch
      File 496:The Sacramento Bee  1988-1995/Sep 12
              (c) 1995 Sacramento Bee
      File 630:Los Angeles Times  1985-1995/Sep 13
              (c) 1995 Los Angeles Times
      File 634:San Jose Mercury  Jun 1985-1995/Sep 06
              (c) 1995 San Jose Mercury News
      File 640:San Francisco Chronicle  1988-1995/Sep 12
              (c) 1995 Chronicle Publ. Co.
      File 716:Daily News Of L.A.  1989-1995/Sep 07
              (c) 1995 Daily News of Los Angeles
      File 732:San Francisco Exam.  1990-1995/Sep 11
              (c) 1995 San Francisco Examiner
      File 739:The Fresno Bee  1990-1995/Sep 12
              (c) 1995 The Fresno Bee
>>>CURRENT2 started


Set       Items        Description
------------------------------
?s raychem/ti
          S1            26        RAYCHEM/TI
?s s1 and (fiberoptic? ? or fiber()optic? ?)
                        26        S1
                        29        FIBEROPTIC? ?
                        6356      FIBER
                        2164      OPTIC? ?
                        1711      FIBER(W)OPTIC? ?
          S2            5         S1 AND (FIBEROPTIC? ? OR FIBER()OPTIC? ?)
?add 636 148
SYSTEM:OS - DIALOG OneSearch
You have 9 files in your file list.
(To see file names, coverage dates, and copyright notices, enter SHOW FILES.)
>>>CURRENT2 started


        Set       Items      Description
        ------------------------
        
Added File(s): 636, 148
Previous sets have been retained; enter DISPLAY SETS to view them.
?repeat
          S1            147       RAYCHEM/TI
                        147       S1
                        729       FIBEROPTIC? ?
                        44416     FIBER
                        26580     OPTIC? ?
                        19275     FIBER(W)OPTIC? ?
          S2            44        S1 AND (FIBEROPTIC? ? OR FIBER()OPTIC? ?)
```

SAVE TEMP

Command: **save temp**

This command saves all search steps since a b nn (begin file) command was issued. DIALOG assigns a SearchSave number to the search strategy and retains it for seven days. To run the saved search again, type exs <SearchSave number> and DIALOG executes all search steps. Use SAVE TEMP when you have refined a search and want to repeat it in other files. Search strategies can also be saved permanently with the SAVE command.

SET
Command: set <option>

The SET command lets you customize your DIALOG session in a number of ways. Some of the most commonly-used SET commands are:

set hilight <character>	lets you highlight the search terms in the retrieved documents. set hilight * would mark each occurrence of a *search* *term*
set kwic n	sets the number of words displayed at either side of the search term in a Keyword-in-Context display
set notice $n	tells DIALOG that you want a cost estimate before a TYPE, PRINT, or DISPLAY command executes if it would exceed a specified amount
set subacct <name>	lets you track your online costs for a search. Your invoice has a special report for the costs incurred for each subaccount

SORT
Command: sort Sn/all/<field>

Use SORT to rearrange the records in a search set by a specific field or fields, such as author (in bibliographic files), revenue (in company directory files), and so on. For example:

sort s1/all/au,ti	to create a list of articles, sorted by author then title
sort s1/all/sa,d	to list companies by sales in descending order
sort s1/all/wd,d	to sort articles by word count with longest articles first

TARGET
Command: target

TARGET is an alternate to traditional Boolean (AND, OR, NOT) searching. It is best used when you are looking for "a few good articles" rather than doing a comprehensive search for everything written on a topic. You type in the words or phrases to search, indicating which ones are critical and *must* be present in the retrieved records. DIALOG uses a proprietary relevance-ranking algorithm to analyze the retrieved records, and then sorts them into a set of the 50 most relevant ones. You can browse the resulting set and display the full text of the records you need, or further modify the search. See Figure 12 for an example of a TARGET search.

FIGURE 12
TARGET Search

?target
Input search terms separated by spaces (e.g., DOG CAT FOOD). You can enhance your TARGET search with the following options:
- PHRASES are enclosed in single quotes
    (e.g., 'DOG FOOD')
- SYNONYMS are enclosed in parentheses
    (e.g., (DOG CANINE))
- SPELLING variations are indicated with a ?
    (e.g., DOG? to search DOG, DOGS)
- Terms that MUST be present are flagged with an asterisk
    (e.g., DOG *FOOD)

Q = QUIT   H = HELP

? 'genetic engineering' *strawberries
Your TARGET search request will retrieve up to 50 of the statistically most relevant records.
Searching 1993-1995 records only
...Processing Complete
    Your search retrieved 50 records.
Press ENTER to browse results C = Customize display Q = QUIT H = HELP
?
DIALOG-TARGET RESULTS (arranged by percent RELEVANCE)
———— Item: 1 -------------------------------------
DIALOG(R)File 16:(c) 1995 Information Access Co. All rts. reserv.

BUILDING A BETTER SNACK

Snack Food   May 1995
----- Item: 2-------------------------------------
DIALOG(R)File 148:(c) 1995 Info Access Co. All rts. reserv.

For a stronger fruit industry. (Column)
Agricultural Research
Nov, 1993
---- Item: 3 -------------------------------------
DIALOG(R)File 148:(c) 1995 Info Access Co. All rts. reserv.

Fruit that swim? (*genetic* *engineering*)
Financial World
June 7, 1994
--- Item: 4 -------------------------------------
DIALOG(R)File 148:(c) 1995 Info Access Co. All rts. reserv.

Small fruits make it big.
Agricultural Research
Oct, 1994
---- Item: 5 -------------------------------------
DIALOG(R)File 148:(c) 1995 Info Access Co. All rts. reserv.

Supercows and flounder berries. (innovations in agricultural biotechnology)
(includes related article on *genetic* *engineering* of female corn earworms)
Industry Week
Dec 6, 1993

TARGET can also be used to home in on the most relevant articles in an existing set of records. For example, you might run a search for specific subject terms, limit that to full-text records only, then run TARGET on the resulting set. The syntax is target sn (where sn is the search set number).

The following DIALOG publications provide helpful information on how to get the most out of DIALOG's search tools.

"10 Tips to Cut Time & Save Money: DIALOG Cost Management & Support Tools"
    DIALOG publication 800075
"10 Tips to Cut Time & Save Money: DIALOG Search Features"
    DIALOG publication 800073
"Getting Started on DIALOG: a Guide to Searching"
    DIALOG publication 0610011-1
"DIALOG Pocket Guide"
    DIALOG publication 0800002-8
"Super Searching: Tips for Power, Precision, Performance"
    DIALOG publication 800017

DIALOG also offers publications for specific commands such as TARGET, RANK, and REPORT TITLES. Request item 4000 from the ASAF service for a list of system documentation materials available via fax.

PRICING

DIALOG charges a yearly maintenance fee of $75 and an initial set-up fee of $295. Users are charged for connect time and per record displayed or printed. Most databases fall into one of five price "bins," set at $15, $30, $60, $90, and $120 per hour. Per-record charges range from free (usually for indexing and title displays) to $35 or more. Most databases that consist of full-text articles charge around $2 per full-text record.

DIALOG also offers two flat-fee pricing plans, the Open Access Plan and the Budget Plan. If you have a fairly predictable usage pattern and use DIALOG frequently (or would, given a favorable pricing structure), you might benefit from one of these plans.

Open Access Plan

Fixed monthly fee that covers all connect time and telecommunications charges and DIALMAIL. User pays output (per record) charges. Renegotiated yearly.

Budget Plan

Fixed monthly fee that covers all connect time and telecommunications charges, DIALMAIL and output (per record) charges (with a ceiling on usage—not completely unlimited access). Renegotiated yearly.

OTHER DIALOG FEATURES

One of the principals of copyright law is that, with electronic versions of articles as with print versions, you are not permitted to make multiple copies without paying a royalty fee to the copyright holder (except within the bounds of "fair use"). DIALOG was the first major online service to offer a simple method of paying for multiple copies of an article, either for redistribution within an organization or for archiving in an electronic format. **ERA (Electronic Redistribution and Archiving)** pricing allows you to electronically purchase rights to extra "copies" of an article at a fraction of the cost you would pay to download the article the specified number of times. The multiplier ranges from three times the cost of a single record (for 15 copies) to 14 times the cost of a single record (for unlimited copies within an organization).

DIALOG offers a one-way listserv via the Internet. At this point, traffic on it is light; you can subscribe without fear of having your electronic mailbox overwhelmed with messages. To subscribe, send an electronic mail message to majordomo@www.dialog.com. In the text of the message, type subscribe dialog-info.

Search output options include display on the screen, mail delivery of printed copies, delivery via facsimile, or electronic delivery. DIALOG's internal electronic mail system, DIAL-MAIL, can be used for delivery, or the results can be sent to other electronic mail systems. Electronic mail delivery is usually within two to four hours. A nice "oops" feature is the opportunity to cancel your print command within 30 minutes after issuance of the command. On the other hand, if you want your information sooner, you can override the 30-minute hold. After issuing a PRINT VIA FAX or PRINT VIA ELECTRONIC MAIL command, type send and the print command is executed immediately rather than being held for 30 minutes.

DIALOG's **Alert** service enables searches to be re-run automatically every day, week, or month in most regularly updated databases. Once the search is saved and the frequency and delivery options specified, the search is run against the records added to the database since the last Alert. The resulting records are delivered via DIALMAIL or other Internet-addressable electronic mail system, via fax, or by first class mail.

Cost estimates are provided automatically when the user ends a session or changes databases. Search costs can be displayed during the search session with the COST command.

Training is available at regional DIALOG offices throughout the world. A one-day system seminar for new users is available for a fee. Search technique and subject-specific training sessions are also offered on a regular basis. New subscribers can also request a temporary password to provide free access to a number of training files on DIALOG.

Online help is available at any prompt. You can request help on a specific command (e.g., help target), or on a specific database (e.g., help file 100 or help field 100), or for the rates for a specific file (e.g., help rates 100).

EVALUATION OF DIALOG

DIALOG is one of the oldest online services and one of the most robust. It uses a fairly arcane command language (who would think that b 100 would be the command to start a search?), but it also offers a number of search tools unavailable anywhere else. In short, DIALOG is a professional searcher's online service.

DIALOG offers excellent coverage of news sources, medical and scientific literature, company information, and industry news. Although most databases are created in and focus on the U.S., DIALOG has broadened its sources in the past few years and offers a number of files that cover non-U.S. news and companies as well.

DIALOG has attempted to make it easier for new and infrequent searchers to use the system. Menus are now available to walk the searcher through the search and display process. However, most documentation, online help, and training courses assume that the user is using commands rather than menus to navigate the system. To get the best value for the cost on DIALOG, users do need to become comfortable with DIALOG's command language.

What do I like most about DIALOG?

- I like the many (often free or low-cost) update sessions available locally. DIALOG adds new features and files frequently and I appreciate the chance to update my search repertoire with these short training courses.

- I like the EXPAND command, which allows me to go behind the scenes and see word variants and misspellings.

- I like DIALOG's power search tools—RANK, SORT, TARGET, OneSearch, duplicate detection, and MAP—and preformatted reports.

- I like the ability to SET so many of my profile parameters—notification of any print command costing more than $XX, predefined print formats, and prompting for a billing subaccount code.

- I like having search sets I can combine and re-use. Many online services do not allow searchers to reference prior search statements and this is one of the best ways to tweak a search until you get just what you want out of the database.

What do I like least about DIALOG?

- I wish there was a more friendly front end for DIALOG. The menus don't offer a cost-effective option for inexperienced or infrequent searchers, and the learning curve to efficient use of DIALOG is too steep for the occasional searcher. Knight-Ridder is working on developing an interface for new users, to be released some time in 1996.

- I wish DIALOG had an across-the-board "free" format similar to its sister company DataStar. Although many of the bibliographic files in DIALOG have made formats 6 and 8 (title and title/indexing terms respectively) free, this is not true with the nonbibliographic files. I find it particularly annoying to be searching a file I'm not as familiar with and having to scramble to look up the *Bluesheet* to find out how to print out records in a free format.

Dow Jones News/Retrieval

CONTACT INFORMATION

NAME   Dow Jones & Company, Inc.

ADDRESS   P.O. Box 300
                            Princeton, NJ 08543-0300

TELEPHONE   609/452-1511

CUSTOMER   Monday through Friday 8:00am - midnight Eastern time
SERVICE HOURS   Saturday 9:00am - 6:00pm Eastern time

EMAIL   through Internet: djnr.support@cor.dowjones.com

WEB HOME PAGE   http://bis.dowjones.com/djnr.html

SERVICE   24 hours a day; 7 days a week
AVAILABILITY

DESCRIPTION OF INFORMATION AVAILABLE

Dow Jones News/Retrieval (DJN/R) focuses on business and financial information resources—not a surprise as it is produced by the publishers of the *Wall Street Journal*. In addition to the full text and abstracts of articles from about 2,000 magazines, newspapers, newsletters, and regional business journals, DJN/R has newswire stories, an extensive database of current and historical stock quotes from U.S. and foreign companies and mutual funds, and company financial information. You navigate through DJN/R by a series of menus (in terminal or plain ASCII mode) or by clicking on [Menu Choices] (with DJN/R proprietary software).

Access to Dow Jones publications—*Wall Street Journal, Barron's* and the Dow Jones newswires—is available exclusively on DJN/R. (Prodigy provides access to the current two weeks of Dow Jones wires, but has no back files.) DJN/R also offers same-day full-text coverage of the *New York Times* (with back files of the most recent 90 days and selected articles dating back to 1980), the *Financial Times* of London, and the *Los Angeles Times*.

DJN/R's primary database of articles is the Text Library and its primary database of newswire stories is WIRES. There is a fair amount of overlap between these two; the past few months' of the *Wall Street Journal* and several other newspapers, Dow Jones newswires, and press releases are available in both databases.

ROADMAP OF RESOURCES

Dow Jones News/Retrieval organizes its services into large groupings—Industry News, Quotes and Market Data, Electronic Clipping Service, and so on. Oddly, the service groupings in the initial terminal mode (plain ASCII) menu are different from those in the initial screen of the DJN/R software. See Figure 13 for the terminal mode main screen. See Figure 14 for the DJN/R software main menu. (Dow Jones will roll out a redesigned version of the DJN/R software by the end of 1996. This version, 5.0, is expected to have a more intuitive interface than the most current version as of early 1996, v3.2.)

Following are the groupings of services listed in the main menus of the terminal mode and DJN/R software:

- The terminal mode menu lists two headlines from today's news, which you can select by number. In the DJN/R software menu, the headlines appear in a special box; click on the [News] menu item to select either of these headlines.

- Business & World Wires (DJN/R software menu only)—search newswire stories by subject or industry, ticker symbol, company name, or by specific wire service.

- Clipping Service (terminal mode) or Dow Jones CustomClips (DJN/R software menu)—electronic clipping service scans most DJN/R news sources and selects items matching the search words you specify.

- Company News and Information (terminal mode only) gives you a choice of Company News (//COMPANY—stories from the Dow Jones Business Newswires); Current Quotes (//CQE); or Company Reports (//REPORTS—Corporate Ownership Watch, Disclosure, Dun & Bradstreet, Investext, etc.).

FIGURE 13
Terminal Mode Main Menu

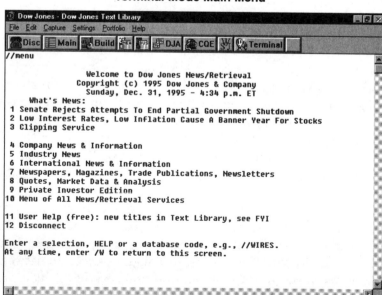

FIGURE 14
DJN/R Software Main Menu

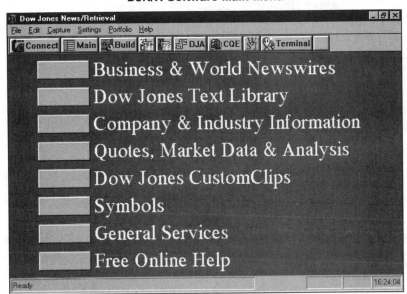

- Industry News (terminal mode only) contains stories from the Dow Jones Business Newswires, broken out by broad industry category (consumer cyclical, consumer non-cyclical, technology, utilities, and so on).

NOTE: In DJN/R software, the preceding two selections are combined in a single menu option, Company & Industry Information. If you select this option, you see a second menu of company report options. Curiously, you cannot access the newswires or current quotes directly from this option; it includes only the options listed under the //REPORTS menu.

- International News & Information (terminal mode only) brings up a submenu of international newswires, WORLDSCOPE, other sources for company financial information, and the TEXT library.

- Newspapers, Magazines, Trade Publications, Newsletters (terminal mode) or Dow Jones Text Library (DJN/R software) brings up a submenu of //TEXT, //TEXTM (the same Text Library, but with more limited search options for the new user), and //CLIP.

- Quotes, Market Data & Analysis (in both terminal mode and DJN/R software) brings up a submenu of stock quote services, market analyses from Innovest and MMS, and Wall $treet Week Online.

- Private Investor Edition (terminal only) brings up submenus for news, stock quotes, market analyses, and the Text Library. Most of the services listed in this option are available through other main menu options as well.

- Symbols (DJN/R software only) lets you look up the market symbol for stocks, bonds, mutual funds, and the Dow Jones Industry Codes used to code articles in

WIRES and TEXT. This option is also available through the DJN/R software under the Free Online Help option.

- General Services (DJN/R software only) gives you a submenu of other DJN/R services such as book and movie reviews, an encyclopedia, a gateway to MCI Mail, sports and weather news, and so on.

- Free Online Help (DJN/R software) or User Help (terminal mode) gives you submenus to the online user guide, online newsletter, invoice information, and the LOGIT function, which lets you indicate a client or charge-back code for the current online session, to appear on the invoice.

TIPS FOR USING DJN/R'S FINDING AIDS

One of the more useful, albeit confusing, features of DJN/R is its bundling of information services. Among the most valuable of these groupings are QuickSearch, Business & Finance Report, and the Dow Jones World Report.

- QuickSearch can be accessed by typing //QUICK in terminal mode or by clicking on the [Company & Industry Information] option on the DJN/R software main menu, then selecting [Quick]. You type in a company name or stock symbol; for privately-held companies, you can only search by company name. QuickSearch presents you with nine report sections from which you can select. For example, a search in QuickSearch for General Mills results in the following menu:

```
                    DOW JONES QUICKSEARCH
             GENERAL MILLS INC.

PRESS           FOR

  1        CURRENT QUOTES
  2        LATEST NEWS ON GIS
  3        FINANCIAL AND MARKET OVERVIEW
  4        EARNINGS ESTIMATES
  5        COMPANY VS INDUSTRY PERFORMANCE
  6        INCOME STATEMENTS, BAL SHEETS
  7        COMPANY PROFILE
  8        INSIDER TRADING SUMMARY
  9        INVESTMENT RESEARCH REPORTS
------------------------------------------------------------------
```

You can order the entire report for a flat fee of $49 or you can order individual sections of the QuickSearch report. If you order separate sections, you are charged for the information units displayed ($1.50 for every 1,000 characters) plus per-section charges for sections 3, 6, 7, 8, or 9. Unless you only need one or two sections, it may be more cost-effective to order the entire report. The information in the QuickSearch report is compiled from a number of DJN/R sources including Standard & Poor's, Dow Jones stock quotes, Media General, Disclosure, and Investext.

- The Business & Finance Report can be accessed by typing //BUSINESS in terminal mode. You can select it through the DJN/R software within the Business & World Newswires, but it takes several menu selections to get to the search menu.

Fortunately, the default settings for the DJN/R software include a small icon on the tool bar of a man holding the business section of a newspaper. Click on that icon and you are at the main Business & Finance Report menu. Following is the terminal mode version of the main //BUSINESS menu:

```
        BUSINESS AND FINANCE REPORT
        FRONT PAGE AT 11:59 P.M. FRIDAY
        COPYRIGHT (C) 1995 DOW JONES & CO.
PRESS FOR
1   McDonnell Douglas Sells Pentagon
            $18 Billion Of C-17 Transports
2   Barron's: Soros Continually
            Proves To Be A Savvy Investor
3   Straight-Forward Stock Picking
            Can Be Road To Simple Success
4   Technology Roundup: Apple Reaches
            Licensing Pacts With Two Firms
5   Business News In //NEWS, //WIRES
-------------------------------------------
N   ADDITIONAL BUSINESS NEWS
F   FINANCIAL NEWS & STATISTICS
J   ALL STREET JOURNAL HIGHLIGHTS
```

The DJN/R software contains the same information; each option is a button to click instead of a number or letter to type.

In addition to providing you with the top business news headlines (and the option to display the full text of the stories), //BUSINESS provides access to the top 10 to 15 stories from the last five issues of the *Wall Street Journal*. This is one instance where using the DJN/R software is much easier than terminal mode. If you select "Wall Street Journal Highlights," the DJN/R software displays the headlines and you can simply click on the article you want. In terminal mode, you get the following instructions on how to obtain the full text of a headlined story:

```
(For stories, enter //TEXTM 1 (Return), then enter the number that appears in parentheses after the headline
you want and follow the instructions to display the story.)
                PAGE ONE
    In a signal to Japan, U.S. bars Daiwa Bank and indicts institution. (951103-0066)
...
```

In other words, once you see a headline you want, you must type //TEXTM 1, then type in the ten-digit number, e.g., 951103-0066, to display the story.

- The Dow Jones World Report can be accessed by typing //NEWS in terminal mode. The World Report is most easily available on DJN/R software by clicking on the small icon on the tool bar that has a picture of a man with the news section of a newspaper.

The top menu of the World Report lists the headlines of five breaking national and international news stories along with headlines of 5 to 15 additional national news and international news stories. The full text of each story is available by typing or

FIGURE 15
Dow Jones World Report (//NEWS) Menu

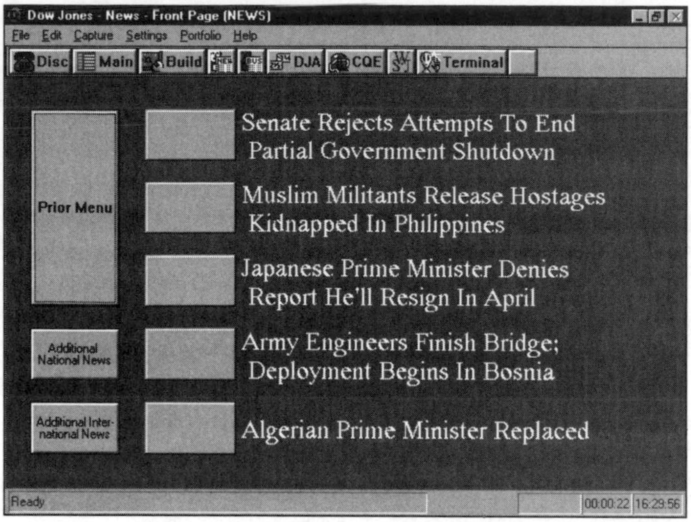

Dow Jones - News - Front Page [NEWS]

File Edit Capture Settings Portfolio Help

Disc   Main   Build   DJA   CQE   Terminal

Prior Menu

Senate Rejects Attempts To End
Partial Government Shutdown

Muslim Militants Release Hostages
Kidnapped In Philippines

Japanese Prime Minister Denies
Report He'll Resign In April

Additional
National News

Army Engineers Finish Bridge;
Deployment Begins In Bosnia

Additional Inter-
national News

Algerian Prime Minister Replaced

Ready   00:00:22 16:29:56

clicking on the number corresponding to that story. See Figure 15 for the top World Report menu through the DJN/R software.

Be aware of the overlap of sources among DJN/R services. As noted earlier, QuickSearch compiles information from a number of sources; if you ordered a QuickSearch report and then searched the newswires for recent news, you would wind up paying for the same information twice. Likewise, if you search the press release wires in the Text Library, be careful if you then run a search in the WIRES (//WIRES or Business & World Newswires). Unless you specifically eliminate the press release wires from that subsequent search, you may be looking at (and paying for) the same material twice.

Many professional online searchers use DJN/R only for the Text Library and the wire services. DJN/R is also a source for a variety of investment-related information. It offers access to several Dun & Bradstreet files, the Disclosure SEC Database and SEC Online, corporate profiles from Media General and Standard & Poor's, and the Corporate Ownership Watch, which tracks insider trading activity.

DJN/R also offers current and historical quotes and averages, a tracking service that monitors news and quotes on up to 125 companies in your portfolio, and foreign exchange rates. The Tradeline service contains 20 years of historical information on stocks, bonds, mutual funds, and indexes. Since these resources are menu-driven, they are particularly easy to use for the occasional searcher.

Although you can access any of DJN/R's services through the menus, in terminal mode you can also go directly to any service by typing //[access code]—e.g., //WIRES to get to the newswires, //TEXT to search the Text Library, or //HQ to search historical stock quotes. Once you become familiar with DJN/R's services, you may want to sidestep the DJN/R software menus and go directly to the terminal mode commands. From within the DJN/R software, you can either click on [Terminal] from the [Settings] pull-down menu or add an icon to the tool bar that lets you toggle between Terminal and DJN/R software mode. See "POWER TOOLS," later in this section, for details on customizing the tool bar.

Commonly-Used Commands

Begin a search	**//[access code]** e.g, //TEXT
Search terms:	
x AND y	x **AND** y
x OR y	x **OR** y
x BUT NOT y	x **NOT** y
x NEXT TO y	x y
	x **W/1** y (x must precede y)
	a **NEAR1** b (x next to y, in either order)
x WITHIN n WORDS OF y	x **W/n** y or x **ADJn** y (x must precede and be within n words of y)
	x **NEARn** y (x within n words of y in either order)
x SAME SENTENCE y	not specifically available—use x **NEAR15** y
x SAME PARAGRAPH y	x **same** y
x SAME FIELD y	not available
Date Searching	**YYMMDD.PD.**
	PD=YYMMDD
	DATE [AFTER] MM/DD/YY
	DATE FROM MM/DD/YY TO MM/DD/YY
Field Searching	**word.co.** or **word.hl,lp.**
Truncation	**word$n** (word with up to n additional letters)
	word??? (word with *exactly* 3 additional letters)
	w?rd (to retrieve w**a**rd, w**o**rd)
Display results	**DISPLAY 1-3,5** (display records 1-3, 5 in complete format)
	DISPLAY BIBLIO 1-3 (display bibliographic citation for records 1-3)
	DISPLAY=5 hit 1,3 (display records 1 and 3 from search set 5 in Keyword-in-Context format)
	DISPLAY 1,3 hl,pd (display headlines and dates for records 1 and 3)

Commonly-Used Commands (continued)

	Use **PAGE** command instead of **DISPLAY** for page-by-page viewing

Help   **//GUIDE** (for online manual)
[**Carriage Return**] at any menu (for context-sensitive help)

Cost:

for session charges up to this point   **//USAGE** (see note which follows). Be careful; this command moves you out of whatever information source you were in and discontinues your search.

for database rates   **//GUIDE**

for total cost when logging off   **//USAGE** (see note which follows)

Log off   **DISC** or **LOGOFF**

Note: //USAGE displays the total number of information units (see "PRICING," later in this section), but does not calculate any special fees incurred.

GETTING CONNECTED

via Tymnet: Please log in: **dow1;;** [No Carriage Return]
         What service please? **djns**

via Sprintnet: **@dow**
         What service please? **djns**

via Internet: **telnet djnr.dowjones.com**
         What service please? **djns**

You can also access Dow Jones through MCI Mail; type dow at the Command: prompt. Your DJN/R charges appear on your MCI Mail invoice.

DJN/R supports speeds from 1200bps through 14400bps. Modem settings should be:
TTY emulation
FULL duplex
1 stop bit, 7 data bits, even parity OR 1 stop bit, 8 data bits, no parity

In addition to plain ASCII dial-up access, DJN/R provides a point-and-click software package for users who prefer this type of interface. Both Windows and Mac versions are available from DJN/R customer service. When in the DJN/R software, you can drop into terminal (plain ASCII) mode by pulling down the [Settings] menu and selecting [Terminal].

System requirements for DJN/R software:
IBM-compatible PC running Windows 3.1 or OS/2 2.1 or higher OR Macintosh
5MB free disk space

POWER TOOLS

DJN/R's primary information resource for most online researchers is the Text Library, available by typing //TEXT or //TEXTM in terminal mode or clicking on the [Dow Jones Text Library] menu option on DJN/R software. It contains full-text articles and abstracts from about 2,000 publications. The database can be searched with Boolean logic in command mode or with menu-driven options.

//TEXT (or the "Text Search with Windows Menus" option in the DJN/R software) is the most straightforward method of searching the Text Library. The terminal mode main //TEXT menu appears as follows:

DOW JONES TEXT LIBRARY
Copyright (c) 1995 Dow Jones & Co.

Major News Publications	Business Newswires
1 The Wall Street Journal	13 Dow Jones News Service
2 The New York Times	14 PIR, CMR, Federal Filings
3 The Washington Post	15 Press Release Wires
4 Los Angeles Times	
5 The Dallas Morning News	Business & Trade Publications
6 Chicago Tribune	16 Major Business Publications
7 Top U.S. Newspapers (in top 50)	17 Industry & Trade Publications
8 Major News Sources	
U.S. Publications by Region	International Publications
9 Northeast & Mid-Atlantic	18 Newspapers & General Publications
10 South	19 Newswires
11 Midwest	
12 West	

You can select any combination of source groupings. The default is to search the most recent two years of text; to search all years, precede your selection of sources with the word TOTAL. For example, to search all years of major news sources and business and trade publications, type TOTAL 8, 16, 17. DJN/R also has codes for publication groupings, both the ones displayed in this menu and additional groupings, such as all Dow Jones publications (DJPUBS), all energy-related publications (ENERGY), and "small newspapers" (SMALL). In addition, you can select individual sources by their code; if you want to search only *Managed Healthcare News* and *Managed Care Alert*, you would type mhcn, hlmu. Refer to the Publications Directory for the list of publication and group codes.

The DJN/R software TEXT menu is somewhat less straightforward than the terminal mode menu. See Figure 16. The menu does not display all publication groupings on one page and, although it includes additional groupings not displayed on the terminal menu, the list of options is confusing. You select the grouping(s) you want by clicking on their descriptions. To search individual publications, you must go

FIGURE 16
DJN/R Software //TEXT Menu

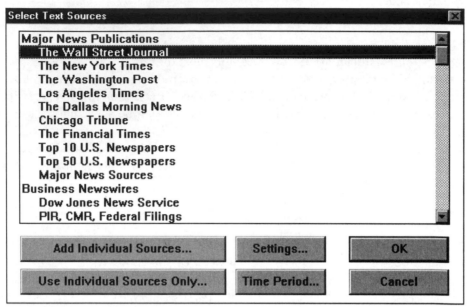

through the list of all 2,000 sources, whereas in terminal mode you can just type in the code for the individual sources you want.

Once you have selected the sources you want searched, you type in your search using DJN/R's connectors (AND, OR, NOT, ADJ, and so on). One nice feature of the DJN/R software's menus is the [Settings] button. You can sort your search results by word count (convenient if what you really want are a few in-depth articles on a topic), by headline, by date, and so on. It is a lot easier to sort by clicking on options than it is to remember the equivalent terminal mode commands, e.g., to sort by word count in descending (i.e., decreasing) order, sort wc d.

Be careful when you display the results of your search. The default display options for the DJN/R software include headline, byline, column, date, full bibliographic citation, and lead paragraph. DJN/R charges you for every character that displays on the screen, so you may want to set the display options to something less character-intensive, say headline, date, and source name. In terminal mode, you can either use a preformatted display option (cite, full, and so on) or you can specify the fields you want displayed (e.g., page hd, pd, sn, cc to display, a page at a time, the headline, publication date, source name and character count for the retrieved articles).

Keep in mind that, before displaying the full text of documents, it's a good idea to display the character count (CC field code) of the items you want. Divide the character count by 1,000 and multiply by $1.50 to determine the cost of the document; this avoids unpleasant surprises when you inadvertently display an article that was much longer than you expected.

The "executive" format is particularly nice if you usually word-process the results of a search to eliminate non-essential elements such as indexing terms and field codes. Following is an example of an article displayed in executive format:

```
              DOCUMENT 2 OF 13 PAGE 1 OF 6
Return to simplicity is growing lifestyle trend
Advocates paring down lives so values, commitment come first
___
MARK GUIDERA
07/30/95
The Star-Ledger Newark, NJ
     Iona and John Conner are downwardly mobile and loving it.
     They have joined the small but growing ranks of Americans
eschewing the pursuit of possessions for what is called "voluntary
simplicity." They have traded secure government jobs, comfortable
homes and a lifetime of collected clutter for pared-down lives.
     "It's good for the Earth and good for the soul," Iona Conner says
of her new life. "I've never been happier."
     The Conners' relatively Spartan lifestyle is taking root even
within the fast-paced, consumption-driven Baltimore-Washington
corridor - a region associated with high ambitions, high incomes and
high costs of living.
     Their two-bedroom Columbia, Md., apartment has no TV, microwave,
...
```

You might want to eliminate that initial line indicating that this is document 2 of 13, but otherwise, this display option gives you a document devoid of those mysterious ISSN numbers, Descriptors, and accession numbers that puzzle nonsearchers.

The //TEXTM version of the Text Library offers very limited search options and should not be used for any but the most straightforward and simple searches. You cannot limit your search terms by field, you cannot use any connectors such as ADJ or NEAR and you cannot combine search sets. Once you have typed in the search terms, your only choices are to display the retrieved documents, delete your last search terms, narrow the search by date, or start a new search. The DJN/R *User's Guide* suggests you use //TEXTM to "do simple searches for background" or "retrieve current and historical information on a subject." I can't see how you could efficiently do either with //TEXTM—an experienced searcher would prefer to use //TEXT. (See Figure 17.)

FIGURE 17
Dow Jones TextM Search

Enter the first word or phrase you want to look for and press (Return).

For example, enter UNITED PARCEL SERVICE (Return) to find all articles
  containing the name of the privately held company.

Enter /HELP (Return) for help, /T (Return) to select a different file.

US WEST appears in 6351 documents.

Add another word or phrase to narrow your search, or

```
Press  to
1      Delete your last search term.
2      Specify or change the dates you want to search.
3      Display the documents found.
4      Start a new search.
```

Enter /HELP (Return) for help.

Your request is being processed; please wait.

US WEST and SERVICE QUALITY appear in 35 documents.

Add another word or phrase to narrow your search, or

```
Press  to
1      Delete your last search term.
2      Specify or change the dates you want to search.
3      Display the documents found.
4      Start a new search.
```

Enter /HELP (Return) for help.

```
Press  to
1      Display the headline and first page of each document.
       You will be able to select documents to display in full.
2      Display the full text of each document.
3      Resume your current search.
4      Start a new search.
```

Enter /HELP (Return) for help.

```
        Document 1 of 35   Page 1 of 26
AN      CGT9610000027
HD      FCC REVISION
BY      REED E. HUNDT
WC      4659 Words
CC      30877 Characters
PD      03/27/96
SN      Congressional Testimony by Federal Document Clearing House
CY      (Copyright 1996 by Federal Document Clearing House, Inc.)
LP
   Statement of Reed E. Hundt
   Chairman Federal Communications Commission
   on Oversight of the FCC
   before the Subcommittee on Telecommunications
   and Finance Committee on Commerce
   U.S. House of Representatives
   March 27, 1996
TD     Good morning Mr. Chairman and Members of the Subcommittee.  Thank
   you for this opportunity to testify before you as part of your
   oversight of the Federal Communications Commission.  We are fortunate
   to be here at a truly historic and exciting moment.  The
```

Enter S to Save, (Return) for next document, X to end review, or /HELP

You can customize the DJN/R software by adding additional service icons to the tool bar along the top of the screen. The first thing I added to my tool bar was an icon to toggle between terminal mode and DJN/R software. If you always want to identify the session by client or billing number, you can add an icon for //LOGIT. If you check your mutual fund regularly, you can set up an icon to go into //CQE and look up the current quote for that mutual fund. You can identify the icon by words (e.g., log-it for the //LOGIT icon) or by a picture. The DJN/R software provides a number of icon images from you can select for each customized service icon, including six different pictures of space aliens. (See upper right icon on Figure 15.)

PRICING

Dow Jones News/Retrieval charges $1.50 for each "information unit," i.e., every 1,000 characters that cross your screen. This includes menus, spaces, and carriage returns as well as the characters within articles or other reports. The Welcome, Guide, and FYI services are free of information unit charges. Unlike many other professional online services, there are no connect-time charges—your invoice is tied directly to the volume of data you receive.

Special fees are charged for a number of DJN/R services. For example, Dun & Bradstreet credit reports cost between $27 and $106 each, depending on the format; company profiles from Disclosure or Standard & Poor's cost $9 per document; stock price tracking services cost between $0.15 and $5 per report.

DJN/R also has a yearly service fee of $19.95. The initial sign-up fee of $29.95 includes the first year's service fee.

OTHER FEATURES

DJN/R offers access to several unique files, most notably the full text of the domestic and international editions of the *Wall Street Journal*. It is also the only online service that carries *Barron's* (another Dow Jones publication), and "Wall $treet Week" transcripts. The Text Library has a wide variety of local newspapers, some of which are available only on DJN/R and DataTimes. Over 60 newspapers are available online on the day of publication.

Prior to 1994, DJN/R and DataTimes offered gateways to each other's systems. DataTimes no longer offers access to Dow Jones, but DJN/R subscribers can still search DataTimes' newspaper files. Unfortunately, this feature is barely mentioned in the DJN/R documentation. Subscribers using terminal mode can search the DataTimes files in the Text Library by using the publication group code DT, e.g., //text dt, to go to the Text Library and begin a search in the DataTimes newspaper files.

DJN/R's **electronic clipping service** is accessed by typing //clips in terminal mode or by clicking on [Dow Jones CustomClips] at the DJN/R software main menu. The process for indicating what news sources to monitor and the search terms to use is menu-driven and straightforward. You name each clipping folder and indicate how you want the clipped articles delivered. You can have the articles held until you have logged on and scanned the headlines, you can have the articles delivered to an Internet-accessible email account, or you can have the articles sent to your fax machine. Oddly, the search commands are slightly different for CustomClips than for regular Text Library searching. For example, to limit a CustomClips search to terms in the headlines, you precede the word with HL/ (e.g., HL/Clinton); to limit the search to certain types of articles in the *Wall Street Journal*, you add J/HST (to limit the search to the "Heard on the Street" column) or J/LMJ (to limit the search to major bylined articles.

DJN/R provides **client code billing** through //LOGIT in terminal mode or by clicking on [LOGIT] from the Free Online Help Menu in DJN/R software. When you select [LOGIT], you are prompted for a client name, project number, or other code of up to 25 characters. Your monthly invoice shows the total charges for each LOGIT code you assigned during an online session. You can request that your account be set to require a LOGIT code when you sign on; this feature must be set by contacting DJN/R Customer Service.

DJN/R offers beginning and advanced training sessions in major cities in the U.S. and selected cities abroad.

Dow Jones produces a four-page monthly subscriber newsletter called *Dowline*, primarily directed to the information needs of users in the investment and business community. DJN/R expects to begin producing a new quarterly magazine some time in 1996, focusing on the needs and interests of professional online searchers.

DJN/R also offers an online newsletter, *FYI*, accessible by typing //FYI in terminal mode or by selecting [FYI] from within the Free Online Help menu through DJN/R software. During one month, the newsletter highlighted the addition of the *New York Times* back files, a description of the newly-introduced DJN/R software, and a discussion of new section codes that facilitate the searching of columns in the *Wall Street Journal*. The search tips and techniques are usually very useful and well-written. It's a shame that no written notice goes out to subscribers, though, as the occasional user may never learn about new features or software.

DJN/R provides new users with printed documentation—a 130-page *User's Guide* (unfortunately, it only describes terminal mode searching, not how to use the DJN/R software), a separate booklet on searching the Text Library (again, only for terminal mode searching), and a publications directory. There is also a good online help system with lists of commands, DJN/R codes, the database update schedule, pricing information, and descriptions of each DJN/R service. There are also online lists of the information sources available on DJN/R to supplement the printed publications directory.

EVALUATION OF DJN/R

Dow Jones News/Retrieval manages to maintain a good balance of services and options of interest to both the investment community and professional business researchers. By putting most of the searchable databases in a single Text Library, and by making all the other information resources menu-driven, DJN/R combines ease of use with search power.

What do I like most about DJN/R?
• I like the variety of information available on DJN/R. Granted, it's limited to information of greatest interest to the business, finance, and investment communities, but it offers breadth and depth for those markets.

- I like the menu-driven services. Most options are no more than one or two levels deep, so I don't usually feel like I have to wade through page after page of options before I can get to the information I need. On the other hand, the menus keep me from having to remember search commands for services I may not use frequently.

- I appreciate the flexibility in customizing the display format of retrieved records. I can specify which fields I want displayed and in what order, which eliminates much of the need to word-process the retrieved documents after downloading them.

- I can limit my Text Library search to specific sources; if I really need to search only the major stories from the *Wall Street Journal* and stories from five specific local newspapers, I can.

- DJN/R's proprietary software is easy to use and more stable than most other professional online services' software packages.

What do I like least about DJN/R?

- DJN/R promotes its information unit pricing as one in which "you pay only for the information you receive from Dow Jones." Well, sort of. You accrue information units when you display service menus and when you browse headlines and indexing terms as well as when you display the full text of articles or reports. Searchers accustomed to being able to browse the headlines and subject terms or Keywords-in-Context of retrieved documents at no or minimal charge may find this pricing particularly burdensome. I find research on DJN/R is often significantly more expensive than comparable searching in other professional online services, particularly if I need to review a number of headlines before selecting the items I want.

- As of early 1996, DJN/R did not have any regular magazine printed for its subscribers who are researchers or heavy online users. Subscribers who fail to read the online FYI newsletter each month may miss important information about new sources, search tips, and system upgrades. I wish DJN/R at least archived the back issues of FYI for a few months for those subscribers who don't check the online newsletter regularly.

- The initial menus in terminal mode and DJN/R software don't coincide. Given that all printed documentation is solely for terminal mode users, DJN/R software users can get puzzled about how to navigate through the system.

- Some DJN/R features, such as the *New York Times* Same-Day Stories, are difficult to find through DJN/R software menus. It takes four menu selections before you finally can search the *New York Times* Same-Day Stories. Through terminal mode, it can be accessed simply by typing //TEXT 7.

- There is inadequate description of exactly what information vendors' products are available in the Text Library. Professional online searchers are always trying to compare functionality, cost, and timeliness of information available on competing online services. I can't tell from looking at the online menus or the printed documentation which of the Text Library options give me access to the PROMT files, Business Dateline, or Trade & Industry Database, for example.

LEXIS-NEXIS

CONTACT INFORMATION

NAME LEXIS-NEXIS, a member of the Reed Elsevier plc group

ADDRESS P.O. Box 933
Dayton, OH 45401

TELEPHONE 800/346-9759; 513/859-5398
800/227-4908 for new accounts

CUSTOMER SERVICE HOURS 24 hours a day; 7 days a week except Sunday between 2:00am and 10:00am Eastern time

EMAIL no direct email access

WEB HOME PAGE http://www.lexis-nexis.com/

SERVICE AVAILABILITY 24 hours a day; 7 days a week except Sunday between 2:00am and 10:00am Eastern time

DESCRIPTION OF INFORMATION AVAILABLE

LEXIS-NEXIS began as an online service providing access to court opinions for the legal community. First, it expanded its LEXIS service to include state statutes, case law from other countries, administrative agency rulings, and public records. Then it grew to include the NEXIS collection of full text and abstracts of magazines, newspapers and newsletters, as well as databases of financial information, market research reports, and profiles of countries. Until early 1996, LEXIS-NEXIS was the only source for the back files of the *New York Times*. Since then, the *Times* has made its electronic archives dating back to 1980 available to non-U.S. DIALOG subscribers; subscribers to DIALOG and some other professional online services in the U.S. are limited to a few months' back issues and still rely on LEXIS-NEXIS for comprehensive searches of the "newspaper of record."

LEXIS-NEXIS also has exclusive rights to the CNN transcripts, available the day of the broadcast. CNN is a valuable source of news coverage, particularly of international news events.

LEXIS-NEXIS divides its resources into "libraries" and "files." A file can be an individual database, such as NYT (the *New York Times*). Unlike most other professional online services, LEXIS-NEXIS considers each online magazine or newspaper to be a separate file. So, for example, *The Boomer Report* can be searched by itself in the BOOMER file or within the NWLTRS newsletters group file. A group file can also be a group of databases organized by characteristics such as TODAY (English-language news sources available the same day they are published) or CURNWS (articles from a variety of news sources published within the past two years). You can select several files to search at once, although there are some files that do not permit multiple-file searching.

A library is a collection of files, organized by type of information, such as news (NEWS library), by topic, such as the entertainment industry (ENTERT library), or by geographic area, such as European news (EUROPE library). LEXIS-NEXIS creates new group files when they see a number of users repeatedly combining certain sources together for a search. See Figure 18 for the initial screen of the library selection menu and Figure 19 for the initial screen of the NEWS file selection menu.

LEXIS-NEXIS is the only major professional online service that focuses on user groups outside the library and information professional communities as well as on information professionals. For a number of years, it encouraged subscribers to use proprietary LEXIS-NEXIS terminals that enabled users to search its databases without needing to type any system commands; its online help still refers to dedicated function keys ("press the <Stop> key").

LEXIS-NEXIS has moved away from dedicated equipment and now provides subscribers with proprietary search software. Unlike most other services' software, though, LEXIS-NEXIS' Research Software is not particularly context-sensitive. For example, it allows you to click on a command that, in fact, is not valid at the current menu. This can be confusing for a user accustomed to having commands automatically disabled when they are not appropriate.

FIGURE 18
Library File Selection Menu

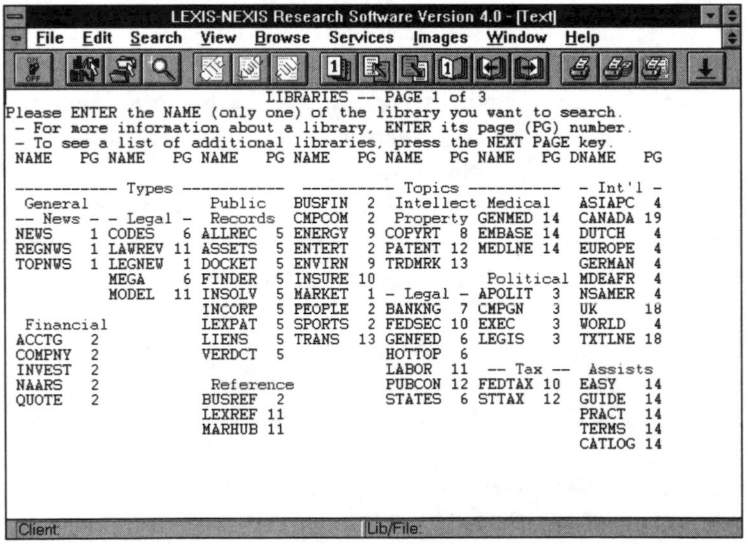

FIGURE 19
File Selection Menu (from the NEWS library)

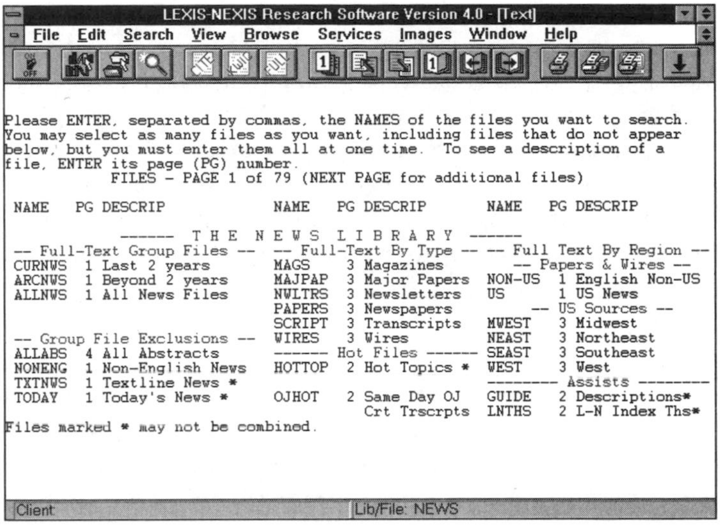

```
┌─────────────────────────────────────────────────────────────────────┐
│              LEXIS-NEXIS Research Software Version 4.0 - [Text]    ▼ ♦ │
│  □  File  Edit  Search  View  Browse  Services  Images  Window  Help ♦│
│ ┌──┐┌──┐┌──┐┌──┐┌──┐┌──┐┌──┐┌──┐┌──┐┌──┐┌──┐┌──┐ ┌──┐┌──┐┌──┐  ┌──┐   │
│ │  ││  ││  ││🔍││  ││  ││  ││ 1││  ││  ││ 1││  │ │  ││  ││  │  │ ↓│   │
│ └──┘└──┘└──┘└──┘└──┘└──┘└──┘└──┘└──┘└──┘└──┘└──┘ └──┘└──┘└──┘  └──┘   │
│                                                                       │
│ Please ENTER, separated by commas, the NAMES of the files you want to search.│
│ You may select as many files as you want, including files that do not appear │
│ below, but you must enter them all at one time.  To see a description of a   │
│ file, ENTER its page (PG) number.                                            │
│            FILES - PAGE 1 of 79 (NEXT PAGE for additional files)             │
│                                                                              │
│  NAME   PG DESCRIP          NAME   PG DESCRIP        NAME   PG DESCRIP        │
│       ------- T H E   N E W S   L I B R A R Y -------                         │
│  -- Full-Text Group Files --  -- Full-Text By Type -- -- Full Text By Region -- │
│  CURNWS  1 Last 2 years     MAGS   3 Magazines             -- Papers & Wires --  │
│  ARCNWS  1 Beyond 2 years   MAJPAP 3 Major Papers   NON-US 1 English Non-US      │
│  ALLNWS  1 All News Files   NWLTRS 3 Newsletters    US     1 US News             │
│                             PAPERS 3 Newspapers           -- US Sources --       │
│                             SCRIPT 3 Transcripts    MWEST  3 Midwest             │
│  -- Group File Exclusions --  WIRES  3 Wires        NEAST  3 Northeast           │
│  ALLABS  4 All Abstracts    ------ Hot Files ------ SEAST  3 Southeast           │
│  NONENG  1 Non-English News  HOTTOP 2 Hot Topics *  WEST   3 West                │
│  TXTNWS  1 Textline News *                          -------- Assists --------   │
│  TODAY   1 Today's News *    OJHOT  2 Same Day OJ    GUIDE  2 Descriptions*      │
│                                     Crt Trscrpts    LNTHS  2 L-N Index Ths*      │
│ Files marked * may not be combined.                                             │
│                                                                              │
│ ┌────────┐                 ┌──────────────┐                                 │
│ │ Client │                 │ Lib/File: NEWS│                                 │
│ └────────┘                 └──────────────┘                                 │
└─────────────────────────────────────────────────────────────────────┘
```

LEXIS-NEXIS is also one of the few professional online services that uses a screen-by-screen display; that is, rather than having information scroll off the screen, it displays a single formatted screen of information at a time. Because of the underlying structure of the system, LEXIS-NEXIS "feels" much different from other professional online services such as DIALOG, DataStar, or Dow Jones News/Retrieval. The most notable difference is that you cannot easily combine search sets, as LEXIS-NEXIS considers each search to be an entirely new search process, unrelated to earlier searches. See "POWER TOOLS," later in this section, for a discussion of how to work around this limitation.

This chapter focuses on LEXIS-NEXIS' news and general information sources rather than on the legal files. The system commands and finding tools can be used in both areas of LEXIS-NEXIS; however, I do not cover the specialized tools that can be used only by LEXIS searchers. In addition, there are several price schedules, depending on whether you are a business customer or a LEXIS (legal industry) customer. The prices quoted here are for business customers. Check with your account representative for the price list that applies to your subscription.

ROADMAP OF RESOURCES

LEXIS-NEXIS provides new subscribers with an introductory booklet on searching, a brief overview of the online services available, and an order form for additional information. The NEXIS *Reference Guide* is an essential tool for anyone planning to do more than the most rudimentary searching; it includes information on how to use system commands and how to make the most efficient use of LEXIS-NEXIS. The *Guide* is not regularly updated when new system commands are developed or when old commands are enhanced; fortunately, you can request updates via fax—a very useful service. See "OTHER FEATURES," later in this section, for information on the fax bulletin service.

For more detailed information about each file or database, you can purchase the four-volume NEXIS *Product Guide* ($65). This *Guide*, which is updated monthly, includes two or three pages of information on each file, along with an overview of how to search LEXIS-NEXIS, and subject and alphabetical indexes to the files. The *Product Guide* also includes Gold Sheets—special descriptions of sample searches and tips written by users particularly skilled in searching a specific file. The Gold Sheet for the *New York Times*, for example, includes pointers on how to search for all articles written in a series, how to find the best-seller list, and how to search for information contained in the *Sunday Magazine*. Unfortunately, not many files have accompanying Gold Sheets.

LEXIS-NEXIS offers an **online guide** to its services, consisting of a description of each file and library, along with search tips, a list of contact names and numbers, and training schedules. Type .GU or click on [Guide] to suspend your current activity and jump to the online guide. The online guide for each group file lists the sources included within the group, a helpful feature. This online guide does not provide the same in-depth information on each file that is available in the printed *Product Guide*, so be sure to consult the printed guide if you need detailed information on a file. I also find that the online guide is not particularly user-friendly—it's often easier to go to the printed version of the *Guide* than the online one.

Take advantage of LEXIS-NEXIS' **specialized group files**. The Hot Topics group file (HOTTOP) has collections of preformatted searches on five or six issues of current interest; in late 1995, those included terrorism in the U.S., the O.J. Simpson murder trial, and the Whitewater hearings. There are also group files for editorial columns, page one stories, and the 1996 presidential campaign press materials. These are useful tools when you want to search a specific concept or you need to search specific sources otherwise difficult to identify.

TIPS FOR USING LEXIS-NEXIS' FINDING AIDS

The primary means for selecting the source(s) to search is to use the library and file selection menus. Unfortunately, the organization of information within the menus is confusing to some users. The screen appearance of the library selection menu makes selection difficult, and the overlap of group files can puzzle even experienced searchers. To be safe, one is tempted to select the broadest categories possible—the NEWS library and the ALLNWS group file. However, searches in the ALLNWS group file cost $42 each under the transactional pricing option, not a very cost-effective choice unless you truly need to search all sources for all years. Take time to learn the group files that best fit your needs or call Customer Service and get some guidance on selecting the most appropriate files.

The online guide (accessed by typing .GU or pulling down the [Help] menu and clicking on [Guide]) may help you select the appropriate source(s). You can enter the Guide at any point during an online session except when you are using BROWSE or FOCUS. If you enter [Guide] while you are in a specific file, you are automatically dropped into the [Guide] page for that file. To return to where you were when you entered the [Guide], type =1 or .EX.

Commonly-Used Commands

NOTE: The search term connectors can be used in Boolean searching but are ignored in FREESTYLE (Natural Language) searches.

You can use typed "short-cut" commands to navigate through LEXIS-NEXIS. In addition, the proprietary Research Software package lets you use either function keys (DOS version), clickable buttons, or pull-down menus (Windows and Mac versions) for most navigational commands. For the sake of simplicity, this chart lists the short-cut command and the name of the command as it appears in the Research Software.

Begin a search
Menu-driven at initial logon
To start a new search: **.NS** (or use the [New Search] button)
To change library: **.CL** (or use the [Change Library] button)
To change file: **.CF** (or use the [Change File] button)

Search terms:
x AND y   x **AND** y
x OR y   x **OR** y
x BUT NOT y   x **AND NOT** y
x NEXT TO y   x y
x WITHIN n WORDS OF y   x **W/n** y (x within n words of y, in either order)
     x **PRE/n** y (x must precede y)
     x **NOT W/n** y (x cannot appear within n words of y)
x SAME SENTENCE y   x **W/S** y (x and y in the same sentence, in either order)
     x **PRE/S** y (x must precede y in the same sentence)
x SAME PARAGRAPH y   x **W/P** y (x and y in the same paragraph, in either order)
     x **PRE/P** y (x must precede y in the same paragraph)
x SAME FIELD y   x **W/SEG** y
     x **NOT W/SEG** y (x cannot appear in the same segment as y)

Date Searching
DATE = yyyy
DATE BEF August 9, 1995
DATE > mm/dd/yyyy
DATE = mm/yyyy

Field Searching
HLEAD (x) (word in the headline or lead paragraph)
SUBJECT (x)

Commonly-Used Commands [continued]

Truncation	word* (for single-character truncation)
	word*** (for as many characters as there are asterisks)
	wom*n (for woman or women)
	word! (for unlimited number of characters)
Display results	**.FU** (full format) (or use the [Full] button)
	.KWIC (Keyword-in-Context) (or use the [KWIC] button)
	.CI (citation) (or use the [Cite] button)
	.LE (citation and lead paragraph) (no comparable button)
	.NP (next page of document) (or use the [Next Page] button or <Page Down> key)
	.PP (previous page of document) (or use the [Prev Page] button or <Page Up> key)
	.ND (next document) (or use the [Next Document] button)
	.PD (previous document) (or use the [Prev Document] button)
	See note which follows re: printing and downloading.
Help	**H** (or use the [Help] button)
Cost:	
for session charges up to this point	**.CO** (or use the [Cost Summary] button)
for database rates	**.PRICE** or **.SE** (or use the [File Price] or [Segments] button). Can be used only at the [File Selection] menu.
for total cost when logging off	**.CO** (or use the [Cost Summary] button) This is a rough estimate and does not include print charges. For a more accurate estimate, use the PAYBACK ID (described later on in "OTHER FEATURES.")
Log off	**.SO** (or use the [Sign Off] button)

NOTE on displaying and printing records: Most online services allow you to download or print retrieved records as they are displayed on the screen. If you turn on the Research Software's [Session Record] feature (which downloads everything displayed on the screen), you are able to capture each record you view without incurring print or display charges. The downloaded record has headers at the top of each page as well as hard carriage returns at the end of each line. The following is an unedited version of a record downloaded with [Session Record].

LEVEL 2-11 OF 23 STORIES

Copyright 1983 The New York Times Company
The New York Times

August 25, 1983, Thursday, Late City Final Edition
Correction Appended

SECTION: Section D; Page 21, Column 2; National Desk

LENGTH: 685 words

HEADLINE: SCOTT NEARING, ENVIRONMENTALIST, PACIFIST AND RADICAL, DIES AT 100

BYLINE: By GLENN FOWLER

BODY:
    Scott Nearing, a prominent pacifist and radical In the early part of the century who later became an ardent environmentalist, died yesterday at the farm overlooking Penobscot Bay in Harborside, Me., where he lived with his wife, Helen. He was 100 years old.

    Dr. Nearing, a leader of the "back to the land" movement after World War II, had been in failing health since early this summer. A family spokesman

The New York Times, August 25, 1983

said he died in the simple stone house the couple built a few years ago on

....

Fortunately, the Research Software comes with a utility called LEXFORM. This program takes any downloaded session, strips off the headers at the beginning of each screen, as well as the page numbers, page breaks, and hard carriage-returns at the end of lines within paragraphs. This feature is a real time-saver for anyone who needs to deliver the results of a search to someone else and wants to be able to reformat and repaginate the downloaded documents. (It also seems to work well with downloaded records from other online services.)

Another option for downloading or printing documents is to issue a PRINT DOC command (.PR or use the [Print/Download Document] button). All documents marked for printing are printed or downloaded after you issue the SIGN OFF command. At that point, you are prompted to indicate the filename and path to which you want the information downloaded. If you are using LEXIS-NEXIS' software, you can specify that you want to have LEXFORM run on the downloaded file. You only incur per-document or per-line charges if you issue a PRINT DOC command.

If you change your mind after you've entered a PRINT DOC command, you can cancel the request with the Print Manager command (.PM or select [LEXIS/NEXIS Print Manager] from the [File] pull-down menu). A list of the print requests is displayed; you can delete any you no longer want to print.

GETTING CONNECTED

In LEXIS-NEXIS' early days, the only way you could access the service was through special LEXIS-NEXIS terminals. Fortunately, we've moved away from that model (remember when you leased your telephone from Ma Bell?). LEXIS-NEXIS now provides access through either its proprietary Research Software (for Windows, DOS and Mac computers) or through a plain ASCII connection. I highly recommend using Session Manager; the ASCII connection requires non-standard settings and is a much clumsier interface than the Research Software.

Logging on to LEXIS-NEXIS via plain ASCII connections:
via LEXNET: type in your terminal type .VT100P
via Tymnet: Please log in: **nexis** or **lexis**
via SprintNet: @ c lexis
via CompuServe Network: Host Name: **nexis** or **lexis**
via Internet: **telnet nex.lexis-nexis.com** or **lex.lexis-nexis.com**

LEXIS-NEXIS supports speeds from 1200bps to 38400bps. Settings should be:
VT100 emulation
HALF duplex
Auto wrap ON
Line feed OFF
1 stop bit, 7 data bits, even parity
Local echo ON

The Research Software automatically configures your communications settings and logs you on to LEXIS-NEXIS. System requirements for the LEXIS-NEXIS proprietary software vary, depending on which version you use.

POWER TOOLS

One of the major limitations of LEXIS-NEXIS is its lack of support for separate search statements. Often, you want to explore several alternative search strategies and then combine them as needed based on what you find, such as:

#1: a AND b
#2: c W/5 d
#3: HEADLINE(a)
#4: #1 and (#2 or #3)

With LEXIS-NEXIS, however, each new search incurs a separate charge—from $6 for a search of a single newspaper to $38 for a combined search of most NEXIS files. If you mistakenly search for sattelite instead of satellite or search for DATE = 1/1/1995 instead of DATE AFT 1/1/1995, you are charged the full cost for that search. This means that you need to carefully think out your search strategy before logging on.

Design your search strategy so that the initial search is just narrow enough to collect records that are possibly relevant, but not overly restrictive. Be sure that all the search terms are typed correctly, and be sure to enclose the initial search in parentheses to give you the most latitude possible in any later modifications of the search. After your initial search, use the tools described later to further refine the search—you incur a new per-search charge only when you use the NEW SEARCH command and *not* when you modify an existing search.

Transactional pricing subscribers in particular need to carefully structure their searches so as to minimize the total number of new searches. Transactional pricing charges are based primarily on the total number of "new searches" executed. As a result, LEXIS-NEXIS power searchers are pros at extracting a lot of information from a single search and its modifications. The flat-fee subscription pricing plan also rewards smart searchers, as the yearly subscription price is based on what the costs would have been under transactional pricing. That means that even flat-fee subscribers are best off using the power tools listed here to minimize the number of new searches they execute.

One key to minimizing search charges is to take advantage of MODIFY and FOCUS. These commands are used after an initial search has been run; they do not incur additional search charges. MODIFY allows you to add additional search phrases to your initial search. FOCUS lets you, in essence, run a search within a search, looking for those documents within the retrieved set that match a further search criterion. To understand how to use MODIFY and FOCUS, it is helpful to look at examples.

For starters, always enclose your entire search statement in parentheses. This enables you to add additional search terms and connectors without losing the logic of the original search. To use the search example mentioned earlier, your initial search would be written as (a AND b). When you have the results of this search, modify the search (type M or use the [Modify] button) by adding the second search statement, again enclosing it in parentheses: (AND (c W/5 d)). To express this in the terminology of the search sets listed earlier, this is equivalent to #1 AND #2. You can browse the retrieved documents in the CITE or KWIC format, issuing print commands for the items you find useful.

At this point, you decide that you might want to see those records that contain both A and B and in which A appears in the title. This is where you use FOCUS to specify that you want to look at only those retrieved documents of your initial search that also have term A in the headline. You change the display back to your initial (Level 1) search by typing .DL1 (or using the [Change Search Level] button). Now you invoke the FOCUS command (.FO or use the [Focus] button) and specify that you want to see only those documents retrieved in your initial search that also have A in the headline—HEADLINE(a). This is equivalent to #1 AND #3 in the search sets listed earlier.

Skilled LEXIS-NEXIS searchers can wring several distinct searches out of a single per-search charge. Say you need to find articles about welfare reform and you need a few overview articles on Shell Oil Co. Start the search in a fairly broad library and file, say the NEWS library and the MAGS file. The initial search includes *both* search concepts, e.g., ((welfare w/3 reform) or hlead(shell oil)). Then use the FOCUS command to sift through the resulting set for articles on welfare reform, using [Session Record] to download articles as you go or using the PRINT command to download all the selected articles at the end of your session. Next, repeat the process, using FOCUS to find articles within your initial search set that mention Shell Oil. Thus, you can get two searches for one search fee. This only works if the searches you wish to combine can cost-effectively be run in the same file(s).

Keep in mind that MODIFY does in fact modify your search; you wind up with a second search level that is distinct from your initial search. FOCUS, on the other hand, sorts through the retrieved records, displays the ones that meet your FOCUS search criteria, and then returns you to your original search set. The advantage of FOCUS is that it allows you to start with a fairly broad search, then filter through the resulting documents—sort of like looking at the search set through different tints of glasses.

Granted, using MODIFY and FOCUS is more convoluted than using numbered search sets as in the initial example. The advantage of becoming proficient in MODIFY and FOCUS is that you can get a lot of searching done for a modest online charge. Remember, you are charged just once for every "new search" run, along with a low telecommunications charge and the per-document or per-line charges. This pricing scheme encourages you to use MODIFY and FOCUS, neither of which is considered a "new search." In addition, the minimal connect-time charges encourage you to cast a fairly wide search net and spend time browsing through documents for the ones you want, rather than try several different search strategies in order to find one that retrieves exactly what you want.

One of the other components of your total online cost is the per-line or per-document charge. Unlike other online services, you can avoid those charges entirely if you download the documents as you view them on the screen using the [Session Record] feature. You only incur the document charges if you issue a PRINT command to download or print documents. There is a trade-off here, of course. If you retrieve lengthy documents, you may find that the connect charges and your time are more of a factor than the per-document charge of $1 to $4. As noted earlier, take advantage of LEXIS-NEXIS' LEXFORM software utility that removes extraneous material from the [Session Record] documents.

In addition to Boolean searching, LEXIS-NEXIS offers FREESTYLE, a Natural Language Search alternative. To begin a FREESTYLE search, type .FR or use the [Freestyle] button. (To return to Boolean searching, type .BOOL or use the [Boolean Search] button.) You type your request in plain English and the system analyzes the request to determine the most significant search terms.

I typed in the question, What is Congress doing about campaign reform? in FREESTYLE. See Figure 20 for the response from LEXIS-NEXIS, identifying the terms to search and giving me the opportunity to specify any terms that *must* be in any retrieved document.

FIGURE 20
FREESTYLE Search

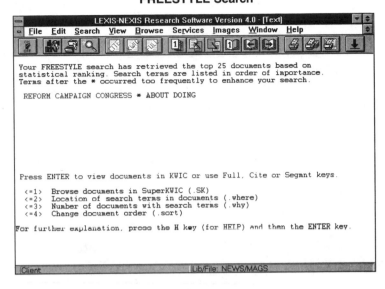

After the search is finished, LEXIS-NEXIS lets you see how many search terms appeared in each of the retrieved documents (the .WHERE screen) and lets you see how it ranked each of the search terms (the .WHY screen). Following are the .WHERE and .WHY screens for my campaign reform question:

LOCATION OF SEARCH TERMS IN DOCUMENTS (.where)

Document numbers are listed across the top of the chart.
Terms are listed down the side in order of importance.
Asterisks (*) indicate the existence of terms in documents.
To view a document, enter the document number.

```
                           1                   2
          1 2 3 4 5 6 7 8 9 0 1 2 3 4 5 6 7 8 9 0 1 2 3 4 5
REFORM    |* * * * * * * * * * * * * * * * * * * * * * * * * |
CAMPAIGN  |* * * * * * * * * * * * * * * * * * * * * * * * * |
CONGRESS  |* * * * * * * * * * * * * * * * * * * * * * * * * |
```

NUMBER OF DOCUMENTS WITH SEARCH TERMS (.why)

Documents	Documents Retrieved	Term Importance Matched	(0-100)
REFORM	25	109644	3
CAMPAIGN	25	208655	1
CONGRESS	25	190745	1
ABOUT	--	--	--
DOING	--	--	--
Total Retrieved:	25		

This .WHY feature is particularly valuable, as it gives you some feedback on how LEXIS-NEXIS interpreted your query. No other major online service offers this option; Natural Language Searching tends to feel like you're operating with a black box that takes your query, does something mysterious to it, and spits out documents. I appreciate being able to see how LEXIS-NEXIS understood and processed my search.

FREESTYLE defaults to retrieving the top 25 documents based on statistical ranking, but you can change the number to any value from 1 to 1,000. FREESTYLE works best with fairly broad conceptual issues rather than specific searches on a well-defined topic. I find it useful when I'm searching an area with which I am not familiar, as it lets me scan some relevant articles for additional search terms or industry buzzwords.

Another interesting Natural Language Search tool is MORE. This command lets you tag a particularly useful document and ask for "more items like this." It can be used while you are using either Boolean or FREESTYLE searching, although the MORE command itself uses the FREESTYLE search logic. Be careful, though; although the documentation is cagey about it, you incur the charge for a new search when you use .MORE. It's annoying that this isn't made more obvious to users, as this can add significantly to the total cost of a search.

In my search for articles on campaign reform, I typed .MORE while viewing a highly relevant article. LEXIS-NEXIS returned with the following screen:

FREESTYLE(TM) SEARCH OPTIONS

Press ENTER to start MORE search or .em to return to original document.
Search terms were added to the end of your Search Description.

Search Description:
WHAT IS CONGRESS DOING ABOUT CAMPAIGN REFORM, PAC, CAMPAIGN-FINANCE, WALDMAN, "WHITE HOUSE", LEADERSHIP, PUBLIC-INTEREST, CONTRIBUTIONS, SPECIAL-INTEREST, CAMPAIGN-, "BILL CLINTON", VOLUNTARY, INITIATIVE, NAFTA, HEALTH-CARE

Press   ENTER to start search.
<=1>   Edit Search Description
<=2>   Enter/edit Mandatory Terms
<=3>   Enter/edit Restrictions (e.g., date)
<=4>   Thesaurus
<=5>   Change number of documents Current setting: 25

I edited the search to eliminate terms I did not think would be helpful (NAFTA, HEALTH-CARE), but kept terms such as CAMPAIGN-FINANCE, CONTRIBUTIONS, and SPECIAL-INTEREST. This was a very useful way of identifying additional search terms most likely to yield additional relevant articles.

Although MORE is a FREESTYLE search, when you are finished viewing the documents retrieved with the .MORE search and exit the [More] feature (.EM—no corresponding button in the Research Software), you are returned to Boolean searching if that was your original search mode.

LEXIS-NEXIS has a good collection of precision search tools that help you fine-tune your search. The most useful of these tools are:

- **ATLEASTn**, which lets you specify how many occurrences of a term must appear in the retrieved documents. ATLEAST20 (x AND y) requires that terms x and y must each appear at least 20 times in the document, for example. This tends to eliminate shorter documents in which it's highly unlikely that any relevant term is repeated 20 times. On the other hand, this may work to your advantage if you are trying to eliminate short articles from your retrieved set.

- **ALLCAPS(word),** which indicates that the word within the parentheses must occur in all capital letters. This is useful when you are searching for acronyms that also appear as regular words, such as ERA (Equal Rights Amendment) or AIDS.

- **NOCAPS(word)** is the opposite of ALLCAPS and requires that the search term not have any capital letters. This is useful if you want, for example, articles on foreign aid and not AIDS.

- **CAPS(word)** requires that at least one letter of the word be capitalized. This tool is useful when searching for company names that are also common words, such as Visa, Tab, Sun, or Windows. It also retrieves common words that are capitalized at the beginning of a sentence, but you can combine it with the ATLEASTn command to ensure that your search finds relevant articles.

One factor to keep in mind with any of these capitalization commands is that files are not entirely consistent. Some files put their subject terms in all capital letters, some files such as the TASS news service are entirely in upper case, and the Xinhau file (a Chinese newswire), and some public records files are entirely in lower case.

LEXIS-NEXIS automatically searches for singular, plural and possessive forms of words, providing the plural is formed in the normal manner—adding an S or ES at the end of a word, or changing a Y to IES. Sometimes, though, you only want the singular or plural form of a word. In this case, you can use the **PLURAL(word)** or **SINGULAR(word)** search tools to limit the word to one or the other.

LEXIS-NEXIS' electronic clipping service is called **ECLIPSE** and is one of the more straightforward of the professional online services' clipping services. You select the library and file in which you want the ECLIPSE search to run and you type in your search. Once the search has been run, you type SAV (or use the [Save Eclipse] button) and indicate the frequency of the clipping service (daily, weekly or so on). The first time and each time thereafter that you log on after the new ECLIPSE search has been run, you are notified if there are new documents available.

PRICING

LEXIS-NEXIS has several pricing plans: its traditional transactional or per-search pricing, hourly pricing, and flat-rate subscription pricing. The transactional pricing structure is based on search processing, so you are charged between $6 and $38 per search depending on the sources you've selected, in addition to telecommunications charges of $13/hour ($18/hour for the LEXNET 800 number), plus $26/hour connect-time charges for NEXIS or $33/hour for LEXIS. There are also per-document printing charges that apply if you issue a print or download command (but not when you use the PRINT SCREEN or SESSION RECORD commands)—$4/document for LEXIS and $2.50/document for NEXIS (except Predicast documents, charged at $4/document). SEC filings, Investext reports and public records are charged at different prices.

The hourly pricing structure is more familiar to users of DIALOG or DataStar; it includes the telecommunications charge plus a higher connect-time charge, but no per-search charges. This pricing scheme also includes per-line charges for any documents printed or downloaded (but does not charge you per line for documents displayed on the screen).

The third and most common pricing option is subscription pricing. Users have a 90-day trial program during which they pay a fairly low flat fee. During this time, they are introduced to LEXIS-NEXIS services, receive training, and begin to identify those libraries and files they are likely to use most frequently. At the end of the 90-day trial, a flat fee based on their usage and anticipated needs is established. The subscription price is recalculated every year, based on usage as calculated by transactional pricing. Thus, even subscription plan users should be cost-conscious when using LEXIS-NEXIS.

Infrequent LEXIS-NEXIS searchers may be better off using the hourly or subscription pricing structure, particularly if you are accustomed to trying a number of different searches and combining results. Searchers familiar with the tricks and techniques that allow you to combine several searches in order to avoid the per-search fee benefit from the transactional pricing.

LEXIS-NEXIS encourages users to establish several IDs based on their search needs—for example, a subscription price ID that allows access to the libraries most frequently searched and a transactional price ID for access to the other libraries.

OTHER FEATURES

In addition to downloading or printing, you can request that your print be redirected to a fax, or to any email address that can accept Internet email. The Research Software prompts you for your print options; you select either fax or email. You can also set up the defaults for an ID to automatically send all prints to a fax or email address.

You can save searches and re-execute them later that day with the .KEEP and .LOG commands. After you have run a search and have finished browsing through documents and selecting any you want to print or download, type .KEEP (or use the [Keep Search] button). Be careful, though—this command ends your current search and returns you to the library selection menu. The KEEP command stores both the search strategy, including modifications, and a record of the library and file in which the search was run. To run the search again the same day (until 2:00am Eastern time), type .LOG (or use the [Open Search Log] button). All kept searches are displayed and you can select which one you wish to run again. For example, after KEEPing two searches, the .LOG command returned the following:

```
<=1>    KEPT SEARCH: TOPNWS;2WEEK
        CAMPAIGN W/P REFORM (LEVEL 1-243 STORIES)
<=2>    KEPT SEARCH: NEWS;CURNWS
        ROSS PEROT W/P CAMPAIGN AND FINANC! AND DATE = 1995
        (LEVEL 1-785 STORIES)
```

You can track search costs by specifying the client or subaccount code when you first connect to LEXIS-NEXIS. You can set your ID to require a client code; the default is to prompt for one, but not require a code. You can change the client code during the search by typing C (or using the [Change Client] button).

The [Cost Estimate] feature of LEXIS-NEXIS is just that—an estimate. You can display the cost estimate by typing .CO (or using the [Cost Summary] button). If you need to see your exact charges, you can request a PAYBACK ID from your account representative. When you log on using this separate ID, you can display the prior eight weeks' invoiced charges. You cannot see the current week's costs, though; there is a delay of a week before the invoice information is available on the PAYBACK ID.

LEXIS-NEXIS offers a fax-on-demand service called **Faxline**. You can call either 800/34NEXIS for NEXIS, or 800/25LEXIS for LEXIS, and request an index of available documents. The index is sent to your fax machine almost immediately. In addition to press releases and information on new system features and information products, you can order descriptions of specific NEXIS or LEXIS applications (e.g., how to search for company intelligence or how the entertainment industry uses NEXIS).

LEXIS-NEXIS also offers a **Fax Bulletin** service. You can receive faxed notification of new files, changes in library groupings, new commands, and other system-related information upon request. Contact your account representative or fax a request to 513/865-1780 to be added to the distribution list for the Fax Bulletins.

LEXIS-NEXIS has developed a series of Reference Information booklets that describe how best to search a certain set of files—investment house reports, Predicast files, full-text market research reports, and so on.

The LEXIS portion of LEXIS-NEXIS has other power tools such as LINK, which marks citations in the text of documents and lets you move directly to the case, statute, or other document marked; LEXSEE, which takes you from the document you are viewing to any legal document; LEXSTAT, similar to LEXSEE, but with statutes instead of cases; and LEXCITE, which lets you quickly look up any citation of a particular case in subsequent cases. LEXIS-NEXIS uses LINK for a few NEXIS files as well, such as the Directory of Corporate Affiliations and Access Disclosure.

LEXIS-NEXIS offers extensive user support—in local sales offices, over the telephone, and with computer-based training programs. There are frequent user training classes, both basic and advanced, offered in most major U.S. cities and free to existing LEXIS-NEXIS customers. They have also established an information professionals support group—representatives who focus on the needs of the library and information community.

It also produces a number of newsletters for its various user groups, including *Information Professional Update, LEXIS-NEXIS Insight, Political Insight, Marketing Insight, Media Insight, Public Relations & Corporate Communications Insight* and *Corporate Counsel In-House.* No other online service offers such specialization in its newsletters.

LEXIS-NEXIS maintains an Internet home page that contains recent news releases, an online directory of libraries and files, the full text of recent newsletters, a searchable list of local access phone numbers, and frequently-asked questions on searching and technical issues—http://www.lexis-nexis.com/.

EVALUATION OF LEXIS-NEXIS

LEXIS-NEXIS is one of the few online services that, while providing a wide variety of information sources, is still designed primarily for users who are not information professionals. It provides extensive training and documentation to assist both veteran and new online searchers in designing efficient and cost-effective searches and has knowledgeable customer service representatives available 24 hours a day. If you learn how to maximize each search and carefully plan your file selection, you can get a lot of information for your search dollar.

What do I like most about LEXIS-NEXIS?
- Downloading documents is streamlined, assuming you use LEXIS-NEXIS' Research Software. The LEXFORM feature, which strips off hard carriage-returns, line-feeds and other extraneous material, makes post-search word-processing a snap.

- LEXIS-NEXIS offers a number of valuable search tools not available in most online services. Features such as FREESTYLE and MORE, FOCUS, ATLEAST, and ALLCAPS give you a lot of flexibility and power.

- If you really need to cover a lot of material efficiently, LEXIS-NEXIS' ALLNWS (all full-text sources in the News library) or CURNWS (all full-text sources for the most recent two years) do so very gracefully.

- LEXIS-NEXIS was designed as a full-text search system, unlike the other professional online services which added full-text sources after their search systems had been developed. Therefore, LEXIS-NEXIS has a very powerful search engine and hashes through huge quantities of text more quickly and smoothly than its competitors.

What do I like least about LEXIS-NEXIS?
- I find it very frustrating that I can't combine search statements as I am accustomed to in other professional online services. Yes, there are work-arounds, but it's

difficult to shift between LEXIS-NEXIS and any other professional service because of the radically different ways you construct a search. Transactional pricing (which ultimately applies to subscription price customers as well) penalizes searchers who are used to being able to try a number of search strategies. LEXIS-NEXIS tends to be the last choice for searchers who are infrequent LEXIS-NEXIS users because of its inflexibility and the fact that you're penalized for typos, logic errors, and experimentation.

- I wish I could use an EXPAND or BROWSE command to see all the terms in the database. In other professional online services, I can browse an index to see if AT&T Corp. is spelled AT&T, AT and T, A T & T, or even American Telephone and Telegraph Co. On LEXIS-NEXIS, I have to try all possible alternatives and I feel like I'm searching blindly. Some databases do try to map some equivalencies (particularly common terms such as U.S.), but I'm never sure what I've missed.

- It is very difficult to select the appropriate file(s) to search. The library and file selection menus are confusing, particularly for users accustomed to having all the databases listed in a single directory or index. LEXIS-NEXIS keeps changing the organization, trying to make it better—they get credit for working on it, but I wish they would do a real overhaul and make file selection more straightforward.

CONTACT INFORMATION

NAME	NewsNet Inc.
ADDRESS	945 Haverford Road Bryn Mawr, PA 19010
TELEPHONE	800/345-1301; 610/527-8030 800/952-0122 for new accounts
CUSTOMER SERVICE HOURS	Monday through Friday 8:30am - 6:00pm Eastern time
EMAIL	through NewsNet: mail newsnet at the main menu through Internet: custserv@newsnet.com
WEB HOME PAGE	http://www.newsnet.com/
SERVICE AVAILABILITY	24 hours; 7 days a week

DESCRIPTION OF INFORMATION AVAILABLE

NewsNet made a name for itself when it opened its doors 13 years ago by providing exclusive access to the full text of industry newsletters. These six- to eight-page publications that often cost subscribers $500 or more a year contain in-depth, focused information on a single facet of an industry such as computer workstations or directory publishing. In the past seven or eight years, other professional online services and individual database vendors have signed agreements with some of the newsletter publishers, but some are still available only on NewsNet.

Magazine and newspaper articles provide overview information on an industry, but only a newsletter with its tightly-focused viewpoint provides you with an insider's look. NewsNet provides access to such titles as *Aircraft Value News, Blood Weekly,* and *Washington Beverage Insight*. NewsNet might not be your first choice to find general business information or an elementary article about a topic, but this is the place to find current, industry-specific articles. Each newsletter offers depth rather than breadth, which may be exactly what you need. NewsNet currently has about 800 newsletters, of which 200 are exclusive to NewsNet. Some newsletters are made available on NewsNet before the print version is delivered to subscribers.

NewsNet considers the heart of the system to be NewsFlash, its electronic clipping service. It is remarkably simple to set up a profile specifying what newsletters to monitor, the keywords to watch for, and the method of delivery.

In addition to newsletters, NewsNet includes
- American Business Information (brief company profiles and mailing lists)
- Dun & Bradstreet Information (business credit reports)
- Investext (stock brokerage reports on companies and industries)
- Investment ANALY$T (current and historic stock quotes)
- Official Airline Guides
- Standard & Poor's (company profiles and news)
- TRW Business Profiles (business credit reports)

Some of these resources are available through a "gateway" – NewsNet transfers you directly to the producer of, for example, the Official Airline Guides. When you complete your search, you exit the gateway and return to NewsNet. The charges appear on your NewsNet invoice; you need not have separate accounts with OAG, TRW or the other gateway services.

NewsNet also has more than 20 newswires for continually updated news. These include, among others, Agence France-Presse, Associated Press, UPI, and Federal News Service.

ROADMAP OF RESOURCES

You can access NewsNet through its proprietary software, Baton, or through a plain ASCII dial-up connection (called "native mode" on NewsNet). Baton is a graphical,

FIGURE 21
Main Menu in Native Mode

SCAN.....Display headlines	ABI.......ABI business lists and profiles
SEARCH...Search for keywords	DNB.......Dun & Bradstreet reports
DISPLAY.....Display full text	TRW.......TRW Business Profiles
	STOCKS....Stock quotes and analyses
FLASH....Update NewsFlash profile	OAG.......Official Airline Guides`
NOTICES..Display NewsFlash hits	
	$.........Display session estimate
BACK.....Return to prior prompt	HELP......Detailed instructions
STOP.....Stop current activity	LIST......Display titles by code
QUIT.....Return to main prompt	
	PAGING....Display text by screens
<CONTROL>S...Freeze display	PROJECT...Track sessions by tasks
<CONTROL>Q...Resume display	OPTIONS...Change global options
<CONTROL>P...Break function	INVOICE...Recent billing detail
	PASSWORD..Change your password
FIXIT....Report problems free	
MAIL.....To NewsNet or publishers	OFF......Sign off NewsNet
ORDER....Order print subscription	$OFF.....Display costs at signoff

FIGURE 22
Main Menu in Baton

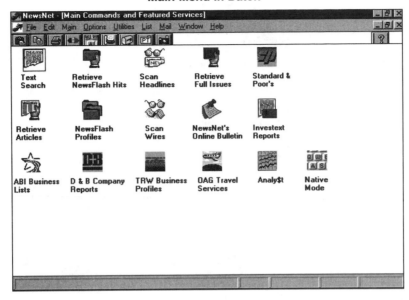

point-and-click software package that streamlines your searching, particularly if you do not search NewsNet frequently. You have the same search and display capabilities with both types of access; the only difference is how the information is displayed on the screen and whether you navigate by typing commands or by clicking on icons. (There is also a "native mode" icon in Baton, so you can toggle between the two interfaces.) Some of the icons in Baton actually drop you into native mode, which can be a bit surprising at first.

When you first log on to NewsNet, you are presented with a main menu spelling out your options. See Figure 21 for the main menu in native mode; see Figure 22 for the Baton main menu. The two main menus appear to offer different services; in fact, they simply word the options differently. For example, the Baton icons [Text Search], [Investext Reports], and [NewsNet's Online Bulletin] all cover functions that are accessed through the SEARCH command in native mode.

NewsNet allows you to search its files by either "concept searching" or Boolean searching. You can set your default search mode to either type of searching by using the OPTIONS command in native mode or by clicking on the desired option in Baton.

Boolean searching uses the traditional AND, OR, NOT connectors, allows truncation, wild-carding, "stemming" and nesting of concepts (i.e., [A OR B] AND C). Concept searching is "plain English" searching—you can search on a topic such as "what is Congress doing to reduce the federal deficit."

Concept searching is best used when you want to cast a fairly wide net, or if you are not familiar with the subject area of your search. Typically, you retrieve a large number of records. The retrieved records are ranked according to relevancy and you can scan the first 15 or 20 to see how the search is working out. You may see additional

FIGURE 23
Baton Concept Search Screen

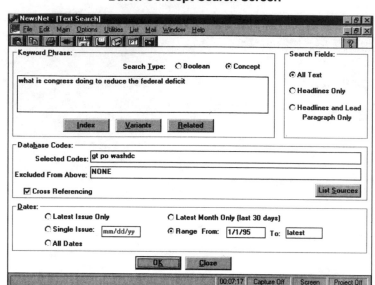

search terms that help focus the search; you may find that you have all the information you need from the top ranked articles. Concept searching also works well for searchers who are not familiar with Boolean searching and don't understand how to formulate a search with AND, OR and NOT. See Figure 23 for an example of the Baton concept search screen.

You can override the search and output options midstream. If your default is set to Boolean searching and you want to run a concept search while in native mode, append /c to the end of your search (e.g., athletes pacemakers /c). If your default is set to concept searching and you want to run a Boolean search, append /b to the end of the search (e.g., athlete* and pacemaker* /b). In Baton, you simply click on the [Boolean] or [Concept] search type button.

If your default is set to Boolean searching, your output is sorted either by issue date or by newsletter title code, according to the options you have selected. If you want the results sorted by relevancy instead, append -sort rank to the end of your search (e.g., athletes and pacemaker* -sort rank). If your default is set to concept searching, your output is sorted by relevance. If you want the results sorted by issue date or by title, append -sort lifo [i.e., Last In, First Out] or -sort alpha respectively.

What often works well for experienced searchers is to use Boolean searching, then sort the results by relevance. You get the search power of Boolean logic, truncation, and nesting of concepts, and you get the benefit of a ranking of the retrieved articles by their expected relevance.

If you want to scan current news without searching on a particular topic, you can scan the current day's wire services. In Baton, click on [Scan Wires]. You can select all wires

FIGURE 24
Scan Wires in Baton

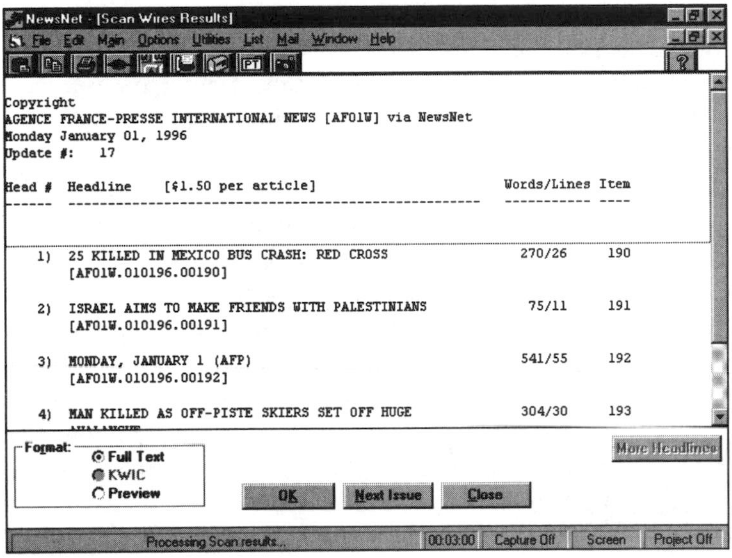

or limit the search to business wires, international wires, or a specific wire source, such as UPI. You can look for prior days' news, all of today's news, or news from any hour of the day. (The updates are dated with a 24-hour clock. To read the news stories from 2:01 pm through 3:00 pm, select [Update #15].) See Figure 24 for a Baton Scan Wires display.

In native mode searching, type scan [database code or WIRES]. For example, scan ap (or abbreviated to sc ap) scans the Associated Press wires; sc wires scans all wire services. You are prompted for the date to scan and the update (i.e., 1 for stories put on the wire from 12:01am until 1:00am, 13 for stories put on the wire from 12:01pm until 1:00pm, and so on). The [Scan Wires] feature is an easy way to monitor the news for a late-breaking story, particularly because it allows you to narrow your scan by the hour of the update. (All times are U.S. Eastern time.)

TIPS FOR USING NEWSNET'S FINDING AIDS

Each newsletter, newswire and other information source on NewsNet is assigned a two-character industry or source code, enabling you to search individual sources or an entire group of newsletters or other sources. A review of the titles within an industry code indicates the degree of specialization in newsletters; within the Food & Beverage industry (industry code FB) are *Food Chemical News*, *Ice Cream Reporter*, *Food Labeling News*, and *Organic Food Business News*.

Each newsletter and newswire is also assigned an individual title code, consisting of two letters indicating the industry it covers and two or three numbers to uniquely identify it within its industry grouping. For example, *North Sea Rig Forecast*'s title code is EY98—EY is the code for energy.

NewsNet also includes "cross-referenced" newsletters within each industry code. These include titles that, while not directly focused on the industry, cover it with a moderate amount of detail. At the beginning of your search, you can specify whether or not you want cross-referenced newsletters included in the search. You can also set your search default options to automatically include or exclude cross-referenced newsletters. Choose [Options] at the main menu, or pull down the [Options] menu in Baton.

In addition to the grouping of newsletters by industry code, NewsNet has special category codes that pull together newsletters regardless of industry grouping that cover a particular topic. The pharmaceutical category PHARMA, for example, includes selected newsletters from the industry groups of Biotechnology, Chemical, Health and Hospital, Investext, Medicine, and Research and Development. Type Help Category at any prompt (in native mode) or click on [List] then [Sources] then [Category codes] (in Baton) for a detailed list of the available categories.

These categories are particularly helpful when you are searching for information in an area with which you are not familiar. You may not think of the possible cross-fertilization among industries and would miss some useful sources.

Commonly-Used Commands

Begin a search	**SEARCH** (in native mode) click on [**Text Search**] (in Baton)
Search terms: x AND y x OR y x BUT NOT y x NEXT TO y	 x **AND** y x **OR** y x **NOT** y x **W/1** y (x next to y in either order) x **ADJ** y (x must precede y) 'x y' (string search; does not allow truncation or stemming within quotation marks)
x WITHIN n WORDS OF y x SAME SENTENCE y x SAME PARAGRAPH y x SAME FIELD y	not specifically available—use x **NEAR/n** y not specifically available—use x **NEAR/15** y not specifically available—use x **NEAR/40** y not available
Date Searching	**MM/DD/YY-MM/DD/YY** **LATEST** (for most recent issue) **MONTH** (for most recent 30 days)

Field Searching	x/**HEAD** (restricts search to headline)
	x/**LEAD** (restricts search to headline and lead paragraph)
	F/n (restricts NewsFlash searches to terms in the first n words)
	no other field searching available
Truncation	word* for multiple-character truncation
	word? for single-character truncation
	w$rd for optional-character wildcard
	(e.g., colo$r retrieves both color and colour)
	[see note which follows re: "stemming"]
Display results	prompted for display option: head, text, KWIC or preview (cite and lead paragraph)
Help	Help (in native mode)
	click on [**Help**] or <**F1**> (in Baton)
Cost:	
for session charges up to this point	$ (in native mode)
	click on [**Utilities**] then [**Session Estimate**] (in Baton)
for database rates	Help [Source Code] or prices [for list of all titles' prices] in native mode
	click on [**List**] then [**Sources**] then [**More Info**] in Baton
for total cost when logging off	$off (you can set this to display automatically by changing [Global Options])
Log off	off in native mode
	click on [**Connect/Disconnect**] icon in Baton

Note: NewsNet offers an alternative to truncation, called "stemming," indicated with the + sign. Stemming looks for other words with the same word root; truncation looks for *any* word that begins with the specified letters. For example, a search for the truncated run* retrieves run, running, runt, and runcible. A search for the stemmed run+ retrieves run, running, runner, and so on, but not runt or runcible. The default settings are for automatic stemming to be turned off for Boolean searching and turned on for concept searching. Both defaults can be reset or can be overridden for a single search. To turn stemming off for a single word when your default is set to stemming-on, use the double quote sign. For example, run" would search only for that word even though you have your default set to automatic stem searching. Use the plus sign to turn stemming back on. To change your default setting (either always include concept stemming or never include it), choose [Options] at the main menu or pull down the [Options] menu in Baton.

GETTING CONNECTED

You can log on to NewsNet using any standard communications software package. You can also use NewsNet's proprietary software package, Baton. This software is a point-and-click GUI interface, available at no extra charge from NewsNet. Unfortunately, it is only available for IBM-compatible PCs at this point; NewsNet is evaluating the demand for a Mac version.

Logging on to NewsNet:
via Tymnet: Please log in: **net**
via SprintNet: **@ c net**
via CompuServe network: host name: **net**
via Internet: **telnet newsnet.com**

NewsNet supports speeds from 1200bps through 19,200bps (2400bps and higher for Baton—9600 or higher recommended). Modem settings should be:
TTY emulation
FULL duplex
1 stop bit, 7 data bits, even or space parity or 1 stop bit, 8 data bits, no parity
(1 stop bit, 8 data bits, no parity for Baton)

The Baton software requires the following:
386 PC or higher (Mac version not yet available)
Windows 3.1 or higher
4MB RAM

POWER TOOLS

ANALYZE

The ANALYZE command reviews your search results and tabulates how many records were found in each newsletter or other source. It lists each title, sorted by title code, along with the number of records from that title. This helps narrow down a search; you can see which sources produced the most hits and can repeat your search in those sources. You can also display the results from selected titles, or exclude selected titles from the display of results.

For example:

Enter HEAd; TExt; Kwic; Analyze; BRoaden; NArrow; or BAck to
enter new keyword phrase
—>**analyze**

*** NEWSNET SEARCH ANALYSIS   Thu 5 Oct 1995   13:38:11 ***
==

Phrase: DATABASE W/1 MARKETING
Database Range: TE
Date Range: 1/1/94-LATEST

CODE	TITLE	OCCURRENCES
AD27	INTERACTIVE MARKETING NEWS	2
EC45	THE REPORT ON IBM	1
EC72	COMPUTERGRAM INTERNATIONAL	6
EC79	COMPUTER WORKSTATIONS	1
FT02	FINANCIAL TIMES FULL TEXT	11
GB55	BUSINESS WEEK	11
IX25	INVESTEXT/TELECOMMUNICATIONS	2
KR02	KNIGHT-RIDDER/TRIBUNE BUSINESS NEWS	20
PB08	WORLDWIDE VIDEOTEX UPDATE	1
PB30	MORGAN REPORT ON DIRECTORY PUBLISHING	4
PB49	DATA BROADCASTING NEWS	1
PB50	COWLES/SIMBA MEDIA DAILY	8
PB51	MULTIMEDIA NETWORKING NEWSLETTER	1
PB99	NEWSNET ACTION LETTER	1
SP01	STANDARD & POOR'S DAILY NEWS	2
TE01	COMMUNICATIONS DAILY	1
TE108	SATNEWSWIRE	1
TE109	TELECOMWORLDWIRE	6
TE11	TELECOMMUNICATIONS REPORTS	2
TE123	DOT.COM	1
TE126	COMMUNICATIONS BUSINESS & FINANCE	1
TE127	M2 PRESSWIRE	29
TE133	COMMUNICATIONS TODAY	2
TE14	TELECOMMUNICATIONS REPORTS INTERNATIONAL	1
TE21	TELE-SERVICE NEWS	2
TE24	EXCHANGE	1
TE26	COMMON CARRIER WEEK	1
TE34	INFORMATION WEEK	11
TE41	INFORMATION & INTERACTIVE SVCS. REPORT	1
TE49	TELCO BUSINESS REPORT	1
TE73	EDGE ON & ABOUT AT&T	2
TE75	TELECOMMUNICATIONS ALERT	1

TOTAL OCCURRENCES. 136

GRAPH

GRAPH provides a graphic indication of the relative relevance of the items retrieved by your search. If you are using the Baton software, this command is unnecessary as Baton automatically displays a graph of relevance for concept searches. See Figure 25 for the relevance graph in Baton. GRAPH is used in native mode to duplicate the bars shown in the Baton search results screen.

FIGURE 25
Relevance Graph in Baton

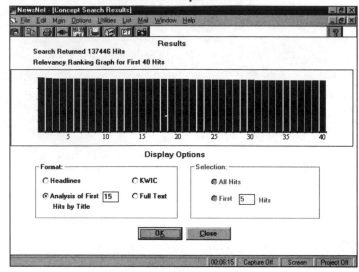

This command can be used only when your search results are sorted by relevance rather than by date or title code. If you used concept searching, your results are automatically sorted by relevance. If you used Boolean searching, you must add -sort rank at the end of your search words in order to have the results sorted by relevance (or change your search options default setting).

The GRAPH command produces the following display:

```
Enter HEAd; TExt; Kwic; Analyze; BRoaden; NArrow; Graph; or BAck to
enter new keyword phrase
—>graph
```

RELEVANCE RANKING BY COMPUTED SCORE

Head # Score
_____

```
 1)    100 ***********************************************************
 2)     97 **********************************************************
 3)     96 *********************************************************
 4)     95 ********************************************************
 5)     93 *******************************************************
 6)     93 *******************************************************
 7)     93 *******************************************************
 8)     93 *******************************************************
 9)     93 *******************************************************
10)     91 ******************************************************
11)     90 ******************************************************
12)     90 ******************************************************
```

I can tell from the graph that records 1 through 4 are quite likely to be relevant, and records 10 and down are slightly less likely.

INDEX

This command takes the word you indicate (by highlighting in Baton or by typing /i [search word] in native mode) and displays the eight or ten words alphabetically before and after it in the file(s) you are searching. For example, searching in the Health & Hospitals industry in native mode:

```
Enter keywords or phrase
—>/i pacemakers

INDEX LOOKUP OF PACEMAKERS

PACEK
PACEL
PACELEY
PACELLA
PACELLE
PACELLI
PACEM
PACEMAKER
*PACEMAKERS*
PACEMAKING
PACEMAN
PACEMARKERS
PACEMEN
PACENTI
...
```

This command is helpful if you are not sure of the spelling of a name or if you think it is likely that the name may have been misspelled (Pacella, Pacelle, Pacelli).

QUERY BY EXAMPLE (QBE)

The theory behind QBE is to allow you to review a set of retrieved articles and identify one article that, although perhaps significantly different from your original search, contains a topic you want to explore. You type QBE at the native mode prompt or click on the [Query by Headline Number] icon in Baton, and specify the headline number of the article on you wish to search. NewsNet proceeds with an entirely new search (be sure you've already viewed all the items you want from your original search). The system constructs the new search from unique terms present in the article you identified, and the results are ranked by relevance.

The idea behind QBE is great; unfortunately, the results are somewhat inconsistent. Some searches turn up very useful articles, while others retrieve quite puzzling results. The search process for QBE often takes several minutes, so use this command only when you are not sure how to construct an expansion or refinement of your search.

RELATED

This command provides a list of words that most often occur within the same articles as the word you indicate. You can either highlight the search word for which you want related terms (in Baton) or precede the search word with /r. This is intended to help you identify related terms, synonyms, and additional search terms to either narrow or broaden your search. With our "pacemaker" example, we see the following RELATED terms:

Enter keywords or phrase
—>/r **pacemaker**

WORDS RELATED TO PACEMAKER

ENCOR
PACEMAKER
69372M
TELECTRONICS
PMED
ACCUFIX
0000585055
0000989922
PACEMAKERS
DEFIBRILLATORS
IPGS
HERTS
INOS
PACING
NEERGAARD
LAURAN
OVERREACTION
WITTERS
WETTLAUFER

Some of the suggested terms make sense and some of the terms are manufacturers of pacemakers. The numbers 0000585055 and 0000989922 are CUSIP (document ID) numbers for Medtronic Inc. and Zoll Medical Corp. However, when I tried a search of pacemaker* and (pmed or herts or ipgs) (three of the "related" terms), I retrieved no documents. I'm at a loss as to why "pmed," "herts" and "ipgs" showed up on the list of related terms. Use this function with a grain of salt.

PRICING

NewsNet charges a yearly subscription fee of $120 if paid annually, or $15 per month. You are charged $15/hour for connect time while you are searching; this rate jumps to $90/hour while viewing headlines or the full text of retrieved records. NewsNet rounds its time-based fees to the nearest second, unlike other professional online services which round to the minute. In addition, you are charged a per-record fee of $.50 for viewing a record in KWIC or PREVIEW, or a fee ranging from $1 to $6 for viewing a record in full-text format. If you download an entire issue by using the RETRIEVE FULL ISSUES command, you are charged a set fee for the entire issue, ranging from $10 to $60. Fortunately, all article and issue costs can be displayed prior to retrieving the full text. The majority of newsletter publishers offer a 40 percent discount off the per-record charge for NewsNet users who also subscribe to the publisher's print newsletters.

Gateway services (Dun & Bradstreet, TRW, American Business Information, OAG, and Analy$t) incur additional surcharges of $90/hour plus per-record charges.

OTHER FEATURES

NewsNet's electronic clipping service, **NewsFlash**, is menu-driven and very straightforward. In Baton, click on [NewsFlash Profiles] to create, edit, or delete a "folder"—that is, the profile of information you want scanned and the sources you want monitored. In native mode, type Flash at the main command prompt, then type Create, Modify or Delete. When you create a folder, you give the folder a name, type in the keywords to search for, indicate if and when the clipping service is to expire, what services to monitor, and how you want the clipped items displayed.

When you want to retrieve the clipped items, you either click on [Retrieve NewsFlash Hits] in Baton or type Notices at the main prompt in native mode. You specify which folder you want to open up and browse, then you can review the headlines, Keyword-in-Context, and/or full text of the retrieved items. After reviewing them, you can save, renew (i.e., change the status from "viewed" to "new") or delete the items in your folder.

You can monitor your search costs during the course of an online session by typing $ at the main menu prompt in native mode or by pulling down the [Utilities] menu, then [Session Estimate] in Baton. The total displayed includes an estimate of all charges except report charges for the gateway services (Dun & Bradstreet, TRW, ABI, and ANALY$T).

You can track your expenses by project with the [Project Tracking] option. In native mode, at any prompt type Project and you are prompted for the name of your project. In Baton, pull down the [Project Tracking] icon on the tool bar. NewsNet keeps track of all charges incurred after that point and groups those charges together on your invoice. You can turn the project tracker off by typing Project Off in native mode or by clicking on the [Project Tracking] icon in Baton. You can also change your [Global Settings] so that you are automatically prompted for a project name each time you log on. In native mode, type Options at the main menu and select [Global Option Settings]; in Baton, pull down the [Options] menu and select [Global Options]. Change the second option [Prompt for project name at signon? (Y/N)] to [YES].

You can have the results of a search redirected to an electronic mail address or to a fax machine. In native mode, append the command –EMS or –FAX to the end of any display command, to have the information sent to a remote location. In Baton, at any display screen, pull down the [Utilities] menu and select either [EMail] or [Fax].

To send the headlines of a search in native mode to a fax machine (the procedure is similar in Baton):

Searching ...

     12 Occurrences

Enter HEAd; TExt; Kwic; Analyze; BRoaden; NArrow; or BAck to
enter new keyword phrase
—>**head -f**
Enter recipient (name, company name, or department, up to 30 characters)
or BACK to return to previous prompt
—>**John Smith ; Corp Planning**

Enter recipient's fax number (10 digits)
—>**202 555-0277**

Enter message for fax recipient (up to 256 characters); or <RETURN> to
send no message
—>**Following are headlines to the most recent articles on the Microsoft Network, as you requested.**

  Fax delivery settings are:

1. Recipient: JOHN SMITH ; CORP PLANNING
2. Recipient's fax number: 2025550277
3. Message for recipient: FOLLOWING ARE HEADLINES TO THE MOST
                                      RECENT ARTICLES ON THE MICROSOFT
                                      NETWORK, AS YOU REQUESTED.

Enter fax delivery option number to modify, List (current settings),
or <RETURN> to accept current settings
—>**<carriage return>**

*** creating outbound delivery file ***

Receipt number: 5826950925124747FAX-PRO00111

*** outbound delivery file queued to be transmitted ***

    Sending a message via email is similar. If you wish to send the results of a search to the Internet address mbates@access.digex.net, you would need to address it to: SITE:INTERNET, ID:<mbates(a)access.digex.net>.

    There is an additional charge of $.50 per fax or email request plus $.01 per line of text.

    One of the challenges encountered by online searchers is the need to distribute multiple copies of an online article and still comply with copyright restrictions. Usually the rule is one search—one copy; if you need three copies of an article, you have to download it three times. NewsNet is one of the few professional online services that enables users to purchase multiple copies of an article for redistribution. That is, you download the article once, specify the number of copies you want, and NewsNet calculates the total cost. Note: this only works in native mode; there is no equivalent command in Baton. If you think you may purchase multiple copies of an article, remember to run your search in native mode.

Once you identify the article(s) you want, append –copies [# of copies] at the end of your full-text display request. For example, to order ten copies of article number three:

Enter headline number(s) to display full text; Kwic; PREview; Broaden; NArrow; or QBE
—>3 –copies 9

Only one copy displays online; your invoice reflects a charge for ten copies (the one copy displayed plus an additional nine copies).

You can purchase redistribution rights for entire issues as well as individual articles, using the same -COPY command.

NewsNet offers a rudimentary electronic mail system, primarily for users to contact Customer Service. In addition, you can send electronic requests directly to the publishers of any newsletters on NewsNet, to begin a subscription or to receive more information about the newsletter. You create email messages by typing Mail or Order at the main menu in native mode or by pulling down the [Mail] menu in Baton and specifying the newsletter title for which you want more information or to which you want to subscribe.

The OPTIONS command (in native mode) or the [Options] pull-down menu (in Baton), allows you to change a number of system defaults. The initial [Options] menu lets you chose to change your Global Options, your Search Options, or your NewsFlash Delivery and Display Options.

If you select [Global Options], you are given the following choices:

Global option settings menu

1. Display session estimates at signoff? (Y/N)	YES
2. Prompt for project name at signon? (Y/N)	YES
3. Signon announcements displayed ONCE per day or at ALL signons?	ONCE
4. Screen and text display options	
5. Modify list of services monitored for update notification	

Most of these settings are self-explanatory. Option 1 displays an estimate of your total session costs when you log off. Option 2 prompts you for a project name, which appears on your invoice itemizing your costs for that project. Option 3 is a useful choice if you log on frequently during the course of a day and do not want to see system announcements each time you log on. Option 4 lets you determine what your highlighting character is, whether you want your search terms highlighted in KWIC format, full format, or both, whether you want the full-text price displayed when you view headlines (be sure to set this to ON), and several other setting options.

If you select [Search Options] at the initial [Options] menu, you are given the following choices:

Search option settings are:

1. Default search type:	BOOLEAN
2. Boolean output sort order:	BY ISSUE DATE: LATEST TO EARLIEST
3. Cross referencing:	YES
4. Boolean stemming:	NO
5. Concept stemming:	YES

As noted earlier, you can override the default search type by appending /c (for concept searching) or /b (for Boolean searching).

If you select [NewsFlash Options] at the initial [Options] menu, you are given the following choices:

The NewsFlash delivery and display option settings are:

1.	Unviewed hits displayed at signon?	YES
2.	Unviewed hits displayed at signoff?	NO
3.	Saved hits displayed BEFORE unviewed hits, AFTER unviewed hits, or on REQUEST only?	BEFORE
4.	SAVE, DELETE, or RENEW hits after viewing?	DELETE
5.	Instant notification of hits delivered during the current session?	NO
6.	Default paging option: HEAD, TEXT, BOTH or NONE?	HEAD: HEADLINES ONLY
7.	Disable monitoring for all folders?	NO
8.	Receive hits from delayed services?	YES

NewsNet offers a remarkable amount of customization for its subscribers. FIXIT is a mechanism to report errors or problems you encounter in NewsNet records. When you see a problem, type FIXIT at the main menu in native mode or pull down the [Mail] menu in Baton and select [Fixit]. You are dropped into NewsNet's electronic mail system where you can type in a description of the problem. The message is sent to NewsNet's Customer Support Center for review and resolution. When the question or problem has been resolved, you will receive a return email message describing the resolution. There is no charge for the time you spend sending a FIXIT request, and you are credited for any other activity associated with the FIXIT request.

NewsNet sends out a monthly newsletter, *Action Letter*, to all subscribers. This newsletter describes new features, highlights a power searching tool with which users may not be familiar, lists new online titles available, and lists recent Customer Service questions and answers. Each issue also contains a list of all the titles available through NewsNet, a helpful feature.

In addition to the *Action Letter*, NewsNet's online publication PB99# contains updates on newsletter title or price changes and information on new features. You can retrieve it in native mode by SEARCHing or DISPLAYing PB99#; in Baton, you click on the [NewsNet's Online Bulletin] icon. Baton drops you into native mode, so be sure to pull down the [File] menu and select either [Begin Capture] or [Print] before you click on the [Bulletin] icon.

Workshops are scheduled regularly in major U.S. and Canadian cities. These training sessions last a half day and cost $60 (and come with a $60 usage credit).

EVALUATION OF NEWSNET

NewsNet is a boutique online service. Its strength is in the breadth and depth of its specialized newsletters; it is not the place to start for general overview articles on a topic. It has no regional business journals, although it has a few business magazines and business sections from 70 U.S. newspapers. On the other hand, if you need focused information on a topic, this is a great resource.

NewsNet also offers access to basic company information in a menu-driven format that is particularly easy to use for users who are not frequent online searchers. The Standard & Poor's services—Daily News, Corporate FirstFacts, and Corporate Descriptions—along with the Dun & Bradstreet and TRW business credit reports, provide all the business information many researchers require without the need for them to use any system commands or Boolean logic.

NewsNet also provides one of the better systems for monitoring late-breaking news by allowing you to view newswire stories separated by hour. It is very easy to log on once an hour, review just the last hour's update, and log off without incurring much cost or spending much time.

What do I like most about NewsNet?
- NewsNet completely reengineered its search software during the spring of 1995, and now offers a lot of search power for such a specialized online system. Both Baton and native mode searching are easy to use, at least for experienced searchers who understand what "sort," "stemming," "index" and "related" mean. There are quite a few options you can set to make the system feel as comfortable as possible—you can default to Boolean or concept searching, you can set the default for how results are sorted (by relevance, in date order latest to earliest, earliest to latest, or by source code), you can be prompted automatically for a project name to appear on the invoice, and so on.

- NewsNet is one of the easiest of the professional online systems for a new user to search, at least if the user is trying a fairly straightforward search. The layout of the commands or icons is intuitive and help is always a keystroke away.

- One important feature of any online system is its customer service. I have subscribed to NewsNet since 1982 and I have never had a bad experience with a NewsNet customer service representative. They have been unfailingly knowledgeable, courteous, and responsive. I always feel that I'm speaking with someone who really knows NewsNet inside and out and wants my search experience to be productive; something I can't always say about some other online systems.

What do I like least about NewsNet?
- Much as I was pleased with the reengineered search software, NewsNet still doesn't offer searchers the flexibility available on other professional online services. I wish I could combine searches (i.e., "combine that first search I tried with this next search") rather than having to rerun the entire search every time I make a modification. Given that the response time on NewsNet is not particularly fast, this can get annoying.

- Searches usually take over a minute and often more than two minutes to complete, particularly if you are searching more than just the current year's information. Although that sounds like very little time, it can be frustrating when you are accustomed to the five- to ten-second response time of most other professional online systems. A particularly long search results in NewsNet responding that it has received no response from you in over a certain amount of time and that it is now disconnecting you from NewsNet! Baton also seems to have a tendency to lock up or crash, most notably during a long search, but also if you are toggling between Baton and another application. NewsNet programmers are working on these problems, particularly the server time-out problem.

- I wish NewsNet had more general business and news magazines to supplement its specialized sources. I find that I usually begin a search in one of the more broad-based online services and then move to NewsNet when I need focused articles targeted to a specific audience of industry insiders.

- NewsNet's pricing structure is confusing and can result in expensive search sessions. As most online services are moving toward a more simplified charging scheme, I find it more and more difficult to estimate how much a search on NewsNet costs. I need to factor in one connect rate while the search is being run, a higher connect rate once I start viewing headlines or the full text of retrieved items, a per-item charge that varies with the amount of information displayed, and surcharges for the gateway services, such as TRW or Investment ANALY$T. Fortunately, I can set my options to have the per-record charges displayed when I review the headlines, and I can review my cumulative costs during the search.

GENERAL
ONLINE SERVICES

America Online

CONTACT INFORMATION

NAME America Online Inc.

ADDRESS 8619 Westwood Center Drive
Vienna, VA 22182

TELEPHONE 800/827-6364; 703/448-8700

CUSTOMER Monday through Friday 9:00am - 2:00am Eastern time
SERVICE HOURS Saturday and Sunday noon - 1:00am Eastern time
Technical representatives are available from
6:00am to 4:00am Eastern time; 7 days a week.

EMAIL through AOL: keyword: Help, click on [Email to
the staff] live online help—keyword: TechLive
(staffed 24 hours a day; 7 days a week) through
Internet: email to fulfill2@aol.com

WEB HOME PAGE http://www.aol.com/

SERVICE 24 hours a day; 7 days a week
AVAILABILITY

DESCRIPTION OF INFORMATION AVAILABLE

America Online, or AOL, provides access to electronic discussion forums, constantly updated newswires, databases of magazine and newspaper articles, full access to the Internet with a proprietary Web browser, live "chat" rooms, and online shopping.

One of the fastest growing of the general online services, AOL distributes its online access software through direct mail, shrink-wrapped with magazine issues, and prepackaged with other software programs. It is one of the easiest services to navigate and has the most comprehensive user documentation available online.

The databases of articles are relatively weak, particularly when compared to those available through another general online service, CompuServe. Its access to the Internet, on the other hand, is one of the best. AOL also provides a good selection of newswires for the day's news.

FIGURE 26
Main Menu

ROADMAP OF RESOURCES

When you first log on to America Online, the main menu presents you with 14 icons from which to choose. See Figure 26. There is a fair amount of overlap among these groupings; you find the same file referenced under several icons. For example, *The Atlantic Monthly* appears in the Newsstand, Reference, Entertainment, and Education groups.

The groupings include, in rough order of usefulness for the online searcher:

Today's News—Reuters newswire, Business Wire, PR Newswire, and Knight-Ridder newswire (updated continuously)

Reference Desk—links to most of the searchable article databases on AOL and an encyclopedia

Newsstand—a collection of all periodicals and publishers on AOL

Internet Connection—information about the Internet; access to WWW, FTP, telnet, gopher, and Internet newsgroups

Personal Finance—current stock quotes, access to discount brokerages, article databases, and business news

Computing—access to computer magazines (usually limited to the current issue and perhaps a short, selected backfile of articles), hardware and software vendor online stores, downloadable software, and discussion forums

Education—basic reference sources (encyclopedia, atlas, thesaurus), and corporate forums

Clubs & Interests—wide variety of forums for special interest groups and associations, and online salons

Entertainment—entertainment industry news and corporate forums (ABC, Disney, Virgin Records)

Travel—airline reservations, travel guides and magazines, and discussion forums

Sports—sports news, statistics and team information, and broadcast networks' forums
Marketplace—online shopping
People Connection—online chat rooms
Kids Only—basic reference sources (encyclopedia, atlas), games, and discussion forums

You can also search the Directory of Services, which contains searchable descriptive words of all AOL's forums, databases, and services. The indexing is a bit erratic; be sure to use several alternative terms for your topics. This is a separate finding tool from the keyword access to resources on AOL, which assigns one or two words to uniquely identify each forum or service.

TIPS FOR USING AMERICA ONLINE'S FINDING AIDS

There is quite a variety of information sources available on AOL; unfortunately, each must be searched separately. The most efficient way to use AOL is to invest some time finding the most valuable resources, then mark them as [Personal Choices]. To add a selection to your [Personal Choices], pull down the [Go To] menu and click on [Edit Go To] menu. You can add as many as ten sites and then jump directly to them by pulling down the [Go To] menu and selecting the source by number, or by pressing <ctrl> <item number>. See Figure 27 for the [Go To] menu with some personal choices listed. If I wanted to scan the top news from today's *New York Times*, I could press <ctrl> <4> and go directly to that screen.

FIGURE 27
Go To Menu

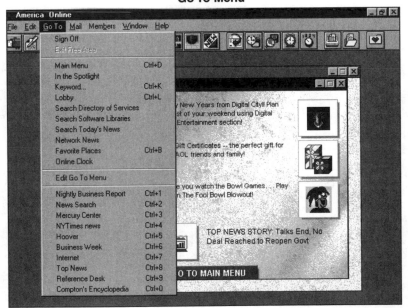

AOL also has an icon for [Favorite Places], which is similar to "bookmarks" on Internet WWW browsers. You can mark any Internet sites you find useful here, and click on the icon to jump directly to one of these sites. Oddly, you can also mark other AOL services and information sources—it duplicates the function of the [Personal Choices] menu, but allows the addition of Internet addresses as well.

Following are notes and comments on the best resources within each of the 14 groups of America Online. When you first set up an account on AOL, use your free time (10 hours, to be used within the first 30 days after you sign on) to explore each area. Save the resources you find most valuable either in your [Personal Choices] list or in the [Favorite Places] icon.

Keep in mind that almost all of the following groups include discussion forums as well as other information sources. Unless the discussion forums are particularly noteworthy, I do not mention them separately in each group.

Today's News

This area contains wire stories of the past several days, photos of recent news events, and links to Internet sites covering current topics. In January 1996 those included a site on the federal government shutdown, the U.S. Department of State home page, the FBI's 10 Most-Wanted list, among other sites. See Figure 28 for a picture of the [Today's News] screen. The design format for this screen is similar to that of the other groups' main screens.

In addition to the customized folders of specific events or issues, you can scan newswire headlines by general topic—U.S. & World, Business, Entertainment, Sports, and Weather. Within each of these sections are selected newswire stories and links to other sources within AOL. For example, within the Business section are links

FIGURE 28
Today's News Screen

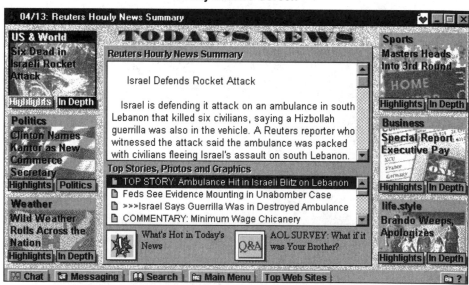

FIGURE 29
Business News Screen

to *Business Week*'s site, Market News, and Portfolio (stock quotes and investment information). See Figure 29 for a picture of the [Business News] screen.

You can select the icon for [Search News] to search all newswire stories. The sources include Reuters and Knight-Ridder newswires and two press release wires, Business Wire and PR Newswire.

There are also icons for [Top Internet Sites] under each [News] icon, which link you to a number of newspapers' home pages.

Reference Desk

Although many of the resources listed in the [Reference Desk] can be found elsewhere as well, this is the most efficient source for scanning almost all searchable databases on AOL. Unfortunately, you still need to search each source separately, so pick the most likely sources first in order to get the most value for your online time. See Figure 30.

The searchable databases are listed alphabetically. Somewhat confusingly, within this list of titles (e.g., *Atlantic Monthly*, *Barrons' Booknotes*, *The Bible*, *Children's Software Information*) is an item called [Magazines]. If you click on this item, you see another list of magazine sites within AOL.

Calling the sites "searchable databases" is somewhat misleading. Many of the sites have very little searchable information. C-SPAN's site, for example, contains lists of its "shoot schedules," but contains no transcripts or other tangible information from its broadcasts. On the other hand, some periodicals such as *Commerce Business Daily* and the *Chicago Tribune* offer extensive archives of back issues. The *Chicago Tribune* has issues as far back as 1985. You can't do very sophisticated searching, but it's often a good way to find a few good articles on a subject. I was looking for a couple of recent articles on Web browsers, so I clicked on [*PC World*] and searched for the phrase "best Web browsers." I found five or six articles right on point (along with five or six articles that were not even remotely relevant).

FIGURE 30
Reference Desk Main Menu

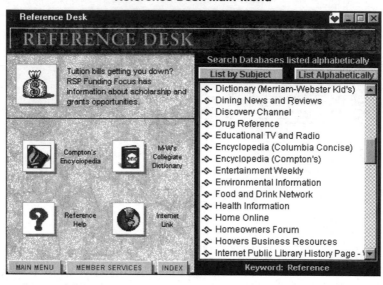

Keep in mind that the information available through AOL may be an abbreviated version of a source's online product. *Congressional Quarterly* has some basic information in AOL—profiles of politicians, white papers on "making Washington work for you," selected transcripts and so on—but there is no mention that *CQ* also offers much more in-depth databases through its own online service.

The [Reference Desk] also contains a dictionary, thesaurus and encyclopedia, as well as links to Internet reference sites such as AT&T's 800 Directory, the Library of Congress, Purdue University's Virtual Reference Desk, and the Yahoo Internet search engine.

Newsstand

The [Newsstand] is a collection of all the periodicals and publishers on AOL. This list is more comprehensive than the [Magazines] selection under [Searchable Databases] in the Reference group, since this list includes publications that do not provide any searchable material, but only the current issue, a description of the publication, and information on how to subscribe. It also includes some searchable databases *not* included in the Reference group, such as "Columnists and Features Online" where you can find anything from opinion pieces on pro-life demonstrations to medical advice columns.

Curiously, it contains some magazines that have searchable back issues but are not, for some reason, included in the [Magazines] selection in the Reference group. *Computer Life*, for example, appears under "Computer Publications" in the [Newsstand] (Publications) list but not in the Reference group, even though it *does* allow searching of back issues.

One surprisingly robust database is the Mercury Center Library, a service of the *San Jose Mercury News*. You can jump to it directly with the keyword MC LIBRARY or you can find it under the *San Jose Mercury News* by clicking on the [News Library] icon at the main [Newsstand] screen. This is one of the few services for which there is a surcharge; the charge is $.80/minute during prime time (6:00am - 6:00pm local time, weekdays) or $.15/minute during nonprime time (6:00pm - 6:00am local time, weekdays, and all day Saturday and Sunday). It offers access to a number of regional newspapers, some going back five to ten years, as well as ten years' worth of the *Mercury News*. The Mercury Center also offers the News Hound, an electronic clipping service of all Mercury Center publications. For $9.95/month, it monitors news sources every hour and sends relevant articles to your electronic mail account.

Internet Connection

In addition to the [Internet Resources] or [Top Internet Sites] icons in each of the other groups, AOL has a separate section for full access to the Internet. In order to access Web sites through AOL you need to use the most recent version of the AOL software. For Windows users this is version 2.5, and for Macintosh users it is version 2.6. (You can get the newest version by going to keyword UPGRADE.) AOL offers the easiest and most straightforward access to the Internet of any of the general online services.

In addition to using AOL's WWW browser, FTP, telnet, gopher services, and Web search engines, you have access to Usenet newsgroups and listservs. Subscribers can also create their own home pages using the AOL Web Page Toolkit.

This area also includes a number of helpful files about the Internet—columns by Internet experts, a database of listservs, netiquette tips, and beginners' guides to the Internet.

Personal Finance

This group includes stock quotes, investment portfolio management, a number of discussion forums on investment topics, and newswire stories on business topics. The main screen shows icons for [Financial Newsstand], [Finance Forums], [Internet Resources], [Quotes & Portfolios], [Research], and [What's Hot].

In addition, the main screen lists [Financial Resources]—a variety of sources including *Business Week* Online, Hoover's Handbooks, *Investor's Business Daily*, and the Fidelity Online Investment Center. You can track the performance of your stock portfolio, get Morningstar's ratings of mutual funds, and read comments about the market from investment analysts. The Hoover's Handbook collection is particularly useful for finding concise overviews of large publicly- and privately-held companies as well as outlooks on a number of industries. Although the financial information is not as up-to-date as I would like, the information on companies' histories and corporate culture and list of competitors is quite useful.

Also available in this group is Disclosure Inc.'s site, offering free access to the full text of companies' filings with the U.S. Securities & Exchange Commission along with information on how to purchase additional material. This is one of the easiest access points to the SEC's EDGAR filings database—you can get to it free of charge by going to http://www.sec.gov/edgarhp.htm, but the formatting is much better through Disclosure on AOL.

The [Financial Newsstand] icon links you to the *New York Times Business Report*, *San Jose Mercury Business*, "Nightly Business Report" transcripts, and so on. It also provides links to several financial publications' sites on the Internet. From a separate [Internet Resources] icon, you can access stock quotes, financial news sources on the Web, the Internet Business Center, and other Internet sources.

The [Research] icon contains a list of many of the same sources listed under the other icons, which is a bit confusing at first. The resources listed here usually do not allow full-text searching, but only permit users to browse one issue at a time. To find a recent article in the Fidelity Online Investment center, I had to click on Fidelity's main screen, then on the [Newsworthy] icon, then on [Article Reprints], then on [Fidelity Focus Current Issue], then on the title of the article I wanted. This seems like a lot of work for a single article. The [Reference Desk] or [Newsstand] groups provide more useful tools for research than this group does.

Computing

This group contains a wide variety of downloadable files, primarily shareware utilities, fonts, and graphics. There are also a number of discussion forums on computer-related topics; this is a great place to find an expert to help you trouble-shoot your installation of Windows 95, design an Excel spreadsheet, or select a CD-ROM drive. A number of hardware and software vendors have online stores and catalogs.

There are also quite a few computer magazines listed here. In addition to current and searchable back issues, you can link to magazines' Internet home pages.

Education

The Education group includes selected magazines and forums for corporations and other organizations in the education industry, such as Kaplan (the test preparation courses), Compton's NewMedia, and National Geographic. These sources include articles, promotions, and discussion forums. Basic reference sources such as an encyclopedia, dictionary, and thesaurus are also available. The [Top Internet Sites] icon points you to Internet resources such as museum Web pages, the Virtual Frog Dissection Web page, the Virtual Online University, and the complete works of Shakespeare.

An interesting feature of the Education group is the Academic Assistance Center. It is designed to help students with homework questions as well as to provide suggestions on how to prepare for standardized exams such as the SAT and to study for end-of-term exams. In addition, it can connect students with teachers who offer online or electronic mail assistance with school questions. This "Teacher Pager" service is available 24 hours; there is usually a teacher available for immediate assistance between 5:00pm and midnight Eastern time. During other times, an electronic mail response is sent within 24 hours.

Clubs & Interests

Although the name of this group suggests hobbyists and social clubs, there are a surprising number of associations, lobbying groups, and special interest groups here as well. Among the discussion forums and information databases are ones for

AARP, the deaf community, entrepreneurs, Gay and Lesbian issues, and the Nature Conservancy.

There are also online salons—discussion groups focusing on current events, books, and other shared interests.

This is a useful people resource—experts and files of information on specific topics. If you are looking for "soft" information, check here for specialists in your area of interest.

Entertainment

Most of the information in the Entertainment group consists of discussion of current entertainment media, critics' reviews of movies, television programs, books, music and games, and information on Hollywood stars.

Under the [ShowBiz News & Info] icon are selected newswire stories on the entertainment industry, arts and leisure news from the *New York Times,* and forums for *Entertainment Weekly* and *Extra.* The "Columnists and Features" described in the NEWSSTAND group is also available through the Entertainment group.

A number of entertainment industry companies have corporate forums in this group, with information on their products, discussion forums, schedules of upcoming events, and online shopping.

Travel

This group provides access to the EAASY SABRE airline reservation system as well as travel guides, travel and tourist magazines, discussion forums on travel-related topics and corporate forums for American Express, *Backpacker* magazine, Travelers Advantage travel club, and other travel industry companies.

For an additional annual fee of $49, you can also access the AutoVantage database of new and used cars.

Sports

The Sports group contains sports news, statistics and scores, discussion forums on all areas of sports, broadcast networks' forums, and fantasy sports leagues.

Marketplace

For those of us who can't survive on just the cable shopping channel and mail-order catalogs, the Marketplace offers online shopping, AOL subscribers' classified ads, and the Shoppers' Advantage shopping club.

People Connection

Unlike other groups, this area contains no databases or discussion forums. It is solely a collection of online chat areas. This is where you can find real-time discussions and banter on everything from games to Hollywood to "Star Trek." Generally, there tends to be little in-depth discussion; if you want thoughtful conversation, head over to a discussion forum.

Kids Only

The name says it all. It's a great place for the 5- to 14-year-old age group, with a number of basic reference sources, discussion forums specifically targeted to children, and online games.

In addition to finding information resources through these groups, you can search the Directory of Services, which includes descriptions of all AOL's information sources and discussion areas. When you type in a word or words encompassing your interest, it searches names and descriptions of forums, databases, and product support forums (e.g., Microsoft Works and Solution Series Support) and displays descriptions of the relevant areas. Unfortunately, the resource descriptions are not written consistently, so remember to use plenty of synonyms. For example, in my search to find medical information I searched for Medicine, Medical, Health, or Physician. I found some good pointers— Emergency Response Club (a forum for Emergency Medical Technicians), Issues in Mental Health, a discussion forum, and AARP Online, which has both a discussion forum and databases focused on caregiving and health issues. But I also retrieved hits for Kaplan (offering test preparation for the MCAT medical school test), and the state of Utah's forum and collection of files.

The Directory of Services works best if you have a fairly specific interest such as investing or politics. If you search for NEWS, you'll get hundreds of hits, many of which aren't relevant, including the Pet Care Forum, The Gadget Guru, and Wine & Dine Online.

There's quite a difference between the Directory of Services and the keyword searching. When you pull down the [Go To] menu and click on [Keyword], you need to type in the name of the area within AOL you want to go to.

If I type in Stock in the keyword screen, I am taken to the StockLink area (current stock quotes). If I type in Stock in the Directory of Services, I am given a list of AOL areas supposedly pertaining to stock. (In addition to pointers to Your Money, StockLink, Reuters News, and Morningstar Mutual Funds, I also retrieved the description to iGOLF, an interactive golf game. Perhaps stocks are customarily discussed during golf games?)

Unfortunately, AOL doesn't provide much in the way of documentation. New subscribers receive a 41-page *Member Guide*, which provides basic information on AOL's features. This guide gives very little information, though, on how a searcher can use AOL to find solid information. There is no help offered on how to compose a search, or whether search terms can be truncated, or how the search results are sorted. There is scant guidance in identifying searchable databases on a particular topic.

Anyone who intends to use AOL for research should purchase *The Official America Online for Windows Tour Guide*, available through AOL. (*See* "Where to Get More Information.") This 500+ page book gives users the information that should accompany the *Member Guide,* but doesn't.

As with most general online services, there are no training courses or update sessions; nor does AOL send out periodic subscriber newsletters, although Steve Case, the CEO of AOL, does post a monthly letter to subscribers.

Commonly-Used Commands

Begin a search	**\<Ctrl\> \<K\>** [**Keyword**] (for the PC) or **\<Command\> \<K\>** [**Keyword**] (for the Mac) or pull down the [**Go To**] menu
Search terms:	
x AND y	x **AND** y
x OR y	x **OR** y
x BUT NOT y	x **NOT** y
x NEXT TO y	"x y"
x WITHIN n WORDS OF y	not available
x SAME SENTENCE y	not available
x SAME PARAGRAPH y	not available
x SAME FIELD y	not available
Date Searching	not available
Field Searching	not available
Truncation	not reliable *
Display results	done automatically when search is completed
Help	click on [**Help**] or [**Member Services**]
Cost:	
for session charges up to this point	not available directly. Click on [**Online Clock**] for length of current session
for database rates	usually no extra charges
for total cost when logging off	not available directly. Click on [**Member Services**] or **\<Ctrl\> \<K\>** [**Billing**] (for the PC) or **\<Command\> \<K\>** [**Billing**] (for the Mac) for the current account balance and prior month's bill.
Log off	**\<Alt\> \<F4\>** (for the PC) or **\<Command\> \<Q\>** (for the Mac)

*AOL automatically searches word stems (e.g., a search for bear also retrieves bears and bearing). This feature cannot be disabled should you want to search for Bear not bears.

Keep in mind that your searches are limited to one specific area at a time. That is, you cannot combine a search in *PC World* with a search in *Computer Life*; you must search each magazine separately.

In some databases, your search statement is limited to about forty characters. In other areas, there is no limit to the number of characters.

In most areas, the results of your search are ranked by relevancy and the first 20 headlines are displayed. You can see each additional set of twenty headlines by clicking on the [More] button at the bottom of the screen.

GETTING CONNECTED

You can access America Online via AOLnet (in selected cities), Sprintnet, Tymnet, or via the Internet. The log-on sequence is done through AOL's proprietary software; you do not need to know the network address or other sign-on commands.

via toll-free call: 800/716-0023 (surcharge of $4.80/hour)
via Internet: via TCP/IP only
AOL supports speeds from 2400bps through 28,800bps via AOLnet; 2400bps through 14,400bps via Sprintnet; 2400bps only via Tymnet.
Modem and terminal settings are handled through AOL's proprietary software.

System requirements for AOL software are:
Mac or IBM-compatible 386 processor or better
4MB RAM
Windows 3.1 or higher (for IBM-compatible)
4MB available on hard disk

AOL offers both incoming and outgoing Internet access.

POWER TOOLS

There are several keyboard shortcuts that save some time in navigating through AOL's screens. For simplicity, I describe the keystrokes for an IBM computer. If you are using a Mac, substitute the <command> key for the <ctrl> key. Use <ctrl> <k> to jump to an area identified by its keyword. Use the <ctrl> <1> through <10> to jump to one of the ten most useful sites that you identified in your [Favorite Places] list. Use <ctrl> <F4> to close down a window, or pull down the [Window] menu and click on [Close all Windows]. (With a Mac, you must pull down the [Window] menu.)

Following are a few other suggestions on how to make the most of your time online.

• Turn on the session log by pulling down the File menu, select [Logging] and select [Open] under Session Log. This saves all documents and files you display on the screen. So, for example, I could log on, use the <ctrl> <6> to jump to *Business Week*, click on the top stories, display the first screen of each story I want to read, log off, then read the articles offline. Alternatively, after closing the session log, I could jump to the Member Services area (keyword HELP), which does not incur any connect-time charges, and review my downloaded articles there.

- If you need to think about a search, answer a phone call, or toggle over to another application, jump to Member Services first to avoid incurring additional time charges.
- Avoid logging on during evening and weekend hours when the system is most heavily used and the response time is slower.
- AOL offers FlashSessions, the ability to set a time for the AOL software to log on, download your electronic mail and any specified files and Internet newsgroup messages, then log off. If you receive a large amount of electronic mail on your AOL account or if you have large files to download (say, the software upgrade to enable you to use AOL's Internet browser), set up a FlashSession to begin at 4:00am when the system is least likely to be busy.
- Bill Pytlovany, a Windows programmer, has written a shareware software package called Whale Express (Whale = W(indows)AOL) that further automates your online sessions and enables you to write extensive scripts. Pull down the [Go To] menu, select [Search Software Libraries], then search for software files that contain the word WHALE for the latest version of this shareware.

Although you may pay a bit more to access the Internet through AOL than directly through an Internet access provider, AOL offers an efficient way of finding useful Internet sites. Rather than use Web searching tools, go into the relevant subject section of AOL and click on the [Top Internet Sites] icon. The group host has done some evaluation, judgment, and checking to confirm that the sites are still active. It takes me a lot less time to find a few good political information sites through AOL than it does for me to use an Internet search engine and wade through the inactive sites, outdated sources, and irrelevant hits to find the few places I really want.

PRICING
The basic fee is $9.95/month for five hours of connect time. Additional hours are $2.95/hour. Some areas incur a surcharge; you are warned of this before entering these areas.

OTHER FEATURES
The America Online FAXLink Service provides information via fax concerning connectivity problems or error messages, and software and hardware incompatibilities.

Call 800/827-5551 from a touch-tone telephone. An automated voice system guides you through requesting the list of available faxes, and prompts you for your fax number. After the list is faxed to you, call the FAXLink number again, and request up to five faxes of interest to you at a time. Both the call and the use of the FAXLink Service are free.

EVALUATION OF AMERICA ONLINE

With the notable exception of the Mercury Center, there aren't very many useful databases for business searchers who need to do extensive research. You can search one magazine at a time, but given AOL's limited search engine, you can spend an inordinate amount of time online with little to show for your efforts.

On the other hand, AOL offers a good selection of wire service stories, conveniently sorted into broad category, in an easy to-use-format. When I heard of the death of Jerry Garcia and wanted immediate confirmation from a newswire, I went online with AOL, knowing I'd be able to find the sad news quickly. AOL also has convenient access to current *New York Times* and *Chicago Tribune* stories.

What do I like most about America Online?

- AOL has one of the most intuitive user interfaces available. When you first log on, you are greeted with a main menu that is clear and uncluttered. Each of the underlying menus is well-organized and understandable.

- Internet access through AOL is convenient and straightforward. I especially appreciated the pointers to relevant Internet sites mixed in with other online resources. I found it much easier to find a few useful Internet sites on a particular topic by going to the appropriate area and clicking on [Top Internet Sites] than to use the search engines available on the Internet itself.

- AOL offers world-class online help services for a general online service. Context-sensitive help is available at virtually every screen; if you have further questions, there is often a discussion forum within each service with additional information. You can also click on [User Services] to access extensive help files at no charge. Not only are there collections of the most frequently asked questions with answers, but there are also bulletin boards for technical topics and a discussion forum called Members Helping Members.

If you want live help, you can call a toll-free number, which is staffed 24 hours a day. It tends to be busy during the peak usage hours, though. Fortunately, AOL also offers Tech Support Live (keyword: TECH LIVE). This live chat area is always staffed with technical support and you can get quick answers to questions here. The chat room is a bit confusing at first—the tech support people are often answering several questions at once, and more questions come in all the time. This is a very convenient way for users to get quick help with simple questions, and adds to the feeling that help is always nearby.

- And finally, AOL is the only online service that offers access to the *Weekly World News*, the supermarket tabloid that first broke the story that 12 U.S. Senators are actually space aliens. I *do* appreciate being able to peruse this tabloid in the privacy of my own office instead of at the checkout stand.

What do I like least about America Online?

- My biggest gripe as an online searcher is that there is very little documentation available. The printed user's guide is woefully inadequate, and the online help does not address the needs of any but the most casual of online searchers. The searchable databases are not presented all in one place, nor is a complete list of online databases available through the finding tools.

- Unfortunately, many of the discussion forums and chat rooms tend to be dominated by adolescents intent on proving their offensiveness and/or ignorance. The occasional thoughtful posting is often drowned out in a flood of boorish comments. If I want to find a forum of professionals discussing business-related topics, I tend to go elsewhere.

- AOL software has been designed to keep most graphic images stored on the subscribers' computers. It is not practical to include all images in the initial software; each time you enter a new area, you wait for the images specific to that area to be downloaded to your machine. This can add a delay of 30 seconds to several minutes when connected at 14,400bps; at a slow speed, this can be a real annoyance. Unfortunately, you cannot stop these downloads once they begin; you simply have to wait out the delay.

A little-known feature does let you turn off the display of graphics which, although not eliminating the image downloads completely, does speed up the screen writing somewhat. At any menu, select [Members] from the menu bar and click on [Personal Choices]. At the next screen, click on [Multimedia Preferences]. You are given three choices of how you want graphics to appear. Select [Off] (only show graphics in documents on request), then click [OK]. Unfortunately, this still doesn't stop all graphics from being downloaded, and tends to lead to unpredictable screen displays. Use it with caution.

- AOL's subscriber policy permits essentially anonymous accounts. This lack of accountability leads to some of the more egregious "flames" in discussion areas and chat rooms and has led, in a few cases, to the sending of unsolicited pornography and other unwelcome email to unsuspecting subscribers. AOL is aware of the problem and is working on ways to solve it. My experience with other electronic forums suggests that one of the best ways to maintain at least a minimum level of civility is to insist on nonanonymous IDs and personal accountability of every subscriber's account holder.

CompuServe Information Service

CONTACT INFORMATION

NAME   CompuServe Information Service

ADDRESS   5000 Arlington Centre Boulevard
                            P.O. Box 20212
                            Columbus, OH 43220

TELEPHONE   800/848-8990; 614/457-8650

CUSTOMER   Monday through Friday 8:00am - midnight Eastern time
SERVICE HOURS   Saturday, Sunday and holidays noon - 10:00pm
                            Eastern time

EMAIL   through CompuServe: 70006,101 or GO FEEDBACK
                            through Internet: 70006.101@compuserve.com

WEB HOME PAGE   http://www.compuserve.com/

SERVICE   24 hours a day; 7 days a week
AVAILABILITY

DESCRIPTION OF INFORMATION AVAILABLE

The CompuServe Information Service offers a variety of resources:

- access to electronic forums (similar to electronic bulletin boards) on topics ranging from chess to desktop publishing to court reporting
- online databases comprising newspaper and magazine articles, company directories, biographical information, trademark information, and other information resources
- investment services including stock quotes, reports from brokerage houses, and stock selection tools

CompuServe also offers an Electronic Mall for online shopping, a real-time "chat" facility, and interactive games, for those times when you need a break from real work.

The information you can glean from CompuServe comes in the form of both 'soft' information—opinions of perceived experts—and "hard" information—financial data, published articles, and the like. The discussion forums are not to be discounted as a source for industry background and pointers to industry experts. CompuServe has promoted itself as an electronic home for professional groups and has a variety of professional interest forums. Researchers looking for guidance on how to begin a project on international trade practices with New Zealand, for example, could post a query in the International Trade Forum and probably receive replies within a few hours from subscribers in or familiar with New Zealand. The PR and Marketing Forum offers regular live conversations with communications experts. A medical researcher could tap into the Attention Deficit Disorder Forum for discussions of current therapies, ADD in the workplace, and new diagnostic tools.

Not surprisingly, a large number of computer hardware and software vendors have a presence on CompuServe, either with their own forums (e.g., NeXT Forum or Semantec Norton Utilities Forum) or by participating in one of the subject-specific forums (e.g., Graphics Developers Forum, or IBM Communications Forum for telecommunications on the IBM PC). Often, vendors upload software patches and updates to the Libraries (file areas) associated with their forum.

And finally, CompuServe provides access to a number of online databases of both current information (weather, news, sports scores) and in-depth collections of articles and business-related information. Resources pertaining to investing and finance are particularly strong. If you are looking for today's wire stories, this is often a cost-effective alternative to the high-powered search services such as Dow Jones News/Retrieval or LEXIS/NEXIS. If you want to do fairly simple searching of back issues of magazines, you can access many of the same databases that are available in the professional online services. The search engines are not always as flexible as the professional services—in most of CompuServe's databases you can't use nested logic (that is, [x or y] and [a or b]), nor can you view the title and Keyword-in-Context of retrieved stories (which means you must make a "purchasing decision" based on title and bibliographic citation alone).

On the other hand, if you want menu-driven access to a database you don't normally search, or if you want to search a source that isn't available elsewhere, you may often find that CompuServe is a reasonably-priced information service.

ROADMAP OF RESOURCES

The CompuServe *User's Guide* is one of the best-organized guides for a general online service. Given the wide variety of services on CompuServe (chat rooms, games, newswires, databases of articles, discussion forums), it is critical that new users have some signposts to guide them. Each chapter of the *Guide* covers a single aspect of CompuServe (news, magazines, sports, finance, and so on) and within each chapter is a description of the relevant information services and forums, along with cross-references to related sources.

CompuServe encourages new subscribers to use its front end software, CompuServe Information Manager (CIM), available in Windows, DOS, OS/2, and Macintosh versions. See Figure 31 for the WinCIM initial screen.

FIGURE 31
WinCIM Main Menu

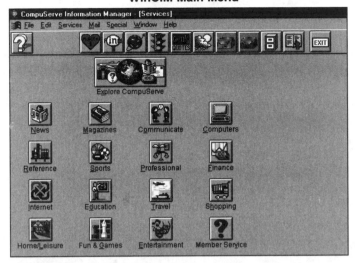

Unfortunately, there is very little documentation to help a user navigate through a plain ASCII online session. New users probably find CompuServe much less confusing when using CIM, but a frequent searcher may want to take advantage of the speed and flexibility of simply typing GO WORK to get to the Working From Home forum rather than having to click on [Services], then on [Go], then typing the name of the forum or remembering what each icon at the top of the screen means.

Some of the services within CompuServe require "terminal emulation"—a CIM user sees a plain screen instead of the point and click environment used in the rest of CompuServe. This mixture of plain ASCII and GUI interactions can be confusing at first, until you remember that many of the services offered on CompuServe are actually gateways to other online services that do not support point-and-click access.

During 1996 and 1997, CompuServe is planning to migrate all its service offerings to a system that does not support ASCII connections. When this happens, users are required to use CIM or other front end software, such as TapCIS or OZCIS (provided by third-party vendors).

If you log on to CompuServe in plain ASCII (that is, using a generic communications software package rather than the CompuServe Information Manager), you can navigate through the system with menu choices. The initial screen offers a first cut of options:

1 Access Basic Services
2 Member Assistance (FREE)
3 Communications/Bulletin Bds.
4 News/Weather/Sports
5 Travel
6 The Electronic MALL/Shopping
7 Money Matters/Markets
8 Entertainment/Games
9 Hobbies/Lifestyles/Education
10 Reference
11 Computers/Technology
12 Business/Other Interests

Enter choice:

If you know which service you want, you can go directly there (GO APO, for example, to jump to the Associated Press Online). If you aren't sure of which resource(s) to search, select the most likely option from the initial menu and the subsequent menus until you have identified the database or forum you want.

If you are using CIM, the initial screen displays the same options in the form of icons instead. You can point-and-click your way through the choices or you can press the [Go] icon (a traffic light) and type in the name of the forum or database you want.

In either CIM or plain ASCII, you can use CompuServe's FIND command to identify databases and forums on a particular topic. Keep in mind that this is not a full text search of either forum contents or online services; this is simply a search of the descriptions of services and forums available, and a fairly rough search at that.

A search for AIDS and HEALTH turned up the following sources:

1	AARP +	[AARP]
2	Aids News Clips +	[AIDSNEWS]
3	CCML AIDS Articles($)	[CCMLAIDS]
4	Health & Fitness Forum +	[GOODHEALTH]
5	Health Database Plus($)	[HLTDB]
6	Health/Fitness +	[FITNESS]
7	HealthNet	[HNT]
8	Holistic Health Forum +	[HOLISTIC]
9	Human Sexuality Databank +	[HUMAN]
10	IQuest($)	[IQUEST]
11	Medsig Forum +	[MEDSIG]
12	Multiple Sclerosis Forum +	[MULTSCLER]
13	NORD Services/Rare Disease DB +	[NORD]
14	PaperChase-MEDLINE($)	[PAPERCHASE]
15	People Magazine	[PEOPLE]

I suspect that AARP turned up because of a reference to medical aids. I could not discern any reason for the Multiple Sclerosis Forum to have been retrieved, nor *People* magazine. Use this finding tool with a grain of salt.

TIPS FOR USING COMPUSERVE'S FINDING AIDS

I have found that, although CompuServe offers a wide variety of types of information (discussion groups, databases, vendor forums), I tend to go to the same few places for most online research. Rather than having to remember the not-always-intuitive names, I add them to the [Favorite Places] icon on CIM. To add an item to the [Favorite Places] list, click on the [Favorite Places] icon, click on [Add], and type in the name and a description of the feature or service you wish to add. I could also create a [Personal Menu] for when I log on via a plain ASCII connection.

Since CompuServe does not send out updated system documentation, it's imperative that users read the monthly *CompuServe Magazine*—this is the only print source for information on new services, search tips, and pointers to redesigned forums.

It is also a good idea to at least scan the [What's New] menu that displays at log on. This list of new services, promotions, changes in rates or billing, and other information is updated weekly.

Commonly-Used Commands

Because CompuServe essentially provides gateway access to information services rather than maintaining its own front end search engine, commands are not uniform across CompuServe's databases. The following are the most common commands used in many of the information services.

Begin a search	**GO [Database Name]**
Search terms:	
x AND y	x **AND** y
x OR y	x **OR** y
x BUT NOT y	not usually available
x NEXT TO y	x y
x WITHIN n WORDS OF y	not usually available
x SAME SENTENCE y	not usually available
x SAME PARAGRAPH y	not usually available
x SAME FIELD y	not usually available
Date Searching	done through menu selection
Field Searching	done through menu selection
Truncation	/ or ?
Display results	done through menu selection
Help	**help** or **?**
Cost:	
for session charges up to this point	sometimes provided during the search session
for database rates	**GO RATES**
for total cost when logging off	not available directly. **GO CHARGES** displays your current account balance and prior months' charges
Log off	**BYE**

NOTE: Knowledge Index (**GO KI**) uses commands similar to the DIALOG system's commands. See the Command/Advanced Searching help screen for more information.

GETTING CONNECTED

CompuServe offers access through its packet-switching network in major U.S. and Canadian cities at no charge. Access outside these areas is available through public packet switching networks such as Tymnet and SprintNet, and through the Internet. There are communications surcharges for access through any network except CompuServe's and the Internet.

CompuServe supports its own front end software, called the CompuServe Information Manager. CIM is available in DOS, Windows, OS/2 and Macintosh versions. CompuServe also permits access through third-party session manager software such as TapCIS and OZCIS. All terminal settings are handled automatically by CIM software and usually are menu-driven with third-party software.

System requirements for CompuServe Information Manager for Windows are:
386 processor or better
2MB RAM (4MB recommended)
Windows 3.1 or higher
4MB available on hard disk

CompuServe provides incoming and outgoing Internet access. Users can telnet into CompuServe (a convenient way to avoid communications surcharges if you are outside the CompuServe network) and can access the Internet through CompuServe. Currently, telnet access to CompuServe supports only ASCII connections; CompuServe expects to provide support for CIM access in the future. Surprisingly, there are few glitches when connecting to CompuServe via the Internet; the <backspace> key works reliably (unlike connections to other online services) and the connection seems to be smooth, clear, and relatively problem-free.

Rates for outgoing Internet access are $2.95/hour after the first five hours of CompuServe usage each month.

POWER TOOLS

Because CompuServe began as a consumer-oriented electronic bulletin board and electronic shopping service, it has not developed the kinds of power tools we expect from the professional online services.

Most forums and databases maintain help files and/or user guides in the Library associated with each forum or database. Often, the main menu includes a pointer to these resources; if it doesn't, you can search the Library for relevant files. If you are connected in ASCII mode, select [Libraries], select the [Library] associated with the database or forum section that looks most relevant, choose [Browse Thru Files], then type in keywords such as GUIDE, INFORMATION, or HELP. This searches through the keyword descriptions of all the files in that Library and displays the filename, size, and

FIGURE 32
Searching within Forum Libraries

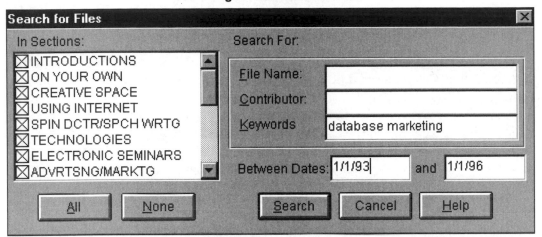

description. You can download or print the relevant files. If you are connected through CIM, click on the [Search Library] icon (a magnifying glass looking at book spines), select [Search], type in keywords such as GUIDE, INFORMATION, or HELP, then select [Retrieve] to download the relevant files. See Figure 32 for a search of a forum Library. Given CompuServe's push over the years to develop and encourage forums targeted to professionals, these forum Libraries can often be excellent sources of background information on industry issues. There are forums on subjects ranging from natural medicine to public relations professionals to women in aviation.

Some of the more comprehensive research databases do offer short-cuts and commands to bypass some of the menus; unfortunately, because access to these databases is through a gateway to an external source, there is no uniformity of commands. If you find that you are consistently searching Business Database or Knowledge Index, for example, it would be worth your while to download the lengthy documentation available and familiarize yourself with any tools available for expert searchers.

PRICING

Under the Standard Pricing Plan, users pay $9.95/month for five hours of access to most services, including discussion forums, newswires, many reference sources, current stock quotes, and games. Additional connect time is charged at $2.95/hour. There are additional surcharges for "Premium services," with either a charge per transaction (per search, per quote, per report, per article) or a charge per minute. These surcharges range from $.05 per stock listing to $50 per issue of the *International Harry Schultz Letter*.

Most Premium services display surcharges at the initial menu; you must accept the charges by hitting the carriage return before entering a surcharged area. The Premium services include such databases and services as Company Screening, TRW Business Profiles, and Business Demographics.

CompuServe also offers a Value Plan which consists of a monthly fee of $24.95 for 20 hours of access and $1.95/hour for additional usage.

For information on rates, type GO RATES. This leads you to a series of menus through which you can select the specific online service for which you want rate information. Unfortunately, CompuServe does not provide a convenient tabular or columnar listing of all rates.

Comparing rates among Premium service databases is a daunting task at best. You must factor in connect charges, per-record charges, surcharges, complexity of the search, and the sources available in each database. *CompuServe Companion*, published by BiblioData, provides an excellent matrix comparing the relative cost for three hypothetical searches: a simple, single query line search, a 15-minute search resulting in four articles, and a complex search. See "Where to Get More Information" for information on how to order this book.

OTHER FEATURES

Most of the information available on CompuServe is in plain ASCII text. However, a number of finance publications are now also available in Adobe Acrobat PDF (Portable Document Format), meaning that the version you receive is formatted to be similar to the printed version. You must download the issue (rather than read it on the screen) and you must have the Adobe Acrobat software in order to view or print the retrieved document. These PDF documents are available in the PUBLICATIONS ONLINE Premium service (GO PUBLONL). These reports can be expensive—surcharges run from $1 to $50 per report—but the ability to view graphical information in its original format is often worth the additional cost.

The IQUEST service, a gateway service provided by Telebase Systems, provides access to a number of commercial online services, including DIALOG, CDE Plus, NewsNet and DataStar. IQUEST also offers live online help; if you type SOS, you are connected in "chat mode" with an information specialist. It's very comforting to see "Hello, this is Joe. How can I help you?" when you are frustrated or confused about how a search is proceeding. The information specialist's answers are usually quick, specific, and complete. This is particularly helpful when you are searching a database with which you are not familiar and what you really need is on-the-spot help. IQUEST is a terminal emulation program, meaning you switch from point-and-click interactions to menu-by-menu interactions. See Figure 33 for a portion of an IQUEST search.

Knowledge Index (GO KI) provides gateway access to over 100 databases on DIALOG at the very competitive rate of $.40/minute and no per-document charges, making a search in Knowledge Index significantly less expensive than searching the corresponding files directly through DIALOG. KI is a limited service, though. Not all DIALOG files are available, and access is available only during nonbusiness hours—Monday through Thursday 6:00pm to 5:00am local time and from 6:00pm Friday through 5:00am Monday. Databases available in KI include many local newspapers, ABI/INFORM,

FIGURE 33
IQUEST Search

After menus, select [Company Research], then [General Business News], then [Trade &
Industry Database Fulltext]

* ENTER SUBJECT WORDS *

SEARCH TIPS: Omit all punctuation and small, common words (examples: the, as,
                 in, on, for, an, of).

SEARCH EXAMPLES: video game/ AND sales
                   videocassette recorder OR video cassette recorder OR VCR
                   Lotus 1 2 3

Type H for more help and examples.

ENTER SUBJECT WORDS
-> disney AND celebration place

Your search in TRADE & INDUSTRY DATABASE FULLTEXT
will use the following search statement:

subject words.................DISNEY AND CELEBRATION PLACE

PRESS   TO SELECT
  1   Add a field
  2   Change terms in a field
  3   Remove one or all fields

  4   Start the Search ... $ 2.00

  5   Database Description and Pricing Information
  6   Consult with a Search Specialist
  7   Cancel Search (Return to Main Menu)

  H   for Help, C for Commands

Total charges thus far: $ 0.00
-> 4

...

There are 19 item(s) that satisfy your search phrase.
We will show you the most recent 5.

You may wish to print or capture this data if possible.

Heading #1   Search: 01-01-1996 20:53

DIALOG(R)File 148:(c) 1995 Info Access Co. All rts. reserv.

08086471   SUPPLIER NUMBER: 17213065 (USE FORMAT 7 OR 9 FOR FULL TEXT)
I-way: AT&T teams with *Disney* for the community of the future.
WORD COUNT: 1400   LINE COUNT: 00135

COMPANY NAMES: Walt *Disney* Co.—Services; American Telephone and
Telegraph Co.—Services

FIGURE 33 (continued)

```
INDUSTRY CODES/NAMES:  TELC   Telecommunications
DESCRIPTORS:  Information superhighway—Services
PRODUCT/INDUSTRY NAMES:  7375000 Database Vendors
SIC CODES:  7375  Information retrieval services
TICKER SYMBOLS:  DIS; T
FILE SEGMENT:  CD File 275


Press <return> to continue.
...


Retrieving 2 full text article(s) will cost:                    $ 15.00
Do you wish to continue? (Y/N): y
```

Trade & Industry Index, and Standard & Poor's Corporate Records. Some other broad-based databases such as PROMT and the Dun & Bradstreet files are not available, though. It is intended for "end-user" searching only, not mediated searching. What does that mean? Essentially, anyone who is doing a search on behalf of another person for which a fee is charged cannot use KI. This includes information brokers and other independent researchers-for-hire who pass along the online charges to their clients.

CompuServe offers electronic clipping services through its Executive News Service (GO ENS). ENS monitors the Associated Press wires, Dow Jones News Service, electronic press releases, UPI wires, and other news services. You can set up a "folder" that continually monitors the wire services for stories containing keywords you specify. Stories are kept for up to 14 days in your folder.

As a general online service, CompuServe does not the offer sophisticated features available through the professional search services, such as redirection of search results to a user's Internet electronic mail account, saving and re-executing of search strategies, and billing account code tracking.

CompuServe provides outgoing Internet access through a variety of protocols. Electronic mail, telnet, FTP, and Usenet newsgroups are available for CIM and plain ASCII users. In addition, with CompuServe's acquisition of SPRY, it is now offering a proprietary World Wide Web browser, NetLauncher. CompuServe has made efforts to educate its subscribers about Netiquette, establishing several discussion forums on Internet use, adding a Netiquette item to the Usenet access menu, and providing FAQs (frequently asked questions) in most access menus.

Tabular data is often difficult to find online. Most online versions of the *Fortune* 500, for example, include the article text but do not include the actual list of the 500 companies. CompuServe offers unique access to the full, current list of the *Fortune* Industrial 500, Service 500, and Most Admired companies in its FORTUNE forum. The complete text of the current issue, plus selected back issues, are also available in the Fortune Library.

EVALUATION OF COMPUSERVE INFORMATION SERVICE

For my money, of the general online services, CompuServe offers the best variety of information resources for your search dollar. The gateways to commercial services, such as DataStar, FT Profile, DIALOG, NewsNet, and Ovid Technologies allow subscribers to access a number of different systems using the same command language without needing to establish separate accounts with each service. Granted, you may often pay more per search if you access these services through CompuServe; on the other hand, if you are searching an unfamiliar database, you may sometimes wind up spending a good deal of time and money trying to get the search statement in the proper syntax, display the records properly, and so on. Having a single command language for these infrequently-searched files is convenient. Of the general online services reviewed in this book, CompuServe provides the greatest depth and best collection of articles, directories, and financial information.

CompuServe has done a decent job of presenting a wide variety of information sources in an organized, logical fashion. Unfortunately, I think it is confusing to many new subscribers. For example, if I select [Magazines] from the initial CIM screen, I am offered such options as [*Fortune*] (which includes a daily update, the current issue and back issues), [*Industry Week*] (which includes both current and back issues, a discussion forum, and opinion polls), [Business Database] (a gateway to a separate online database), and the [Entrepreneur's Small Business Square] (which offers a submenu including the Entrepreneurs' Small Business Forum, information on franchise and business opportunities, and an online catalog of business books and software, all sponsored by *Entrepreneur* magazine—but containing virtually no issues of the magazine itself!).

It's difficult for new subscribers to distinguish among databases of articles, discussion forums, and catalogs. Unfortunately, the section on this icon in the *User's Guide* does not contain any information on more than 50 percent of the items listed in the current [Magazine] menu. As CompuServe continues to add new services, the lack of updated documentation becomes more and more of a problem.

Oddly, the initial screen during an ASCII-mode session does not offer the option [Magazines]. You can find it by typing GO MAGAZINES, but it seems strange to be offered such different choices depending on whether you use CIM or plain ASCII mode.

What do I like most about CompuServe?
- Some of the resources on CompuServe are not available online anywhere else. It is gratifying to see how often new services are added to CompuServe, particularly for the professional (as opposed to consumer) community.

- The discussion forums on CompuServe are moderated by experts in the area on which the forum focuses. The forum participants are often experienced professionals; the signal-to-noise ratio tends to be higher here than it is in other venues. Files can be uploaded into forum libraries by subscribers (after a virus check by the forum leaders) and often contain archived discussions of topics of ongoing concern.

- The CompuServe Information Manager works well, given the fact that CompuServe itself is still (at this writing) operating in plain ASCII mode. For a front end system that has been added to an existing service, it doesn't feel like it has been cobbled together or added on after the fact.

What do I like least about CompuServe? These complaints may seem to indicate that I am expecting more from CompuServe than is warranted. It's a service that has grown up over the past few years from one that caters to the home market to one that is attractive to professional users as well. Unfortunately, its infrastructure has not kept up with the information content.

- There is no systematic effort to keep users informed of new information services or resources. Experienced users tend to skip the opening menu and go straight to the resource they need; CIM makes this particularly easy by allowing users, while still offline, to click on the specific item they want and bypass the opening menu altogether. As a result, users miss any online announcements about new services.

- I requested a new copy of WinCIM, along with any current documentation, in June 1995. The user guides were dated October 1994 and did not contain information on a number of new services available in mid-1995. Perhaps CompuServe could compile an annotated list of the new forums and services added since the guides were published and send a current update along with the guides to new subscribers.

- The *CompuServe Magazine*, while intended to serve the purpose of alerting subscribers to new services, tries to be all things for all people and fails to catch the attention of most experienced searchers. A typical issue has a section on the Electronic Mall, two or three lengthy articles on anything from access to Hollywood stars online to profiles of specific forums to hints on conducting online research (unfortunately, not updated since an article appeared in September 1993). Too many of the articles are not relevant to business searchers, and this tends to create the impression of many professionals that CompuServe is not much more than a place for discussions and online shopping. A separate, targeted newsletter, even one delivered to the electronic mail boxes of business users who request it, would go a long way toward making the professional searcher feel more welcome.

- As with most consumer services, it can often be difficult to get through to a customer service representative. During normal business hours, I often have to try eight or ten times before I get anything but a busy signal. Even after I get through, I can sit on hold for anywhere from 5 to 20 minutes. This can be frustrating for a user who is the middle of an online research project, and is another reason why the live online SOS feature on IQUEST is so valuable.

- I find the organization of forums and databases confusing. Why are Business Database and Computer Database included in both the Magazine and Reference categories, but Knowledge Index and IQUEST are only in Reference despite the fact that they too consist primarily of articles? I have to fight the feeling at the end of a search session that I have somehow missed a great resource because I didn't stumble across it through the menus or by using the FIND command. Since the written documentation is not kept updated, I have no way to be sure I haven't omitted the one source that provides the ideal answer to my research question.

- CompuServe does not offer training courses, which is unfortunate considering the depth and variety of its information resources. A number of books are available to help you search more efficiently, but the little system documentation sent to new users provides virtually no guidance on how to most efficiently and cost-effectively search its information sources. Fortunately, the books produced by third parties are often well written; I wish CompuServe would pay attention to this need and produce more updated print material for its professional searcher user base.

CONTACT INFORMATION

NAME	Microsoft Corp.
ADDRESS	One Microsoft Way Redmond, WA 98052-6399
TELEPHONE	800/386-5550
CUSTOMER SERVICE HOURS	Monday through Friday 7:00am - 2:00am Eastern time, Saturday and Sunday noon - 10:00pm Eastern time
EMAIL	through MSN: Click on [Member Lobby] from the MSN Central screen. Click on [MSN Support]. Click on [MSN Help Desk]. Click on [For More Information], then click on [Ask Member Support]. You are guided through creating an email message to Customer Support.
WEB HOME PAGE	http://www.msn.com/
SERVICE AVAILABILITY	24 hours a day; 7 days a week

DESCRIPTION OF INFORMATION AVAILABLE

The Microsoft Network (MSN) opened for business with much fanfare on August 24, 1995 in conjunction with the roll-out of Microsoft's Windows 95 operating system. The potential MSN subscriber base was initially limited to people who are running Windows 95, which left out the Macintosh community and anyone who didn't have a hard drive with 30 or 40MB to spare. It also left out many people who might connect to MSN through their office PCs, as most organizations are not early adopters of new operating systems and tend to avoid version 1.0 of any software. By the end of 1997, as Windows 95 becomes established within organizations and as more people buy new computers (with Windows 95 installed), the user base of MSN should have a fair amount of depth and breadth. Indications exist that Microsoft may change its marketing strategy and make MSN accessible to anyone with Internet access, rather than limiting it to Windows 95 users.

The value of a general online service is a function of both the information services available and the breadth of helpful experts subscribing to and participating in the service's discussion forums and chat areas. As MSN expands its user base and as its professional-oriented discussion forums become more active, MSN may become more of a resource.

As with other general online services, MSN provides a number of discussion forums, called BBSs, and online chat areas. Most of MSN is divided into broad "Categories," under which are BBSs, chat areas, files, and services. MSN has more of a family and personal-interest feel to it than America Online or Prodigy—almost half of MSN's Categories are oriented toward topics other than work or professional issues. Not only is there a Category devoted to chat rooms, but there are also Categories for Home & Family; People & Communities; Interests, Leisure & Hobbies; and Health & Fitness.

MSN has some newswire feeds and other current news sources, but is weaker than its general online service competitors in terms of providing basic reference sources or collections of articles online. It appears that Microsoft is positioning MSN primarily as an Internet access provider rather than as a source of information independent of the Net. Whether MSN will find it necessary to collect and organize additional information resources as well remains to be seen.

One of the most interesting features of MSN is its almost seamless fit with Windows 95. It feels the same, the tool bar is virtually identical, the help screens are structured similarly. When you click on a [README] file in MSN, the file is downloaded to your machine and, if you have Microsoft Word installed, launches Word and loads the document. You can embed a "Shortcut" file within an email message; when the recipient clicks on the [File] icon, MSN is launched and the user is logged on and taken directly to the file or service in the shortcut file.

ROADMAP OF RESOURCES

You can navigate through MSN's resources in several ways and, depending on your needs and interests, one navigation tool may be better for you than another. The primary ways of finding and going to specific forums or services are through the MSN Today screen, the MSN Central screen, or the Exploring MSN screen. These three displays present MSN resources in quite different lights; this can be confusing at first.

The best way to get an overview of what's available on MSN and understand where to find each service is through the Exploring MSN screen. When you first connect to MSN, this screen and MSN Today are opened as two active windows. See Figure 34 for the Exploring MSN screen and Figure 35 for the MSN Today screen.

The Exploring MSN display is similar to an Internet gopher menu viewed with browser software—you see a list of the broad Categories on the left, then a detailed display of the options within each Category expanded on the right. You can drill down into the Categories efficiently through the Exploring MSN screen, and you may find it very helpful to have a graphic display of what screen you came from to get down to each level. You don't have all the navigational functionality in Exploring MSN that you have when you go directly to each Category, but it is a much easier way of digging through MSN offerings.

FIGURE 34
Exploring MSN Screen

FIGURE 35
Initial MSN Today Screen

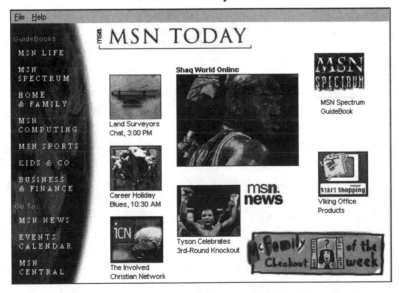

The other default display option for MSN is the MSN Today screen. Most of the screen is taken up by pictures and links to features within MSN. Usually a couple of BBSs are featured, a news item, an ad for a product or service, and links to a chat area or two. Along the left margin are links to "GuideBooks"—online magazines that list some (but by no means all) features, by broad topic. It's tempting to think that the GuideBooks are equivalent to the Categories; they're not, they are simply pointers to

FIGURE 36
MSN News

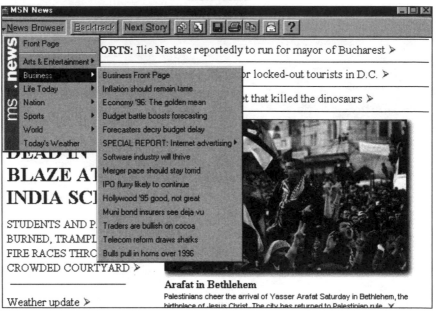

some interesting areas within MSN. GuideBooks include MSN Life, MSN Spectrum, Home & Family, MSN Computing, MSN Sports, Kids & Co., and Business & Finance. Below the GuideBooks are "Go To" links that take you directly to other features: MSN News, Events Calendar, Directory, and MSN Central. Here's where it gets confusing...the Go To MSN News link is different from the MSN News Category. The former is what I expected to see when I first logged on—a nice browser-like display of front-page news along with pull-down menus for other news sections, such as business, sports, and entertainment. See Figure 36 for the MSN News browser with the pull-down menus. The MSN News Category, on the other hand, consists primarily of text-based wire services and news features.

The Event Calendar, as expected, lists upcoming chats with celebrities or with a specific focus, and other special features. The Directory is a listing of all MSN forums, features, BBSs, and chat areas, sorted by Category, topic, and alphabetically by name. Although this finding tool isn't as useful as Exploring MSN for getting a feel for what is available, it's a helpful feature if you remember seeing a forum, but can't remember where, or if you can't remember the keyword that enables you to jump directly to that area. (See "TIPS FOR USING MICROSOFT NETWORK'S FINDING AIDS" later in this chapter for more information on the GO command that uses keywords to move quickly from one feature to another.)

Once you have become familiar with MSN's organization, one efficient way to find your way around is to use the Categories icon within MSN Central. When you click on the [Categories] selection from the MSN Today screen, you see a display of all the MSN services, arranged clearly and logically by broad topic. (See Figure 37.)

FIGURE 37
MSN Categories

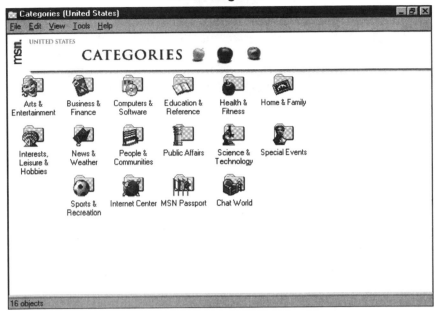

Interestingly, MSN has different Categories (and different content) for different countries. This chapter describes the U.S. Categories; most of the other available country Categories (currently Australia, Canada, France, Germany, Japan, and the U.K.) are similar. The icons are in the native language of each country, as are the BBSs. Some of the information available is different—the French Enterprise et Finance Category included *La Tribune Desfosses*, the Australian Categories included the BBQ Area, and the U.K. Categories included The Village Green (which has within it a BBS called "Princess Diana—Your Opinion").

The U.S. Categories include:

Arts & Entertainment—files and forums on art, books, comics, movies, theatre, and so on.

Business & Finance—business news, BBSs for specific professions, and forums that are essentially promotional areas for business- and investment-related products or services.

Computers & Software—folders for a number of computer-related magazines (very few full-text articles, though) and BBSs on specific hardware and software. This is a good place for information on Microsoft products.

Education & Reference—BBSs for educator-to-educator, primary and secondary school BBSs and chat areas, and access to an abbreviated version of Microsoft's Encarta encyclopedia.

Health & Fitness—BBSs and files on a number of health-related topics, including the medical profession, physical fitness, mental health, and support groups.

Home & Family—BBSs on a variety of family-related topics, such as pets, genealogy, and real estate.

Interests, Leisure & Hobbies—BBSs on everything from arts and crafts to radio-controlled toys, bowling to UFOs, bird-watching to theme parks.

News & Weather—Several files of special reports, access to weather news, links to some Internet news sites, and the MSN News browser.

People & Communities—BBSs and chat areas for men and women, on religion, genealogy, and related topics.

Public Affairs—BBSs on politics, public health, public safety, and the media.

Science & Technology—BBSs and files on a variety of sci-tech topics, such as computers, communications, math, biology, and so on.

Special Events—a listing of upcoming guest appearances and special features, as well as an archive of some prior special events.

Sports & Recreation—a number of sports news services, as well as BBSs and files on professional, college, and amateur sports.

Internet Center—access to Usenet newsgroups, files and BBSs about the Internet, and a downloadable version of Internet Explorer, the MSN Internet browser.

MSN Passport—a central place to find international content. There are BBSs, chat areas, and services specifically targeted to subscribers outside the U.S. The MSN Passport provides links to those areas, arranged by country.

Chatworld—links to all the moderated or themed chat areas within MSN. It also takes you to unmoderated chat areas; you can select a room for two described as being "especially designed for 2 members to chat privately. The cozy atmosphere with soft pillows and greenery adds to the richness of the room. This room is not monitored." Goodness!

TIPS FOR USING MICROSOFT NETWORK'S FINDING AIDS

MSN has a good variety of finding aids and navigation tools. The most useful of these include:

- Exploring MSN
  This hierarchical display of MSN's services offers a bird's eye view of the service's structure. Use this to browse Categories with which you aren't familiar. It is particularly helpful if you want to jump from one area to another—rather than having to go up one level, then select a different icon, and drill down again, you can just click on the appropriate items in the hierarchical display on the left side of the Exploring MSN screen.

- Favorite Places

  The MSN Central screen gives you access to your "Favorite Places" folder—links to individual BBSs, chat areas, forums, or services—and lets you jump directly to any of those areas, sidestepping the need to go from screen to screen. Given MSN's structure in which virtually every file or BBS requires going through three or four menus, Favorite Places is a real time-saver.

MSN Central also has links to the MSN Today news browser, email through the Microsoft Exchange network (which also supports Internet email), Member Assistance (with BBSs and files focusing on customer service and member support information), and the Categories screen.

- Categories

  Within the Categories screen are icons for each of MSN's broad topic Categories. Each Category is subdivided into areas and each of those areas is often subdivided again, which results in users having to click through an annoying number of layers before finding some actual content. Use the Categories approach when you just want to poke around and get a feel for an area. It is also much easier to add an icon to your "Favorite Places" folder if you are navigating via the Categories screen rather than the Exploring MSN screen.

The Business & Finance Category has some interesting material, but the entire Category feels cobbled together. At the initial Business & Finance screen, you see 12 icons for, among others, international trade, Site-Seeing Guide (a collection of commercial sites on the Internet), professional forums, and Business News & Reference. Under the Business News & Reference icon are five more icons: Today's Business News, Business Issues, Business Press, Company News & Profiles, and Business Information Services. Under Today's Business News are eight more icons for specific news features, including MSN News This Just In, "Superhighway News" (a newsletter by Paul Budde Communication covering Australian and Pacific Rim telecommunications and Internet news), a listing of programs on CNBC, and so on. Under MSN News This Just In are seven icons (News Summaries, World News, Business News, and so on) that you can click on to finally view newswire stories from the past few days. The MSN News This Just In service is a useful wire service—unfortunately, it took six icon selections to get to the point where I could see information!

MSN offers Hoover Company Profiles, Disclosure (U.S. Securities & Exchange Commission filings), and American Business Information mailing lists under the Business News & Reference icon. It also has icons for Dun & Bradstreet, Profound, and other business information services, but none of these services offer any products directly through MSN. The icons only provide sample material and information on how to contact the company to purchase further information directly. An icon for IAC Business Intelligence, although presently offering only "400 carefully selected articles" on topics of interest to small business, may eventually contain more extensive searchable databases.

The Business & Finance icon also lists links to "sensational sites" on the Web, but they are not particularly useful or relevant to most business researchers—sites for

Internet usage statistics, a site for historical stock quotes, and a commercial site for a company selling market research. A typical business user would find more use for, say, the EDGAR database of U.S. SEC filings, current stock quotes, or links to government sites that provide current economic statistics.

Curiously, an icon for MSN News Business Statistics, which has news on, among other things, mutual fund high performers, and the impact of pending tax laws on your income tax liability, is not in the Business & Finance Category at all, but under the MSN News icon.

News & Weather is another Category with an extraordinary number of layers. The initial screen contains eight icons including MSN News, NBC News, USA Today, The WeatherLab, and so on. Here's where it gets confusing. When you click on the [MSN News] icon, you see yet another icon also called MSN News, along with MSN News This Just In, MSN News Business Statistics, and five other icons. This second MSN News icon is the one that links you to the day's news in a browser format. (See Figure 36.) MSN News This Just In is the same material as in the MSN Business & Finance Category. If you intend to use MSN for news, be sure to use the Shortcut or Favorite Places feature (described in the "POWER TOOLS" section) to minimize the time required to find and display the news sources.

The MSN Passport Category serves to remind subscribers that this is one online service that is not strictly U.S.-based. There are French areas, conducted in French, with some information sources not accessible except through the French Categories menu. At the end of 1995, there were full-fledged Categories for Australia, Canada, France, Germany, Japan, the U.K., and additional BBSs and files in Swedish, Italian and Spanish. MSN is actively seeking forum managers to assist in expanding the features available for subscribers outside the U.S. This is an area to watch, as it is the only general online service with a significant focus beyond the United States and could be an excellent resource for finding experts and information from throughout the world.

Some of the MSN Categories are of use to researchers primarily as a way of connecting to experts in a particular area. These Categories include Arts & Entertainment, Computers & Software, Education & Reference, Health & Fitness, People & Communities, Public Affairs, and Science & Technology. Education & Reference was rather disappointing when compared to the resources available on America Online, CompuServe, or Prodigy, all of which provide some kind of encyclopedia and basic reference tools. MSN offers an introductory version of its Encarta Encyclopedia (which must be downloaded to disk and takes ten minutes to download). Unfortunately, MSN doesn't compensate for lack of adequate reference sources by providing useful links to Internet sources either; the Reference area feels more like an advertisement for Microsoft products (the Encarta Encyclopedia, Bookshelf, Encarta World Atlas, and Cinemania CD-ROMs) than a real reference tool.

Some Categories are of minimal use to researchers, at least for most information needs. These Categories include Home & Family; Interests, Leisure & Hobbies; Special Events; Chat World; and Sports & Recreation.

- Directory

  The MSN Directory is accessible through the MSN Today screen and lists all MSN folders, BBSs, chat areas, and services, along with their GO words (i.e., the keyword you can use to jump directly to that area). The Directory can be sorted by Category, by title, or by general topic. Most directory listings have brief descriptions of the service, and you can jump directly to a listing by clicking on the title. Use the Directory if you are trying to find files or forums on a particular topic (movies, finance) or if you know the area you want, but don't know how to find it. The only way to get to the Directory is through the MSN Today screen.

- MSN GuideBooks

  The GuideBooks, available from the MSN Today screen and from within each Category, are primarily electronic magazines pointing out interesting features within MSN. They include articles written by the editorial staff—subscribers are encouraged to submit articles as well—and are not intended to be comprehensive guides to MSN, notwithstanding the name "GuideBook." They include pointers to Internet sites; most Categories have not yet integrated Internet sites into their service offerings so the GuideBooks are the primary way MSN subscribers find interesting Internet sites.

The MSN Life GuideBook feature articles describing MSN services ("shop online instead of battling the malls") and personal short stories written by MSN staff members.

The MSN Spectrum GuideBook offers links to each of the Categories, although using the Categories screen from MSN Central is a much easier way to navigate and includes some features not accessible through MSN Spectrum. This GuideBook also includes feature articles with hypertext links to MSN forums.

The Home & Family GuideBook has several topical feature articles (in December 1995, they included New Year's resolutions and gift-giving suggestions), and an annotated mini-index of the MSN features divided into such groupings as Family Health & Well-Being, Home & Garden, Family Interests & Recreation, Home & Family Media, and so on.

The MSN Computing GuideBook provides links to computer- and software-oriented forums and services, including a BBS of computer industry press releases, several feature articles, a few selected articles from Ziff-Davis Net, and links to computer-related Internet sites.

The MSN Sports & Recreation GuideBook includes several feature articles, a pointer to Shaquille O'Neal's MSN site, and links to sports-related Internet sites.

The Kids & Co. GuideBook includes pointers to forums and features of interest to the under-18 set. It includes such items as a feature advertising Kellogg's cereals, a forum on a man sailing around the world, and a riddle in rhyme.

Commonly-Used Commands

The search commands are only available with the Find tool, (described in the "POWER TOOLS" section) which helps you search through MSN file and service descriptions and Usenet newsgroup names

Begin a search   pull down [Tools] menu, select [Find]

Search terms:
x AND y   x y
x OR y   x, y
x BUT NOT y   not available
x NEXT TO y   "x y"
x WITHIN n WORDS OF y   not available
x SAME SENTENCE y   not available
x SAME PARAGRAPH y   not available
x SAME FIELD y   not available

Date Searching   not available

Field Searching   not available

Truncation   word* (for any number of characters)
                                                  word? (for only one character)
                                                  wom?n (for woman or women)

Display results   results are displayed automatically

Help   pull down [Help] menu

Cost:
for session charges up to this point   pull down [Tools] menu, select [Billing], then
                                                  select [Summary of Charges], click on [Get
                                                  Details], click on [Current Period]
for database rates   click right mouse button, select [Properties]
for total cost when logging off   pull down [Tools] menu, select [Billing], then
                                                  select [Summary of Charges], click on [Get
                                                  Details], click on [Current Period]

Log off   pull down [File] menu, select [Sign Out], or
                                                  move mouse to [MSN] icon, press right
                                                  mouse button, select [Sign Out]

GETTING CONNECTED

All communications settings and log-on procedures are done through MSN's proprietary software. Microsoft Network supports speeds from 2400bps through 28800bps in most areas, through 14400 in the rest. If available, 9600bps or higher is recommended.

System requirements for Microsoft Network are:
a Windows-based PC
386 processor or better
at least 4MB RAM
Windows 95
between 20 and 40MB (depending on the number of features you install)

As noted earlier, Microsoft is considering changing its marketing strategy to allow access to non-Windows 95 users, via the Internet.

Internet access: Normal MSN setup includes access to Internet email and Usenet newsgroups. For WWW access, you need to download the Internet Explorer, Microsoft's Internet browser. It takes about 30 minutes to install and requires another 10MB of disk space. It preempts any existing Internet browser software's settings, so be careful. You may need to reinstall any other browser after you install Internet Explorer. Microsoft says it is working with other software developers to make their software compatible with Windows 95 and the Internet Explorer. In the meantime, if you are upgrading your existing setup, plan to either convert to the Internet Explorer or reinstall your browser after installing Windows 95.

POWER TOOLS

One of the most common complaints in the user feedback areas within MSN is that MSN is unbelievably slow. Screens often take close to a minute to load and if you have more than one or two MSN windows active, this delay can get even worse. Microsoft is working on this problem and, in fact, there has been a noticeable improvement in some areas. Customer Support suggests that subscribers make use of navigation shortcuts whenever possible to minimize the number of steps to get to where they want. This is particularly important to remember since it often takes five or six steps to get from the initial sign-on menu down to the BBS or file needed.

- Up One Level
  As you go from level to level, you sometimes need to backtrack and try another icon to find what you need. Most general online services have some icon or pointer on the screen for "go back"—on MSN, you need to pull down the [File] menu and select [Up One Level]. This is the preferred way to go back, as it closes the window of what you are presently viewing. If you do not close each window after you are finished viewing it, the speed with which you navigate MSN goes down significantly.

- Go
The fastest way to get to a specific BBS, file, or service on MSN is to use the GO command. Virtually all MSN features have a keyword (or Go Word) associated with them. You can find a feature's Go Word by looking it up in the Directory or by displaying the feature's "Properties" and noting the Go Word. To display Properties, move the cursor to the appropriate icon and press the right mouse button, or pull down the [File] menu, and select [Properties]. (The Properties feature is standard throughout Windows 95.) This displays the name of the service, its Go Word, the Category (i.e., how to find it through the Categories screen within the MSN Central screen), the type of service it is (Category, folder, chat room, and so on), its Rating (no rating means it is acceptable for general audiences), and a brief description of the service. Properties is a nice feature. Not only can you find out how to jump directly to a place within MSN, but you also get an idea of what to expect when you get there.

- Use the Task Bar
Windows 95 displays a small icon along the bottom of the screen for each open window. Since MSN allows multiple windows to be open at once, you can jump from one place to another within MSN by clicking on the associated icon on the Task Bar. I find that what often works best is to keep the MSN Central screen open along with the Exploring MSN screen. Then if you get confused about where you are, or need to shift gears, you can just jump back to the beginning by clicking on either the [MSN Central] or [Exploring MSN] Task Bar icon.

- Find
"Find" is a surprisingly robust command on MSN, supporting full Boolean logic and truncation. You start the command by pulling down the [Tools] menu and clicking on [Find] or by positioning the pointer on the [MSN] icon on the lower right corner, pressing the right mouse button and selecting [Find]. This command lets you search for any word or phrase in the name, topic, or description of any MSN feature. You can limit your search to forums, BBSs, chat areas, Internet Usenet newsgroups, and so on, or you can search through the entire Network. This feature works best if you are either looking for Internet newsgroups, which aren't listed in the Directory, or for a narrow or vague concept for which you can't guess the appropriate topic or Category.

- Shortcuts
One of my favorite features of MSN is Shortcut. Actually, Shortcut is a new feature available throughout Windows 95, but it is particularly useful with MSN. Shortcuts are icons you can click on to go directly to a specific place within MSN. You can create a Shortcut icon by clicking once on the item you want with the left mouse button, then pulling down the [File] menu and clicking on [Create Shortcut], or by clicking once on the item with the right mouse button and selecting [Create Shortcut]. MSN automatically puts a Shortcut icon on your desktop that, when clicked, connects you directly to the item you marked.

FIGURE 38
Text with a Shortcut Embedded

One of the more attractive and easy-to-use news browsers on MSN is called MSN News. You can GO to it with the keyword READMSNNEWS, or just click here and your PC launches MSN, connects you to the system, and brings up the MSN News screen.

Shortcut to MSN News.mcc

You can embed Shortcut items in text (see Figure 38). If you were reading this page in Microsoft Word and clicked on the [Shortcut] icon in Figure 38, you would automatically be logged on to MSN and connected to the MSN News feature described. You can send email to someone on MSN, telling about an interesting feature and embedding a Shortcut to let the recipient go directly to the feature being described. Or you can keep Shortcuts for the MSN features you use the most on your desktop and click on them rather than logging on to MSN through the MSN icon and having to wade through the MSN Today screen.

- Favorite Places
  These are links to features, files or services you use frequently; the concept is similar to an Internet hotlist or bookmark. To mark a Favorite Place, click once on its icon, then either pull down the [File] menu and select [Add to Favorite Places], or click the right mouse button and select [Add to Favorite Places]. You can get to your Favorite Places folder from the MSN Central screen or by moving the cursor to the MSN icon in the lower right corner, clicking the right mouse button, and selecting [Go to Favorite Places]. At the Favorite Places folder you can click on the icon for whatever place you want.

The main distinction between Shortcuts and Favorite Places is this: you use Shortcuts if you want to get into a specific area of MSN from *outside* MSN or you want to point someone else to a MSN feature, whereas you use Favorite Places within MSN to move quickly from one feature to another. You can jump from one feature to another using the Favorite Places folder; you usually use Shortcuts to go to one specific place since you need a separate Shortcut for each place you wish to link.

- Single Click? Double Click?
  This isn't as much a power tool as a way to save your sanity. Some MSN icons and features need a single mouse-click and some need a double-click. With the delay in seeing the results of your clicking, it's easy to double-click when you shouldn't (and get a General Protection Fault error message) or click once and wind up waiting for something to happen until you realize that you should have double-clicked. Instead, use another of the Windows 95 features: move the cursor to the icon you want, press the right mouse button, and click on [Open]. This always opens the icon, whether it needs one click or two.

PRICING

MSN has two pricing plans—the Standard Monthly Plan, which is $4.95/month for three hours of use and each additional hour at $2.50 or the Frequent User Monthly Plan, which is $19.95/month for 20 hours of use and each additional hour at $2.

Some features incur small surcharges; you are notified ahead of time and must click on [OK] to authorize the expense. Since there are very few value-added services on MSN, you probably will not incur many additional charges.

OTHER FEATURES

MSN has a very well-written and -organized online help facility in the Member Support area. In addition, the standard Help Topics for Windows 95 include MSN help along with other operating system help. There are plenty of "related topics" links to other help topics as well, making navigation through the Help guide fairly painless.

The right mouse button has gained new functionality with Windows 95, and that carries over into MSN. As noted in the "POWER TOOLS" section, you can use the right button to see an icon's Properties, to create a Shortcut or Favorite Places link, and to open an icon.

MSN provides access to the Internet as well as to its own services and features. MSN version 1.x automatically supports Internet email (through Microsoft Exchange) and Usenet newsgroups. You can download Microsoft's Internet browser, Internet Express, for access to the World Wide Web. Although it takes quite a while to install, the process is fairly easy, with "wizards" to walk you through the steps—a nice feature for anyone not familiar with the Internet who is intimidated by the complexity of installing most Internet browsers. Internet Explorer is not 100% compatible with some Netscape Navigator display elements, but as Windows 95 becomes the new operating system standard, we may well find that Internet Express likewise dictates the HTML standard.

EVALUATION OF MICROSOFT NETWORK

What makes MSN unique among general online services is its symbiotic ties to the Windows 95 operating system. The new features on Win95 are also available on MSN, and somehow it feels like MSN is just another Win95 feature on my desktop, like a disk management utility or Microsoft Word. This blending of MSN into the desktop is facilitated by the Shortcut feature; now I can create a daily to-do list, for example, and embed into it a Shortcut to a document that has to be sent out, a presentation I need to prepare, and, oh yes, a Shortcut to MSN News This Just In to check for any late-breaking stories on the company to whom I am giving the presentation.

What do I like most about Microsoft Network?
• Once you're accustomed to the look and feel of Windows 95 and MSN, you find it fairly easy to navigate through MSN's icons and folders. You use some of the same tools such as the Task Bar, Shortcuts, and Properties to get information and open applications.

• I think Shortcuts and Favorite Places are great! I can avoid some of the more annoying delays of the MSN system by liberal use of Shortcuts (when I just want to check one service within MSN) and Favorite Places (when I need to dive in, hit my five most useful sources on MSN, then leave).

What do I like least about Microsoft Network?
• MSN is absurdly slow—it often takes a full minute at 14400bps to load one of the GuideBooks or the MSN Today screen. Browsing from screen to screen is very annoying, as one errant mouse click means another 60 to 90 seconds waiting for the screen to load before I can go back to the prior menu. Microsoft is aware of how subscribers feel about this problem and is working to alleviate the delays. I hope that MSN version 2.x fixes this difficulty.

• MSN is poorly-organized, with far too many screens and menus to drill through to find information. This hierarchical structure works fine when you're organizing data on a hard disk, but it is not the way you want an online service to work.

• There isn't much substantial information in MSN. This is partly due to the fact that the service is still new and MSN is still seeking new information content providers. However, another reason for the lack of any meaty information resources within MSN is its vision of itself as primarily an Internet access provider. It's possible that MSN may decide to focus on making Internet resources accessible rather than on developing any conventional online information resources of its own.

Prodigy

CONTACT INFORMATION

NAME	Prodigy Services Co.
ADDRESS	445 Hamilton Avenue White Plains, NY 10601
TELEPHONE	800/776-3449; 914/448-8000
CUSTOMER SERVICE HOURS	24 hours/day; 7 days a week
EMAIL	through Prodigy: [Jump] Member Help for help files and email to Customer Service. Or [Jump] Live Help for member services chat area
WEB HOME PAGE	http://www.prodigy.com/
SYSTEM AVAILABILITY	24 hours/day except between 4:00am - 7:00am Eastern time on Wednesday and Thursday

DESCRIPTION OF INFORMATION AVAILABLE

Prodigy began as an advertiser-supported conferencing system, which sets it apart from other general online services. It has a wide variety of electronic bulletin boards (called BBs) and chat areas as well as a limited selection of information resources. Its strength for business or professional researchers is in its investment information sources.

Through its proprietary software, Prodigy also provides access to the World Wide Web and Usenet newsgroups on the Internet. A number of companies have their own forums or "features" on Prodigy; this can be either a feature or a bug depending on whether you want to find product and service information on companies when you are looking for other types of information. Prodigy also inserts an advertisement at the bottom portion of most screens; you are encouraged to click on the advertisement and look at the ad copy behind the teaser.

Most of Prodigy's information resources offer only limited searching, but a service called Homework Helper allows users to search through extensive back issues of magazines, newspapers, reference books, and some television and radio broadcast transcripts. Despite its name and appearance, it can be used for some business and professional research as well as for students' homework.

ROADMAP OF RESOURCES

Prodigy's services and features are sorted by general topic on the initial logon screen (Highlights menu). See Figure 39 for the Highlights screen. The topics in rough order of usefulness to online searchers are:

- Business/Finance—current business news from Dow Jones News/Retrieval, company reports, several online stock brokerage services, investment news, and analysis tools
- News/Weather—current national, international, political, and general-interest news, current events BBs and chat areas
- Newsstand—links to about 20 newspapers and magazines available on Prodigy
- Computing—wide collection of BBs, forums, and ordering information for hardware and software products, and a selection of columns on computer topics
- Communicate—access to all Prodigy's BBs and chat areas and to email
- Internet—WWW browser, Usenet newsgroups, FTP, and gopher
- Travel—EAASY Sabre airline reservation system, several travel guides
- Entertainment—wire stories on entertainment topics, BBs on art, television, etc.
- Sports—sports news, extensive BBs, chat areas, and forums on sports topics
- Marketplace—online shopping
- Music—BBs and chat areas on music
- Kids Zone—BBs, chat areas, games, basic reference material and a link to Homework Helper
- Teen Turf—BBs, chat areas, and forums for the 12- to 19-year-old set. A good deal of overlap with the material found in Kids Zone

The Highlights menu also lists Member Help as a separate topic. This connects you to live customer service help in a chat area, several Member Help BBs, a list of frequently-asked questions and answers, telephone access numbers, Prodigy press releases, and software upgrades. Given the lack of printed documentation (and hence, the need for good online help), this is not a particularly useful collection of online help resources. The live chat area is helpful, although somewhat chaotic when several people are asking questions and one Customer Service representative is responding.

What makes the absence of printed documentation more irritating is the fact that when you do telephone Prodigy's Customer Service number and try to navigate through the options to get help from a live person, you are repeatedly reminded that you can get help online by JUMPing to Member Help. In fact, several of the options within the automated telephone answering system tell you where you can find the information online, then disconnect you or give you a busy signal.

FIGURE 39
Highlights (Main) Screen

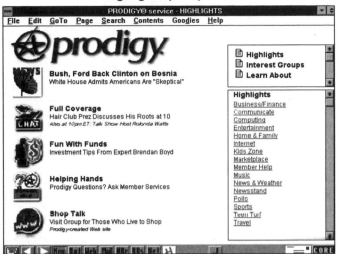

You can click on any of the topics displayed in the initial Highlights screen in order to go to, say, the news and weather features. To go directly to a specific feature, you "jump" there by pulling down the [Go To] menu, clicking on [Jump] (or pressing <ctrl><J>) and typing the name of the feature you want, or the address for an Internet WWW site, an Internet Usenet newsgroup, or an FTP or gopher site. If what you type is not an exact match of a Prodigy feature (or Internet address), Prodigy displays either a list of related features or services (if a list has been compiled) or it displays features that appear alphabetically before or after the term you typed. There are not many lists of related features and many of them are for the recreational Prodigy user, e.g., As the World Turns, Knives, Large Sedans, Parenting.

As an example of a list of related services and features, when I JUMPed Investing, the following feature choices were displayed:

Boyd's on Investments	column
Business Resources	list
Company News	news
Company Reports	info
CR Investments	report
Financial Services	list

...

However, when I typed in Company, Prodigy dropped me into the alphabetical list of options:

Compact Discs	list
Compact Disk Players	list
Compact Disks	news
Company Corporation	apply
Company News	news
Company News Symbols	menu
Company Reports	info

....

This alphabetical "A-Z List" of all Prodigy features and services can also be viewed from the Go To pull-down menu. It lists each service, BB, feature, list, menu, and advertiser's site. Unfortunately, there is no cross-indexing, making it difficult to find resources. For example, Customer Service told me that books about Prodigy were available for purchase through Prodigy. I tried looking for Books under the A-Z List and found book reviews, Books & Writing BB, and books for kids, but no help in purchasing books about Prodigy. I tried looking for Shopping in the A-Z List and was linked to the Marketplace. I tried to find Prodigy products in the Marketplace and could not find them under any of the categories of products listed. I finally gave up, called Customer Service back, and after a ten-minute wait was told to [Jump] Prodigy Shop, where I finally found the listing for Prodigy books. I wonder how many potential purchasers would have been this persistent?

Unfortunately, there is virtually no documentation or printed material describing Prodigy's services. Its proprietary software is sent with a one- or two-page description of places to check out (the MTV forum, the Kennedy Space Center feature, WEB Personals, and the Virtual World). It does not even include the most basic information on how to move from screen to screen, how to jump to a feature, how to *find* a feature, or how to get help.

TIPS FOR USING PRODIGY'S FINDING AIDS

Prodigy's finding tools are fairly rudimentary; the best suggestion is to be persistent in your searching. The "lists" of services and features are usually helpful and pull together a number of related services, provided you can identify a list that covers the topic in question.

Following are descriptions of the resources available within each of the general topic areas accessible through the main Highlights menu.

• Business/Finance—The main screen for this service displays the most recent business news headlines from Associated Press, pointers to several companies' advertising pages (e.g., H&R Block tax information, BillPay USA electronic bill payment service), and links to other business and finance information. See Figure 40 for the Business/Finance main screen. One of the best online values is access to the Dow Jones News/Retrieval wire service through Prodigy ([Jump] Company News). Granted, it's only the most recent two weeks' worth of news, but it's information you pay a premium for when you get it directly from Dow Jones. You can scan the stories by stock symbol or by Dow Jones' industry codes. Again, there is no online documentation to explain Dow Jones' indexing or even to point users to this valuable information source.

Prodigy has a wide variety of information and analysis tools for investors, most of which are available through the Business/Finance section. Be careful, though; many of these tools incur an additional fee on top of your monthly Prodigy charge. You can order *Market Guide* company profiles ($1.95 for a 5-page quick report, $3.95 for a 10- to 12-page full report). You can get a daily summary of news items tailored to your interests from the Heads Up service ($29.95/month or $695/year). You can read

FIGURE 40
Business & Finance Main Screen

columns from Kiplinger's *Personal Finance*. (But beware! This service only includes the current issue and issues from 1990 to 1993. I can't help but wonder how accurate his finance and investment advice is now, given all the changes in the tax laws. It seems misleading to present such dated material to investors.) You can search Dun & Bradstreet's company profiles (basic company and financial information, not credit reports—$2.50/company). There are several online stock brokerage firms along with services that track and analyze the performance of stocks and mutual funds, most of which involve a per-report or per-transaction fee. For a list of investment resources, [Jump] Investing.

The Business/Finance section also has links to some Internet resources, including the EDGAR filings with the U.S. Securities and Exchange Commission and a number of corporate home pages.

• News/Weather—This area provides current news—national, international, political, and general interest. Sources include the AP Wire and States News Service. There are also quite a few photos available, many more than through America Online, the other general online service that provides current news photos.

If you click on [More About News], you see links to BBs on current events topics and chat areas. There are also some good Internet WWW links to sites such as the *San Jose Mercury* Center and Reuters News Online (for news summaries). There are also links to a seemingly random selection of Usenet newsgroups—when I last looked, the list consisted of sci.aeronautics, sci.space, cnn.newsroom, news.misc, alt.true-crime, alt.war, alt.iraqi.dictator.bomb.bomb.bomb, alt.military.police, and soc.history.war.vietnam.

(And this wasn't even during a week in which the news was particularly focused on the military!)

Prodigy provides access to some local newspapers' sites available on the AT&T Interchange Network. These are "****" or premium services, incurring a charge of $4.95/month plus $2.95/hour in addition to the monthly Prodigy fee. These services offer access to some back issues of the newspapers and some local information, and are primarily of interest to local residents rather than to most Prodigy users.

As the name implies, this area also has an extensive collection of weather maps and other weather information.

- Homework Helper—This is a service targeted to elementary and secondary school students, although it also has limited usefulness for business and professional searchers. (Ironically, the quarter-page screen advertisement for Homework Helper describes it as "the most powerful research tool of it's [sic] kind.")

To access Homework Helper, you need to download special software. There is no charge for the required software. Then you can either [Jump] Homework Helper or click on the separate Homework Helper icon on your desktop.

The charges for Homework Helper are either $6/hour for pay-as-you-go use or, on the Basic Plan, $9.95/month for two hours of connect time, with additional hours at $2.95/hour.

See the "OTHER FEATURES" section later in this chapter for additional information on Homework Helper.

- Newsstand—This links you to magazines and newspapers on Prodigy. There are about ten magazine titles, plus Internet WWW links to other magazines' home pages. This area also links you to the newspapers that are included in the News/Weather area; again, they are not the full text of the newspapers but selected features along with other local information of interest to residents of the newspaper's city.

- Computing—As expected with any electronic information system, this area has a wide variety of BBs, forums, and chat areas for hardware and software companies. ZD Net, a service provided by Ziff-Davis for an additional $3.50/month, provides access to hundreds of shareware programs, current computer industry news, and the current issue and some back issues of Ziff-Davis magazines such as *Computer Life, Mac World,* and *PC Magazine.* In addition, many computer companies have services in the Computing area through which subscribers can order products or additional information on hardware and software. This area also has links to corporate WWW home pages, selected computer-oriented Usenet newsgroups, and columns by Larry Magid and John Edwards. Unfortunately, the columns can be scanned by date but not searched by keyword.

- Communicate—This is the area in which you can find all Prodigy BBs and chat forums. The featured topics on one day were discussions on domestic violence, a chat area with Sydney Biddle Barrows (the Mayflower Madam), astronomy, Godzilla movies, and Italian heritage. You can also link to Prodigy's email function from this area.

- Internet—This area not only links you to Prodigy's Internet WWW browser but also helps Internet newcomers learn about netiquette and the ins and outs of Internet use. There are BBs about the Internet, a list of frequently-asked questions, and a Usenet newsgroup browser. Prodigy's browser supports http (WWW), FTP, and gopher protocols.

- Entertainment—This area focuses on comics, movies, celebrities, television, and books. There is no substantial news on the entertainment industry, although there are lists of celebrities' birthdays, movie reviews, *TV Guide*, and commentary on recent developments in comic strips. There are also BBs on arts, movies, books, and so on, along with links to WWW home pages and Usenet newsgroups on entertainment topics.

- Travel—The Travel area includes a link to EAASY Sabre, the airline flight and reservation service, several features on traveling (including a feature from the British Tourist Authority), and online access to the *Mobil Travel Guide* and the *Zagat Restaurant Survey*.

- Sports—This area has sports news and a bulletin board or forum for virtually all professional and college sports. There are sports statistics and fantasy football and baseball games. This area also has links to WWW home pages for individual teams and sports and Usenet newsgroups focusing on sports.

- Marketplace—You can access any advertiser's feature through Marketplace. The companies are listed by broad category and alphabetically.

- Music—This area has BBs and chat areas on various kinds of music, links to WWW home pages, and Usenet newsgroups focusing on music, and links to other entertainment-related services on Prodigy.

- Kids Zone—This area has loads of BBs and chat areas, games, features from organizations such as National Geographic and Nickelodeon, some basic reference materials such as a dictionary and thesaurus, and a link to Homework Helper.

- Teen Turf—As with Kids Zone, this area has plenty of BBs and chat areas, games, reference material, *TV Guide*, and a link to Homework Helper. It also links to selected WWW home pages and Usenet newsgroups. Some of the BBs limit access—the Teen Girlz Limited BB checks your account profile for appropriate age and gender—but it is fairly simple to change your account information to reflect the expected criteria.

Commonly-Used Commands

Begin a search	**[Jump] {feature name}** e.g., [Jump] company reports
Search terms:	[these commands are available with "Search" only, which searches current AP news. You generally cannot search for information within Prodigy features or services]

Commonly-Used Commands [continued]

x AND y	x y
x OR y	x **OR** y
x BUT NOT y	x **AND NOT** y
x NEXT TO y	'x y'
x WITHIN n WORDS OF y	not available
x SAME SENTENCE y	not available
x SAME PARAGRAPH y	not available
x SAME FIELD y	not available
Date Searching	not available
Field Searching	not available
Truncation	not available
Display results	done by clicking on headlines
Help	**[Jump] Member Help**
Cost:	
for session charges up to this point	**[Jump] Usage** (includes time spent in CORE and PLUS; does not include additional fees incurred in "****" services)
for database rates	displayed when you request information for which there is a fee
for total cost when logging off	**[Jump] Usage** (includes time spent in CORE and PLUS; does not include additional fees incurred in "****" services)
Log off	**<Alt><F4>** or pull down the **[File]** menu, select **[Exit]**

GETTING CONNECTED

Prodigy offers access through its own packet-switched network and through the IBM Advantis network. Access via a toll-free call is available at $0.10/minute in addition to regular charges. All communications settings are done through Prodigy's proprietary software; the only changes you make are to identify a local telephone number and to set the modem speed. Prodigy's software is required; it is available at no charge from Prodigy. You can either call the customer service office and request a copy of the software on diskette or you can download the software from Prodigy's Internet home page—http://www.prodigy.com/.

Prodigy supports speeds from 1200bps through 28800bps. Modem speed of 14400 and above is available through special setup. You may experience noticeable screen delays with speeds below 9600bps.

System requirements:
IBM compatible PC 386 or higher and Windows 3.1 or higher or Mac SE or higher
4MB RAM
4MB hard disk space (3.5MB for Mac)

POWER TOOLS

Prodigy allows you to build Hot Lists of favorite Prodigy features and services as well as Internet WWW, FTP, and gopher sites. To add an item to your Prodigy Hot List, pull down the [Go To] menu and click on [Add to Hot List]. To add an item to your WWW, FTP, or gopher Hot List (while using the Prodigy Internet browser software) click on the [Hot List] button (or pull down the [Navigate] menu and click on [Hot Lists] and then click on [Add to Hot List]). You can jump from one item in your Prodigy Hot List to the next by pressing the <F4> key. When using the Prodigy Internet browser, click on the [Hot List] button, highlight the site you want to go to and click on [Go].

There are a number of shareware and freeware software packages available to help speed up and simplify your interaction with Prodigy. Many of these packages relate to managing your investments and tracking stock prices. There are also products designed to help you read BB messages offline and a surprising number of utilities designed to make interesting sounds. It took quite a bit of looking to find this library of software packages; [Jump] Utilities.

Journalist

A third-party software package produced by POINTCast Inc., Journalist allows you to specify the information sources you want tracked regularly, logs on to Prodigy, downloads the information, and formats it into an electronic newspaper. You can track and maintain a database of stock prices, download tables, and retrieve the day's business news or computer industry columns. You can schedule the time when Journalist logs on and downloads the information to ensure that it connects to Prodigy when the response time is quick, thus cutting down on your total connect time. There appears to be some doubt, however, whether Journalist can continue to function on Prodigy as Prodigy makes its transition to its new interface. POINTCast has discontinued support for Journalist on Prodigy; Prodigy customer service says it is providing support. Unfortunately, the fact that the software producer is no longer supporting the product is NOT included in the online order form for the Journalist software, which seems a bit misleading. Journalist can be purchased through Prodigy and costs $49.95 for Prodigy members.

Tool Bar

In addition to pull-down menus along the top of each Prodigy screen, you can edit the navigation tools along the bottom of the screen. Pull down the [Goodies] menu and select [Tool Bar Setup]. You can select which functions you would like displayed: commands such as jump, print, menu, or exit; features such as Usenet newsgroups, Quote Track, and Homework Helper; or user-defined macros.

PRICING

Prodigy offers three pricing plans. For any but the most casual user, the Value Plan is probably the most economical of the three plans.

- Basic Plan is $9.95/month for five hours of usage. Additional hours are $2.95/hour.
- Value Plan is $14.95/month for unlimited time in the CORE areas, and five hours in the PLUS areas. Additional hours are $2.95/hour. (See information that follows for explanation of free, CORE, and PLUS areas.)
- 30/30 Plan is $29.95/month for 30 hours of usage. Additional hours are $2.95/hour.

A billing indicator appears in the lower right corner of each Prodigy screen indicating whether you are in a free, CORE, PLUS, or "****" area for billing purposes. Free areas are those in which your connect time is not counted toward your allotment of hours included in the monthly fee (5 hours for Basic and Value plans, 30 hours for 30/30 plan). Free areas include the member help and shopping areas. CORE areas include weather, news, sports, and business news features. Value Plan members have unlimited time in the CORE areas. PLUS areas are timed; the time you spend in a PLUS area is counted against your monthly allotment of hours. PLUS features include bulletin boards and chat areas, Quote Check, EAASY Sabre, and Usenet. "****" areas are features that incur additional fees, either per-minute or per-transaction or both. Fees are usually modest, but there are a surprising number of services to which these additional fees apply. You are usually notified of the additional fees before you incur any charges. Time spent in the "****" areas is usually not counted against your monthly allotment of hours. Extra-fee features include Strategic Investor, all the online newspapers, Company Reports, and Homework Helper.

Each Prodigy account permits six individual logon passwords, presumably for different household members. The primary account (identified by an A at the end of the account ID) can control the access of the other accounts (identified by a B through F at the end of the account ID). The primary account holder can block the B through F accounts from using any of the PLUS services, including chat areas and bulletin boards, as well as accessing Usenet newsgroups.

OTHER FEATURES

Prodigy Search

You can search the past two weeks' newswire stories in any of the Prodigy features by pulling down the [Search] menu and clicking on either [Quick Search] or [Power Search]. Power Search allows you to limit the search by section (AP National news, People Stories, AP Health/Science, and so on), or to search all newswire categories, and limit the search by date. You can use basic Boolean searching, although there is no truncation or field searching. The results can be displayed chronologically—either earliest to latest or latest to earliest—or in order of computed relevancy. Quick Search works similarly, but does not allow for date searching or for specifying how the results are to be displayed; the retrieved articles are sorted by computed relevancy.

FIGURE 41
Homework Helper Search Screen

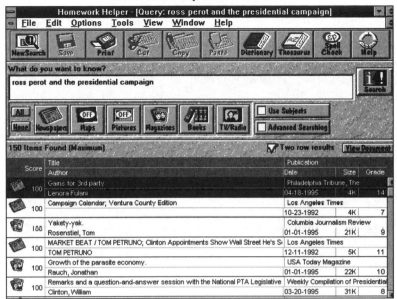

Homework Helper

Homework Helper is the one area within Prodigy in which you can search an extensive collection of magazines, newspapers, reference books, and related material. You can either [Jump] Homework Helper or click on the [Homework Helper] icon. See Figure 41 for the Homework Helper search screen. Once you connect to Homework Helper, you select which types of material you want searched. Your options are:

- chapters and sections from 2,000 reference books (almanacs, encyclopedia, classic works of literature, and history books)

- articles from 650 magazines and newsletters (covering business, industry, and general interest—no indication of how extensive a back-file of issues is included)

- 100 newspapers (some local newspapers—although not many major newspapers—a large number of special interest newsletters such as *Armenian Reporter, Hispanic Engineer, Hyde Park Citizen*)

- 300 maps and 1,500 pictures

- transcripts from several television and radio programs, primarily National Public Radio broadcasts

You select which of these categories of sources you wish to include in your search (or you can search all categories). Then you type in your question, using keywords to describe the topic. Homework Helper uses Natural Language searching so you do not use Boolean connectors. Since the search engine takes all the search terms and looks for records that contain the most occurrences of those terms, you get the best results by *not* using synonyms but just typing in one word for each concept. For example, in my search for articles on the use of pacemakers by runners and other athletes, I retrieved more (and more relevant) records by searching for either "athletes and pacemakers" or for "runners and pacemakers" than I did when I searched for "athletes or runners and pacemakers." Although there is no documentation to guide you in more sophisticated searching, Homework Helper appears to perform some rudimentary truncation or word-stemming. A search for hottest also retrieved items with "hotter." On the other hand, it considers "7" to be distinct from "seven."

When a search is completed, the results are ranked by calculated relevance and the headlines are displayed along with an indication of the reading grade level of each item—another reminder that this product is intended for students, not business or professional searchers. You select the items you want to view one at a time; the record is displayed with the search terms highlighted.

You can focus your search by clicking on the [Advanced Searching] icon. This lets you search by author (which is not searched in a regular Homework Helper search), title, publication name, and date. You can also focus your search by clicking on the [Subject] icon. This useful feature allows you to limit the search to broad categories: business, arts and entertainment, interesting and fun facts, literature, science and technology, sports, or history. You can select as many or as few of the categories as you wish. Reminder: don't forget to reset the categories if you decide to conduct a search in a new topic. There is no onscreen reminder that you have limited your categories, and this results in puzzling results if you try a new search in an area not covered by the previously-selected categories.

I found Homework Helper to be useful when searching for fairly broad topics and when all I needed were a few good pieces of material on a topic. I did not find it as useful when looking for narrowly-defined subjects such as database marketing or even a nonbusiness search such as backpacking in the Wind Rivers area. The search sometimes takes quite a bit of time to process, so given the searching limitations, Homework Helper is best used when you want to make a first pass through the literature, not when you want an exhaustive or finely-tuned search.

EVALUATION OF PRODIGY

Prodigy has some valuable resources for individual investors and has an adequate search function for recent news stories. It also offers a wider variety of third-party information services than most other general online services.

On the other hand, Prodigy looks and feels as if it is focusing almost exclusively on the home computing market. Its screens are brightly colored and the lettering is in a large block print. There is very little documentation to help a business user who has limited time to explore the service. A recent letter to subscribers was telling; Prodigy's head of public relations described what he used Prodigy for and the features he mentioned were CMJ/Sonic Net, Health and Fitness, Food, Virtual Vineyards, Trivia, Religion, Comics, MIDI/Music, Skiing, Travel, and Hockey. I wish that the letters to subscribers always included some reminder of the business- and investment-related features on Prodigy.

Prodigy has made a serious effort to make its service "family-friendly." The master subscription holder (the person responsible for paying the bill) can limit the access of all subaccounts of other household members. All BB postings automatically include the account number of the person posting the message, making subscribers responsible for what they say online. Unfortunately, the chat areas allow anonymous postings, which tends to encourage irresponsible messages by some users. Prodigy responds that at least with this system, the parent (who holds the master subscription) can be notified of the behavior of the child and, presumably, restrict that child's access to chat areas. This doesn't help if the main account holder is the one posting irresponsible messages in chat areas.

Prodigy has run into some problems because of its policy of monitoring and censoring BBs for content it considers obscene or indecent. This policy makes Prodigy more attractive to parents who don't want their children to be exposed to adult language or topics. However, it also creates the impression that Prodigy is taking responsibility for what is posted in its BBs. Prodigy was sued for libel by a company that was accused of fraud by a subscriber on Prodigy. The company claimed that, by monitoring its BBs for content and removing messages it considered obscene or indecent, Prodigy was acting as a publisher of information rather than merely a passive conduit.

What do I like most about Prodigy?
- Prodigy has a very strong selection of information and analysis tools for investors. By accessing third-party products such as Dun & Bradstreet's company information, daily summaries of news by Heads Up and Wall Street Edge, and company profiles from Market Guides, Inc., subscribers can tap into a fairly broad array of information to make investment decisions.

- Although it is not advertised or promoted, Prodigy subscribers can access recent news from the Dow Jones Newswire, *Wall Street Journal*, and *Barron's* magazine without paying a premium charge. If you usually search Dow Jones for recent news rather than for information dating back more than two or three weeks, this is much more cost-effective than a subscription to Dow Jones News/Retrieval.

- Prodigy's Internet Usenet newsgroup reader software is easy to use, flexible, and more intuitive than many of the newsgroup readers available.

What do I like least about Prodigy?
- Prodigy makes little effort to help its subscribers find their way around the service. Initial screens of text provide little information. There is no coordinated attempt to streamline access to information for business or professional users. Subscribers can easily use up their ten free hours simply trying to figure out what information is available and where it is.

- The interface, with its bright colors and large but thin print, makes Prodigy difficult to look at for more than a few minutes, at least for those of us who have seen the far side of 30. It was not easy to find how to change the font to one that was slightly more readable; it can be done by JUMPing Change Display. Due to the large size font, each screen of text contains much less information than a comparable screen of text on any other online system, which means that users must frequently go from screen to screen to screen trying to locate the information they need.

- Along with inadequate printed user documentation, the online help is skimpy and the telephone customer service is frustrating. Often after you spend several minutes making selections and being kept on hold it either tells you to find the information online or yields a busy signal.

- Often the "information services" within Prodigy are actually companies' promotional material rather than information sources. I would have preferred to have all the promotional features in a single place, or at least clearly marked on every menu and listed as advertisements, not information sources.

Internet

This chapter does not bear much resemblance to ones profiling other online services. The Internet per se has no centralized customer service telephone numbers, hours of service, or headquarters address. Likewise, there is no single set of system commands, training classes, or documentation. This chapter does not attempt to cover all the resources available on the Net; rather, it provides you with finding tools, key resources, and guidelines to make searching the Internet as straightforward as possible. The Internet sites listed in this chapter are accurate as of early 1996; keep in mind that addresses are likely to change. For current links to all the sites described in this chapter, see http://www.access.digex.net/~mbates/. This chapter assumes that you have at least a passing familiarity with the Internet. See "Where to Get More Information" for a list of useful books on Internet basics.

An evaluation of the Internet as an information source needs to be tempered by the realization that it is a completely different beast from general or professional online services. There is very little overlap between the Internet and other online services; you won't find the full text of last year's *Wall Street Journal* on the Internet and you won't find the full text of the 1996 U.S. federal budget on a general or professional online service. Even when there is overlap, the search engines available on the Internet offer much less search power than those available on DIALOG or LEXIS-NEXIS. The price differential reflects this difference in search power; you can sometimes pay much less for an article identified and ordered over the Internet than you would for the same article retrieved through a search on a professional service.

In general, the Internet offers great breadth and little depth, with some notable exceptions. Yes, you can look through the catalog of the Library of Congress, but you can only download copies of a few of the books through the Internet. You can find a surprising amount of detailed information on the treatment of breast cancer, but you'd have a hard time finding much on the current market for nutritional supplements.

DESCRIPTION OF INFORMATION AVAILABLE

The Internet has been depicted variously as a network of networks, the electronic equivalent of the Library of Congress but with all the books on the floor, and electronic anarchy. In a sense, it's all these things.

Most online researchers use the Internet to find and download files (text, graphics, spreadsheets, and so on), monitor and gather information, communicate with peers and subject experts, browse organizations' home pages and library catalogs, and connect to other online services such as CompuServe or DIALOG. They also use the Net to conduct preliminary research—using services such as UnCover (telnet://database.carl.org) to scan the tables of contents of magazines, or to read a discussion group's compilation of frequently-asked questions.

In its minimal definition, the Internet is a network that connects networks of computers throughout the world. Following are examples of searches for information on the Internet:

- I am looking for statistics on the number of commercial airline passengers for the past five years. I connect to the U.S. Department of Transportation's Internet site, find that there is a home page for the Bureau of Transportation Statistics and that I can download an Excel spreadsheet with the information I need. (http://www.bts.gov/ cgi-bin/imagemap/HomeBottom/ *and* gopher://gopher.bts.gov/11/nts/1995/)

- I need information on a bill that was recently introduced in the U.S. House of Representatives regarding Superfund cleanup of hazardous waste. I need to know the bill number, who is cosponsoring it, whether it has been reported out of committee, and a summary of the bill's provisions. I can log on to the Library of Congress and monitor the bill as it works its way through Congress. (telnet://locis.loc.gov *or* http://thomas.loc.gov/)

- I want to find the reference in *Hamlet* to "There's rosemary, that's for remembrance." I can download any of Shakespeare's works and search for specific words and phrases. (gopher://wiretap.spies.com:70/11/Library/Classic/Shakespeare/)

- I want to find discussions of new treatments for Parkinson's disease. I can either use an Internet research tool that searches through Usenet newsgroup postings for the keywords "Parkinson and treatment and new" or I can use a news filtering service that monitors any Usenet newsgroup postings on an ongoing basis for any mention of treatment for Parkinson's disease. (http://www.dejanews.com/ *or* http://sift.stanford.edu/)

- I am working with a colleague in Berkeley and she wants me to see an article she recently completed. She uses FTP (file transfer protocol) to upload the article into a subdirectory on my machine; I can view the article in my word-processing software, having retained her original formatting and graphics.

- I need to gather information about a company. I download its latest financial filings from the U.S. Securities and Exchange Commission, use one of the Net browsers to show its home page and review recent press releases and product announcements, and search a database of magazine articles and order fax copies of recent articles profiling the company. (http://www.sec.gov/ *and* telnet://database.carl.org)

ROADMAP OF RESOURCES, FINDING AIDS, AND GUIDELINES

The Internet seems to have become ubiquitous, what with home pages listed in automobile ads on television, but the Internet hasn't been around in its present form for very long. For some interesting history of the Internet, see Vint Cerf's "How the Internet Came to Be," as told to Bernard Aboba in *The Online User's Encyclopedia*, Addison-Wesley, 1993, and Robert Zakon's "Hobbes' Internet Timeline" at http://info. isoc.org/guest/zakon/Internet/History/HIT.html.

For a sense of the explosive growth of the Internet since the early 1990s, consider the following landmarks in the development of the Internet, extracted from the Hobbes' Internet Timeline:

1972	Telnet protocol developed
1973	File Transfer Protocol developed
1976	Internet email established
1979	Usenet newsgroups established
1982	Transmission Control Protocol and Internet Protocol (TCP/IP) established
1984	over 1,000 hosts on the Internet
1988	Internet Relay Chat developed
1989	over 100,000 hosts on the Internet
1990	Archie (FTP finding tool) released
	Hytelnet (Telnet finding tool) released
1991	Gopher developed
1992	World-Wide Web software released
	over 1,000,000 hosts on the Internet
	Veronica (gopher finding tool) released
1995	AOL, CompuServe, Microsoft Network, Prodigy provide Internet access
	over 7,000,000 hosts on the Internet

Not only is the Internet growing at a phenomenal rate, but the tools we use to navigate through the Net are still in their early stages of development. No wonder it feels like the Internet is in a constant state of change!

The Internet consists of a number of "places" and, like the blind men and the elephant, it's tempting to believe that one view of the Internet encompasses the entire Net universe. Although the bottom line is that you are connecting your computer to another computer, how you make the connection, how you view the available information, and whether and how you can manipulate it depend on the tools you use and the places you go.

The most common form of Internet navigation is through the **World Wide Web** (WWW). You usually use software that supports point-and-click navigation, viewing text, graphics, and images on the screen and clicking on text or icons to move from one screen of text to another. Although a great deal of information is available on the Web, not all resources are.

Telnet is a straightforward way of connecting your computer to another computer, usually in order to search a database. Telnet was developed over 20 years ago and is still a useful means for gaining access to a library's card catalog, connecting to an online service such as DIALOG or CompuServe, or logging on to an electronic bulletin board system.

File Transfer Protocol (FTP) enables you to connect to another computer and download or upload a file. The most common form of FTP—so-called anonymous FTP—allows you to log on to a host computer without having an ID and password for that computer. With anonymous FTP, you have access only to publicly-accessible directories and files. FTP sites are often good resources for lists—of all newsgroups, all FAQ (Frequently-Asked Questions) files, and so on—and for large documents such as book chapters.

Gopher is a program that displays information sources (files, telnet sites, FTP sites, WWW home pages) in an easy-to-navigate ASCII menu. "Gopherspace" refers to all the resources you can access through gopher menus.

Usenet Newsgroups are electronic discussions on a given topic. There are newsgroups on everything from the BBC television show "Absolutely Fabulous" to veterinary medicine to geodesic domes. Newsgroups enable you to tap into the expertise of Internet users from around the world—a great way to expand your circle of friends and colleagues as well as find an authority on just about anything. The messages posted to newsgroups are usually retained for three months to a year, depending on your Internet access provider's policies.

The Internet would be much more confusing and frustrating were it not for the tools that have been developed over the years to help users navigate through the resources and find the information they need. As you search through the Internet for information, remember to try several finding tools and a variety of search terms. Unlike other online services, there is no universal Internet Index or set of standardized subject terms, so try alternate words if your first search proves fruitless.

There are finding tools specific to the WWW, telnet, gophers, and so on, but there are also several excellent Internet guides that cover a wide range of Net resources. Three that I find useful are All-in-One, Business Sources on the Net, and the Clearinghouse for Subject-oriented Internet Resource Guides.

All-in-One
http://www.albany.net/allinone/

The All-in-One page, developed by William Cross, is a compilation of many Internet search tools. He has separate sections for tools to search the WWW or newsgroups, to search for software, people, news, literature, domain names, or reference sources, and so on. If you think there must be a way to find something on the Net, but aren't sure how to search for it, start with the All-in-One page.

Business Sources on the Net
gopher://refmac.kent.edu:70/1D-1%3a2577%3aBusiness

This lists the best Internet business resources in each of 17 areas of business, ranging from accounting to management to environmental resources of interest to businesses. Each section starts with a discussion of the topic, then describes the most useful WWW, gopher, telnet, and FTP sites that cover that subject. These collections do not actually provide links to the URLs listed, so you need to download and read the BSN chapter you want, then try out the sources listed.

Clearinghouse for Subject-oriented Internet Resource Guides
gopher://una.hh.lib.umich.edu:70/11/inetdirs/

This resource is maintained jointly by the University of Michigan University Library and the School of Library and Information Studies. See Figure 42 for the main subject menu. This resource is gradually being migrated over to the WWW, where it can be viewed at http://www.lib.umich.edu/chouse/chhome.html. Each guide is prepared and updated by either a subject specialist or library school student and is quite comprehensive. Some guides are a bit dated, but all have been developed by experts and since each is signed by the author, corrections and additions can be sent to the person responsible for the guide.

FIGURE 42
Clearinghouse for Subject-oriented Internet Resource Guides

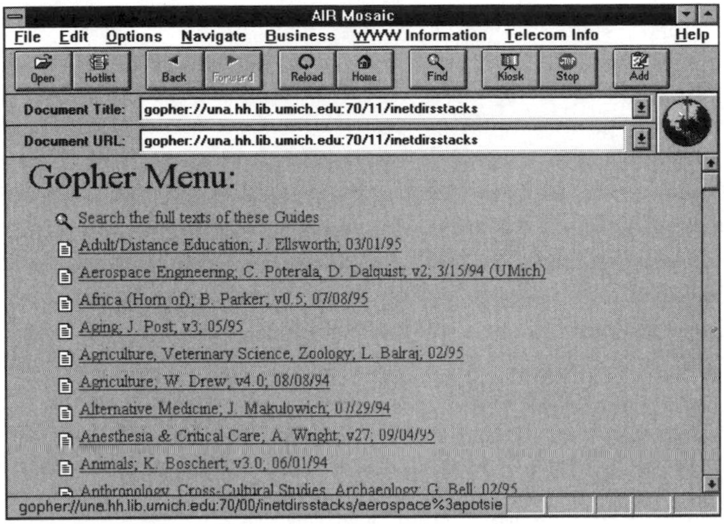

Examples of the subjects covered in the Clearinghouse are Adult/Distance Education, Business News, Journalism, U.S. Politics, and Virology, Viruses, and Microbiology.

WORLD WIDE WEB

The World Wide Web (also referred to as the Web or WWW) allows you to connect to an Internet site and view information in a full-screen point-and-click format. Web documents often have graphic images, files, and other binary applications embedded in them, and they often include sophisticated linking to other documents and Internet sites. The development of the WWW was particularly exciting because it allowed all Internet users to easily create their own publicly-accessible documents, or home pages. Now you can become a publisher by creating a home page that includes information about yourself, copies of articles you've written, pictures of your pets, links to your favorite Internet sites, even sound clips of music. A fascinating story illustrating the impact of the Internet and self-publishing appeared in the January 1, 1996 issue of *The Nation* ("The Cigarette Papers" pp. 11-18). Copies of internal documents from Brown & Williamson (B&W), a tobacco manufacturer, were sent anonymously to a researcher at the University of California, San Francisco (UCSF). He turned the papers over to the UCSF Library, which maintains a special collection of tobacco-related material. The Library became inundated with requests for access to the B&W collection so, to facilitate access, it scanned the documents electronically and made them available on the Internet (http://www.library.ucsf.edu/tobacco/). When B&W attempted to reclaim the documents and suppress Internet access, the California Supreme Court ruled that this constituted prior restraint of publication and that, as with the *New York Times'* publication of the "Pentagon Papers," it was not appropriate for the court to prevent publication. Most publishing companies declined to print the collection of documents, so the material was "published" through an alternate medium. (Another interesting example of alternative publishing is the availability of the Unabomber manifesto, published in the *Washington Post* and uploaded to the Net within a few days.)

Most Internet searchers use a Web browser to view WWW sites—graphical software that greatly facilitates the navigation through linked documents and that takes advantage of the point-and-click features of Web pages. At present, the most popular browser is Netscape; the proprietary software packages provided by America Online, CompuServe, and Prodigy include browsers as well. Microsoft has developed its own browser, Internet Explorer, which requires the Windows 95 operating system. Given the likelihood that many PC users will upgrade to Win95, this may become the default Internet browser.

You can also navigate the WWW in plain ASCII mode. Most Internet service providers (ISPs) provide an ASCII Web browser such as lynx, which enables you to view the text but not the graphics of Web pages. You lose much of the formatting when you use an ASCII browser. Although it is often more difficult to navigate from screen to screen with this type of browser, it usually takes much less time to move from Web page to Web page since the only data being transferred to your screen is the plain text without the graphics. If you access the Internet through an ISP rather than through a general online service, you have the option of either a shell account (which supports only plain ASCII) or a SLIP/PPP account (which supports a graphical browser).

You can also set your graphical browser to load only text; you lose the graphics but it takes much less time to display each screen of text and the overall formatting is preserved. Some Web pages offer both graphics and text-only versions to accommodate both users who have a graphical browser and those who are using an ASCII browser. See Figures 43 through 45 for examples of a WWW page viewed through a graphical browser with images displayed, with images off, and through an ASCII browser.

FIGURE 43
Web Page with Graphical Browser with Images Displayed

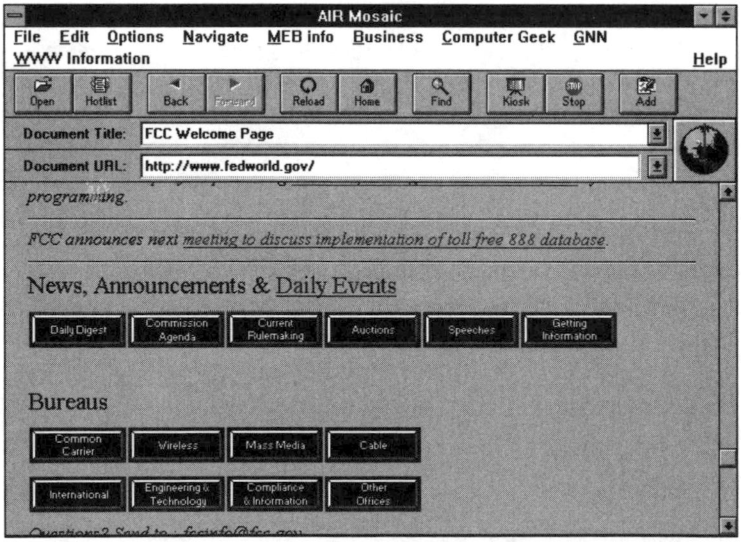

FIGURE 44
Web Page with Graphical Browser with Images Off

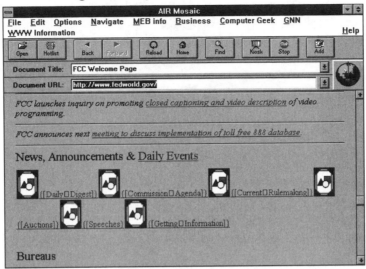

FIGURE 45
Web Page with ASCII Browser

FCC launches inquiry on promoting closed captioning and video description of video programming.

FCC announces next meeting to discuss implementation of toll free 888 database.

News, Announcements & Daily Events

[Daily Digest] [Commission Agenda] [Current Rulemaking] [Auctions][Speeches] [Getting Information]

Bureaus

The push for more government is on
[Common Carrier] [Wireless] [Mass Media] [Cable] [International] [Engineering and Technology] [Compliance and Information] [Other Offices]

Questions? Send to : fccinfo@fcc.gov

Or write: Federal Communications Commission, 1919 M Street N.W.,Washington DC 20554
Or call: Consumer Assistance, 202-418-0200   Updated 12/18/95

There are a number of tools to help you locate information on the WWW. Some are hypertext bibliographies, in which information professionals or subject experts have listed and built links to what they judge to be the most valuable sources on a subject. Other finding tools are search engines that allow you to find URLs (Uniform Resource Locators—standardized Internet addresses such as http://www.fcc.gov/), descriptions of Web pages, gopher sites, FTP sites, telnet sites, and Usenet newsgroups. Be sure to read the description of a search tool to get a sense of how comprehensive its index is—does it contain only information sent to it from owners of Web pages? Does it include WWW sites, but not gopher or FTP sites? Is it updated daily or monthly? The answers to these questions are particularly important if you want to attempt a comprehensive search of Internet resources, since different finding tools search different areas of the Net and have different criteria for what to include. Keep in mind, too, that a "comprehensive" search may be overwhelming. Do you want *every* instance in which the word "history" appears in URL, a Web page, a gopher menu, or a Usenet newsgroup posting? Or do you really want a selection of relevant Internet sites that provide information on Medieval History?

The following are some of the better Web indexes and search engines. There are many others available, and more are being developed every month.

Lycos

http://lycos.cs.cmu.edu/

Be sure to read the Lycos help screens before you run a search; you might miss some of the search features of this finding tool, such as specifying whether you want an exact match or a "loose" match, whether you want to require that the search retrieve only items that contain *all* the search terms or just some of them, and whether you want the search terms truncated or not. Lycos claims to have indexed over 90 percent of the Web, adding over 300,000 home pages a week. The principle advantage of a search engine such as Lycos is that a search is likely to turn up a relevant site. The disadvantage is that you may also retrieve material that is not particularly relevant. Lycos is best-suited for searches in which you need to be comprehensive or for searches on topics that are somewhat undefined or vague.

Yahoo

http://www.yahoo.com/

The Yahoo Guide is another popular tool for finding Web sites. See Figure 46 for the initial Yahoo screen. What sets it apart from most indexes is the fact that it is compiled by humans rather than by machines scanning the Internet for as many publicly-available sites as possible. It breaks out all the Internet resources into broad subject categories (Business, Health, Government) and then subdivides the topics by more specific subject headings. You can either search through all the Yahoo indexes for any occurrence of a word or you can browse through an entry for a specific topic.

The tradeoff with this arrangement of human-designed and arranged resource indexes is that you get a much smaller, but arguably tighter and more relevant, collection of Web resources. On the other hand, Yahoo also includes self-nominated sites, so it may still contain some sites of questionable value. Yahoo is most appropriate for searches in which you need a few of the best Net resources, or for searches that are clearly-defined.

WebCrawler

http://webcrawler.com/

The WebCrawler is owned by America Online and is the default search engine for AOL subscribers. It is one of the faster search engines on the Net. In addition to enabling you to search Web pages, gopher sites, and FTP sites, it compiles a list of the

FIGURE 46
Yahoo Main Screen

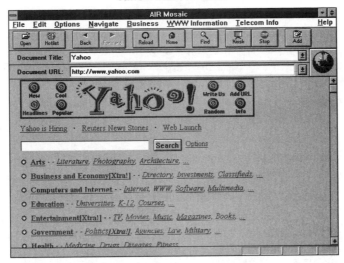

25 most frequently linked URLs on the Web. If a search engine changes its URL and you can't find it with the old address, you can check WebCrawler, assuming that most of the better search engines are among the top 25 URLs. In fact, I wander over to the list once a month or so just to make sure I haven't missed a particularly useful site.

Following is a list of the Top 25 during February 1996 and the number of links to each site:

1. Yahoo (3855)
2. Welcome to Netscape (3609)
3. WebCrawler Searching (3392)
4. Netscape Now (2392)
5. The Lycos Home Page: Hunting WWW Information (2021)
6. The World-Wide Web Virtual Library: Subject Catalogue (1761)
7. Microsoft Corporation (1355)
8. Welcome to the White House (1321)
9. What's New With NCSA Mosaic (1219)
10. NCSA Mosaic Home Page (1180)
11. WWWW - WORLD WIDE WEB WORM (1179)
12. The IBM world wide web home page (1073)
13. USADATA Local Market Data Resource (1055)
14. The World Wide Web Consortium (W3C) (1013)
15. City.Net (1011)
17. Silicon Graphics' Silicon Surf (928)
18. Apple Computer (900)
19. Sun Microsystems (899)
20. Internet Audit Bureau(tm) (895)
21. Virtual Tourist World Map (841)
22. Cool Site of the Day (824)
23. World-Wide Web Servers: Summary (820)
24. Starting Points for Internet Exploration (816)
25. A Beginner's Guide to HTML (793)

Inktomi

http://inktomi.berkeley.edu/

The Inktomi search engine is a fast and reasonably comprehensive tool for searching Web pages. It claims to have more sites indexed than any of the other popular Web search tools; unfortunately, every service counts its URLs differently, so it's difficult to verify claims. Inktomi offers flexibility in searching (you can specify any terms that must appear and any that must not appear) and its ranking of retrieved documents in order of relevance works well.

Alta Vista

http://altavista.digital.com/

Alta Vista is a search engine developed by Digital Equipment Corp. to search Web pages and Usenet news groups. You can limit the search to Web pages or news; you can search for phrases, for terms in ALL CAPS, for items in specific news groups, and for truncated terms. Alta Vista indexes all words in WWW pages, which vastly expands the searchability of the Web. Given its broad range, it is often useful to use Alta Vista's convention of indicating mandatory search terms (those terms that must appear in any retrieved document) with a "+". Alta Vista casts one of the widest nets in the Web; use it when you want a more comprehensive rather than a more focused search.

There are two search engines that, while offering some free information, also charge a small fee for a more extensive search of information. **InfoSeek** (http://www.infoseek.com/) searches through WWW pages, articles in business and industry magazines, newswires, and other sources usually available only in commercial databases. And, unlike most search engines listed earlier, it also searches the past four weeks' worth of postings from close to 20,000 Usenet newsgroups. It offers free searching of Web pages; to retrieve search results from Usenet newsgroups or other sources, you can pay by the search ($0.20 each search) or you can pay a monthly fee, after which each search is charged at a reduced rate. The first month's searching is free when you sign up.

Another for-fee Net search engine (or as the producer describes it, "knowledge access tool") is **NlightN** (http://www.nlightn.com/). NlightN lets you search through WWW pages as well as indexes from a surprising array of commercial databases. These range from indexes of the British Library Document Supply Centre to Conference Papers Abstracts to CNN transcripts to the *World Almanac*. It also provides a link to the Lycos search engine, thus providing a single point for searching much of the Internet and a good (although far from comprehensive) variety of sources not otherwise available on the Net.

NlightN provides links to and extracts from WWW home pages, and lets you purchase the full text of articles, entries in encyclopedias and almanacs, and entire books. Items not available electronically (some articles and all the books) are sent via fax or first class mail. This merging of Internet sites, articles, and book indexes is an interesting idea, but won't be a threat to the for-fee online services any time soon. The searching is rudimentary at best; NlightN's primary advantage is in the ability to search a number of sources simultaneously or sequentially without having to jump from one search engine to another.

WWW Virtual Library

http://www.w3.org/hypertext/ DataSources/bySubject/Overview.html

This is a collection of over fifty subject indexes to Net resources, with topics that range from "Standards and Standardization Bodies" to "Paranormal Phenomena." The organization is not as clear-cut as Yahoo, but some of the indexes are quite good. As with most other Web search engines, the indexes include links that let you go straight to the sources being cited.

Several so-called meta-search engines are also being developed to enable you to simultaneously search a number of Internet search tools. One such meta-searcher is SavvyScarch http://guaraldi.cs.colostate.edu:2000/, developed by Daniel Dreilinger at Colorado State University.

FILE TRANSFER PROTOCOL (FTP)

FTP is the most basic way of transferring any ASCII or binary file between computers. One of the first protocols for connecting one computer to another across the Internet, FTP is still an effective way to move information from one place to another. Much of the information available on publicly-accessible FTP sites can be retrieved through WWW search engines, but some material is most easily accessed through a direct FTP connection. The Massachusetts Institute of Technology maintains an anonymous FTP site with lists of all anonymous FTP sites (ftp://rtfm.mit.edu/pub/usenet/news.answers/ftp-list/sitelist/). **Archie** is the finding tool for FTP files—it is resident on most Internet service providers and searches for words in the FTP filenames. It's a fairly clunky tool, particularly when you consider that many gopher menus and WWW search engines include FTP files in their databases.

GOPHER

Gopher is software that enables subject experts and network administrators to develop menus of resources available throughout the Internet. Before gopher, if you wanted to retrieve files or make a remote connection (telnet) to a computer on the Internet, you had to know the Internet address and, in the case of file retrieval, the subdirectory in which the file you wanted was located. Say I had a list of great astronomy-related Internet resources. The only way I could get to those sites, or tell anyone else about them, was to use a list of the Internet addresses and type in each address to access that site:

Astronomy Images (via Univ.of Rennes, France)
<URL:gopher://roland.univ-rennes1.fr:70/11/Divers%20serveurs%20Ftp/Le%20serveur%20ftp%20du%
20CRI-CICB/Images/ASTRO>

Astronomy and Space Science
<URL:gopher://scilibx.ucsc.edu:70/11/The%20Researcher/Science%20and%20Engineering/Astronomy%20and%20Space%20Science>

Astronomy, Astrophysics, and Physics Journals
<URL:gopher://marvel.loc.gov:70/11/global/sci/astro/journals>

Astrophysical, Planetary and Atmospheric Sciences, CU Boulder
<URL:gopher://apas.Colorado.EDU:70/1>

Images - Astronomy
<URL:gopher://k12.ucs.umass.edu:70/1>

Planetology Resources
<URL:gopher://somalia.earth.nwu.edu:70/11/planet>

The Lunar & Planetary Institute
<URL:telnet://lpi.jsc.nasa.gov@LPI:23>

Obviously, that's a bit cumbersome. Gopher enables me to build a menu for you to use instead of requiring you to type in each of those URLs. An astronomy gopher menu might look like this:

1. Astronomical Institute Tatranska Lomnica/
2. Astronomical Internet Resources Directory from STScI/
3. Astronomy Images (via Univ.of Rennes, France)/
4. Astronomy and Space Science/
5. Astronomy, Astrophysics, and Physics Journals/
6. Astrophysical, Planetary and Atmospheric Sciences, CU Boulder/
7. BUBL Astronomy Section - BH2C3/
8. Facultad de Ciencias Astronomicas y Geofisicas/
9. HST - Hubble Space Telescope Archive <TEL>
10. Images - Astronomy/
11. NASA/
12. NASA Ames GMS vis/IR images/
13. NASA Links/
14. Planetology Resources/
15. Space Telescope Electronic Information System (STEIS)/
16. The Lunar & Planetary Institute <TEL>

You could move your cursor to item 10 and you would be linked to a computer in France that has, among other things, images of Jupiter—and you wouldn't have to type in the full address: gopher://sir.univ-rennes1.fr:70/I9/Astro%20Gopher/jupiter/c1634554.gif.

Some gopher menus list only information available on their own sites; some, such as the Astronomy gopher previously mentioned, include information from many other Internet sites. They can include links to telnet sites, other gopher menus, Web pages, or FTP sites. Gopher menus are easy to navigate—they are ASCII-based rather than graphical, they offer fast connections from one site to another, and the subject-oriented gophers are often well-organized, since they are compiled and maintained by experts.

Keep in mind that neither gopherspace (all information retrievable through gophers) nor the WWW provides a comprehensive view of all the information available on the Internet; a search of both gopherspace and the WWW ensures that you have covered most of the Net.

Veronica (which stands for Very Easy Rodent-Oriented Net-wide Index to Computerized Archives—groan!) is a finding tool for locating information within gopherspace. It searches for words within gopher titles (i.e., each of the entries in a menu). When it was first developed in 1992, it was considered a great tool for finding information. We've become spoiled since then—now it seems clumsy, slow, and crude compared to the WWW search engines. Fortunately, there are a number of gopher sites that are themselves pointers to other gophers. I find that these are more efficient tools for finding information in gopherspace, as they are compiled by information professionals and organized logically by subject. Three **indexes of gopherspace**, arranged by topic, are available at gopher://liberty.uc.wlu.edu:70/11/gophers/subject_gophers.

My personal favorite gopher is **PEG, a Peripatetic, Eclectic Gopher** (gopher://peg. cwis.uci.edu:7000/11/gopher.welcome/peg). It contains links to collections of what its compilers consider to be the best resources on a subject; it also attempts to compile a comprehensive list of government gopher sites. If I can't find the information I need through one of the subject-oriented gophers listed earlier, but I have heard or suspect that a piece of information might be available, I usually start my search in PEG.

Following is the main PEG menu:

```
                 PEG, a Peripatetic, Eclectic Gopher

-->   1.  About PEG, a Peripatetic, Eclectic GOPHER
      2.  Biology/
      3.  Electronic Journals/
      4.  Favorite Bookmarks/
      5.  GOPHERS/
      6.  Humanities/
      7.  INTERNET ASSISTANCE/
      8.  Arvin Weather and world events/
      9.  LIBRARIES/
     10.  MATHEMATICS/
     11.  MEDICINE/
     12.  PHILOSOPHY/
     13.  POLITICS and GOVERNMENT/
     14.  Physics/
     15.  VIRTUAL REFERENCE DESK/
     16.  VIRTUAL REFERENCE DESK UCI SPECIFIC/
     17.  WOMEN'S STUDIES and RESOURCES/
```

TELNET (ALSO KNOWN AS RLOGIN)

Telnet enables Internet users to log on to another computer on the Internet, usually to access a public resource such as a library's electronic card catalog or to search a database. Telnet also allows you to connect to online services such as CompuServe, DIALOG, or DataTimes, provided you have already established an account with the service. The ability to telnet to an online service is particularly useful for people who have local access to the Internet but who must make a long-distance call to reach the nearest node of a packet-switching network such as Sprintnet or Tymnet. Telnet can also be used to log on to electronic bulletin board systems or other Internet service providers.

The best, and best-known, finding tool for telnet is **Hytelnet**, a hypertext index of publicly-accessible telnet sites developed by Peter Scott. Hytelnet can be downloaded and run on your PC or local Internet host (see http://www.lights.com/hytelnet/ for a list of FTP sites) or can be searched remotely (gopher://liberty.uc.wlu.edu/11/internet/hytelnet/ or http://library.usask.ca/hytelnet/). Many ISPs also maintain Hytelnet on their host machines.

USENET NEWSGROUPS

One of the Internet's strong suits is the ability to link people with similar interests or concerns throughout the world. Whether you have an interest in telecommunications regulation, pharmaceuticals, or the Peace Corps, there is probably an electronic discussion going on concerning that topic. Researchers use newsgroups to keep up on their industry, to tap into a group of experts for advice or pointers, and to share their expertise.

Since newsgroups often get the same questions over and over, many have developed files of Frequently-Asked Questions (FAQs) and, of course, the answers to those questions. These FAQs are written by participants of the newsgroup recognized as experts in the newsgroup's field of interest, whether it's urban folklore, amniocentesis, or Islam. These files are pretty accurate—they are read and reviewed by people who are interested in the subject area and errors are usually caught and corrected quickly. I often find that it helps to look for a relevant FAQ when I am beginning research in an area with which I'm not familiar. All current FAQs are available via anonymous FTP at ftp://rtfm.mit.edu/pub/usenet-by-group and are posted to the news.answers Usenet newsgroup.

Obviously, it makes sense to subscribe to the newsgroups you find useful on an ongoing basis. But what if you need to see what's been said recently about a topic you haven't been monitoring? Two newsgroup scanners offer the ability to capture discussions on topics of interest, either retrospectively or on an ongoing basis.

DejaNews
(http://www.dejanews.com/)

DejaNews maintains an archive of Usenet newsgroup postings for at least a month and some groups for up to a year (excluding the following groups: alt.*, soc.*, talk.* and *.binaries). It allows you to search through selected newsgroups, search by author, limit the search by date, and rank the resulting searches by relevance, date, group, or author. DejaNews is particularly useful if you are not sure what newsgroup is likely to be discussing a topic of interest to you, or to identify specific issues that have been discussed within the past year.

InfoSeek (see earlier) also maintains a searchable archive of the past four weeks of Usenet postings.

SIFT
(http://sift.stanford.edu/)

SIFT, formerly known as Stanford University's NetNews Filtering Service, scans items posted in newsgroups and filters them against search terms you specify. You can have the search run once against the current day's new documents (to help you refine and focus your search), then you can subscribe and have the retrieved items delivered to your email account. SIFT is most useful if you wish to monitor a large number of newsgroups for mention of a topic, company, or concept.

GETTING CONNECTED

You can get access to the Internet through any of the general online services such as America Online, CompuServe, Microsoft Network, or Prodigy. These online services provide Web browsers and offer access to the WWW, FTP, and gopher. Some also support telnet (incoming and outgoing) as well. All support both incoming and outgoing Internet email. Most charge several dollars an hour for connect-time while you are accessing the Internet.

You can also get access to the Internet directly through Internet service providers. These ISPs offer both shell (plain ASCII) and SLIP/PPP (graphical, World Wide Web) access. Some give service to customers within a limited geographical area; others provide local numbers throughout the U.S.

If you plan to be on the Internet for more than an hour a day, you will probably pay much less by selecting an ISP rather than using one of the general online services. On the other hand, ISPs usually offer limited customer service and set-up help. You may be left to your own devices when it comes to configuring your Web browser software or troubleshooting the settings of your electronic mail profile.

Most computer magazines have full-page advertisements for companies that offer nationwide Internet access. Accurate, updated, complete lists of ISPs are difficult to find on the Net. One list that appears to be fairly stable is contained in the *EFF Guide to the Internet*, formerly known as *The Big Dummy's Guide to the Internet*. You can find this guide in any of the following electronic homes for the Electronic Frontier Foundation:

on America Online: keyword **EFF**
on CompuServe: **go EFFSIG**
on the Internet: http://www.eff.org/papers/eegtti

Another list of ISPs that appears to be both stable and reliable is called The List and is provided by MecklerMedia at http://thelist.com/. You can search The List by state, area code, country, or country code. As of late 1995, The List contained about 1,600 ISPs. (These sources and additional information are also listed in "Where to Get More Information.")

The following is a list of selected major Internet service providers:

internetMCI
6325244@mcimail.com
800/955-5210; 410/494-6808
http://www.internetmci.com/

NETCOM On-Line Communication Services, Inc.
info@netcom.com
800/353-6600; 408/983-5950
http://www.netcom.com/

PSI (Performance Systems International)
info@psi.com
800/827-7482
http://www.psi.com/

UUNet
UUNET Technologies
800/265-2213
info@uunet.uu.net
http://www.uu.net/

See the chapters on America Online, CompuServe, MicroSoft Network, and Prodigy for information on accessing the Internet through their services.

POWER TOOLS

Every Internet searcher develops her own favorite sites and search techniques. Perhaps the best piece of advice is to keep your eyes open, as new resources and finding tools are being developed virtually every week. Since I don't have a lot of spare time to surf the Net looking for new sites, I rely on people whose job it is to explore the Net and report back.

Two of my primary sources of information on Net developments are Net Happenings and the Scout Report. Net Happenings is available as a newsgroup (comp.internet. net-happenings) or a mailing list, also called a listserv (send email to listserv@ lists.internic.net with the body of the message: subscribe net-happenings yourfirstname yourlastname). Gleason Sackman of InterNIC compiles short descriptions of new WWW sites, gopher sites, listservs, books, telnet-able databases, software, electronic journals, and other Net resources and distributes these descriptions to subscribers. It can be a bit overwhelming at first—each "issue" of Net Happenings can include 20 or 25 items—but it's an easy way of keeping an eye out for new developments.

The Scout Report is a weekly update, prepared by Susan Calcari of InterNIC. Her report is much more selective than Net Happenings and each entry is described in much more detail. She focuses on sites of interest to researchers and educators, so the Scout Report is a source for tools rather than a way of monitoring developments throughout the Net. You can subscribe to the Scout Report by sending email to listserv@lists.internic.net with the body of the message: subscribe scout-report yourfirstname yourlastname, or by reading it at http://rs.internic.net/scout_report-index.html.

A good way to keep track of your favorite Internet sites is to use bookmarks or hotlists. WWW browsers and gopher servers offer the ability to store addresses to

FIGURE 47
WWW Browser Hotlist

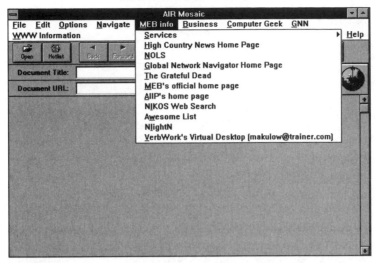

interesting Internet sites for future reference. You can mark any useful site as you find it and then pull up your hotlist later and return to the site.

Most WWW browsers have a button or menu item labeled [Hotlists] or [Favorite Places] or [Bookmarks]—click there when you are viewing a site you want to save. You can pull down the [Hotlist] later and click on a site you wish to see. Since most browsers let you maintain a number of hotlist folders, you can organize your favorite sites by topic: search engines, government sites, resources about the Internet, and so on. See Figure 47 for a very personalized hotlist.

Shell or ASCII gophers and browsers also allow you to create bookmarks. In gopher, type **A** when you are viewing a gopher menu you wish to save, or **a** if you want to save only the gopher menu item highlighted. To view your menu of bookmarked gopher sites and go directly to a site, type **gopher -b**. In lynx, one of the common ASCII browsers, use **a** to save a Web site and type **v** to display your bookmarked Web pages and go directly to a site. Following is a personalized gopher menu created with bookmarks through a shell account:

Internet Gopher Information Client v2.1.3

Bookmarks

1. International Telecommunication Union (ITU)/
2. ITU-DOC circular letters/
3. inetdirsstacks/
4. TelecommInfo/
5. Government Information(Federal Depository Info & Docs)
6. WIRED magazine gopher/
7. InterNIC Information Services Directory/
8. Gopher Jewels/
9. The Internet Wiretap - wiretap.spies.com/
10. Electronic Frontier Foundation Gopher Server/

Bookmarks

11. Internet Guides and Resources/
12. Cygnus Telecom Gopher   - with great Internet Info CD-ROM/
13. NTDB on the Internet/
14. NII - Information Infrastructure Task   Force gopher/
15. search Harvard B-School case study abstracts <TEL>
16. On-Line Ready Reference/
17. Internet Statistics (use /stat)/
18. Federal Register/

Although the Net is moving toward an environment in which all navigation is done through point-and-click tools, you still need to know some basic UNIX commands. UNIX is the operating system for many of the host machines on the Net. If you have a shell account on an Internet service provider, you are probably connected to a UNIX machine. If you use FTP, you are also most likely be connected to a UNIX machine. The following are the bare UNIX essentials you need to survive.

finger [USERID]—this command allows you to get profiles of Internet users (provided they make that information available). **finger** requests a copy of a file called .plan, created by the user. If you do not create a .plan file, **finger** responds with the name, login ID, and a note that the person has "no plan." The following is information on Reva Basch:

access2% **finger reva@well.com**

Login: reva   Name: Reva Basch
Directory: /home/r/e/reva   Shell: /usr/local/shell/picospan
Last login Thu Dec 28 12:10 (PDT) on pts/17 from netcom20.netcom.
Plan:
Mail Address: reva
Registered: 7 November 1988
Computers: Pentium, PowerBook 180c

I'm one of many librarian, ex-librarian, lapsed-librarian and wannabe-librarian types on The WELL. I do online searching, write about online searching, and consult to the online industry. I'm based on the northern California coast; my business name, Aubergine Information Services, is a vestige of my catering days.

For fun, I like to cook. That's why I stopped catering.

I'm married, with cats.

I co-host the Miscellaneous and Berkeley conferences, as well as Women on The WELL (wow) a private conference for - you guessed it - women on The WELL. If you're interested and female, email me for more information.

> "The same thing that makes you live
> can kill you in the end."
>
> -- Neil Young

A corresponding UNIX command to find information about an Internet site is **whois** [DOMAIN NAME]. **whois** tells you basic information about the site, along with a contact name. I use it as a quick way of getting a company's address and telephone number. Following is information on FAXON Corp.'s Internet site:

```
access2% whois faxon.com
The Faxon Company (FAXON-DOM)
    15 Southwest Park
    Westwood, MA 02090

    Domain Name: FAXON.COM

    Administrative Contact:
        Morency, John (JM196) morency@faxon.com
        (617) 329-3350
    Technical Contact, Zone Contact:
        Heavey, Martin (MH267) HEAVEY@FAXON.FAXON.COM
        (617) 329-3350 ext. 489

    Record last updated on 30-Jun-92.
    Record created on 25-Apr-90.

    Domain servers in listed order:

    THING.FAXON.COM              140.234.1.1
    NIC.NEAR.NET                 192.52.71.4
```

If you have a shell account and need help using a command such as telnet or FTP, you can consult the online manual by using the **man** [COMMAND] command. (**man** is short for "manual.") Following is the first **man** page of information on FTP— obviously, the documentation tends to be written by and for computer experts.

```
access2% man ftp

FTP(1C)                          USER COMMANDS
FTP(1C)

NAME
        ftp - file transfer program

SYNOPSIS
        ftp [ -dgintv ] [ hostname ]

AVAILABILITY
        This command is available with the Networking software installation option. Refer to Installing SunOS
4.1 for on how to install optional software.

DESCRIPTION
        ftp is the user interface to the ARPANET standard File
        Transfer protocol (FTP). ftp transfers files to and from a remote network site.

        The client host with which ftp is to communicate may be
        specified on the command line. If this is done, ftp immedi-
...
```

My final UNIX command, and my personal favorite, is **ls -al |more**. This command is roughly equivalent to the MS-DOS DIR command (a list of all files and subdirectories at your current location), and it specifies that the listing be displayed a screen at a time (so it doesn't scroll off the screen before you can read it). This command is particularly useful when you are using FTP to go to a site, find a useful file, and download it to your computer.

The following is an example of the use of **ls -al |more** on the ds0.internic.net site:

```
ftp> ls -al lmore
200 PORT command successful.
150 Opening ASCII mode data connection for /bin/ls.
total 72755
drwxr-xr-x        4 welcome        26112 Dec 29    04:57    .
drwxr-xr-x       24 welcome          512 Dec 13    15:36    ..
drwxr-xr-x        2 welcome          512 Apr 30    1993     .cap
-r—r—r—          1 welcome         6362 Dec 28    14:53    fyi-index.txt
drwxr-xr-x        2 welcome          512 Oct 6     03:58    rfc-editor
-r—r—r—          1 welcome       256775 Dec 29    04:57    rfc-index.txt
-rw-r—r—         1 welcome         3348 Oct 15    1992     rfc10.txt
-rw-r—r—         1 welcome       315315 Oct 15    1992     rfc1000.txt
-rw-r—r—         1 welcome       154427 Oct 15    1992     rfc1001.txt
-rw-r—r—         1 welcome       165250 Mar 21    1993     rfc1002.txt
-rw-r—r—         1 welcome        19405 Mar 13    1987     rfc1003.txt
-rw-r—r—         1 welcome        20952 Apr 21    1987     rfc1004.txt
-rw-r—r—         1 welcome        68051 May 7     1987     rfc1005.txt
-rw-r—r—         1 welcome        30798 Jun 15    1992     rfc1006.txt
-rw-r—r—         1 welcome        49925 Jun 11    1987     rfc1007.txt
-rw-r—r—         1 welcome       200357 Jun 11    1987     rfc1008.txt
-rw-r—r—         1 welcome       125039 Jun 6     1987     rfc1009.txt
-rw-r—r—         1 welcome        75628 May 29    1987     rfc1010.txt
-rw-r—r—         1 welcome        71630 May 29    1987     rfc1011.txt
—More—
```

For more help on basic UNIX commands, see the **UNIXHelp for Users** service, funded by the Information Technology Training Initiative at the University of St. Andrews, Scotland. It's well-organized and explains UNIX commands in plain English (http://cssun7.vassar.edu/~info/Unixhelp/TOP_.html).

The most important "power tool" you can bring to Internet searching is your experience and common sense. Sources on the Internet can be unreliable; a copy of the Periodic Table of Elements with only 84 elements was available on a number of sites before the mistake was noticed. (There are 109 elements, some yet unnamed, at last count.) Other outdated or simply incorrect sources that are not so obvious can also be found on the Internet. People who post responses in newsgroups may be industry experts...or they may have only a passing knowledge of the subject, if that.

Use common sense when evaluating information obtained on the Internet. Is this a site that's referenced in any of the subject guides to Internet resources? Is there any corroboration to what this person is saying? Does this white paper indicate the date it was written, and by whom?

Another way to determine the reliability of a piece of information is to examine the source. For example, a great site for information on local telecommunications is maintained by the Alliance for Competitive Communications (http://www.bell.com/ or gopher://gopher. bell.com/). You might not immediately realize that this site is produced by the seven Baby Bell companies who definitely have an opinion on the regulation or deregulation of local telecommunications services. I think their site is useful and reasonably balanced, but it is important to keep in mind who is producing the "Competition Fact Sheet" available on this site and that it may be less than completely impartial.

Read the onscreen documentation for each search engine you use. Many now offer you the ability to truncate search terms, use Boolean logic, and sort the retrieved information by date, relevance, or source. Be sure you understand *what* you are searching—does this search engine look at FTP sites or just WWW sites? Does it include newsgroups? How comprehensive is its index?

One of the joys of the Internet is that it does a good job of self-documenting. In addition to the onscreen help described earlier, there is extensive documentation on all aspects of Internet management, protocol, and use. The primary sources for information are RFCs (Request For Comments) and FYIs (For Your Information), maintained by the Internet Engineering Task Force. According to FYI17, the IETF "is a loosely self-organized group of people who make technical and other contributions to the engineering and evolution of the Internet and its technologies." The RFCs and FYIs are excellent starting points if you need information on how to register a domain name, how to locate people on the Internet, or if you want a description of the file transfer protocol or the basics of Hypertext Mark-up Language (HTML). You can obtain RFCs and FYIs at gopher://ds2.internic.net/11/.ds/.internetdocs or ftp://ds0.internic.net/rfc/ and ftp://ds0.internic.net/fyi/.

And finally, remember that common courtesy goes a long way. If you ask for help in a newsgroup, remember to thank the people who helped you. Consider compiling the information you received and posting it to the newsgroup for others to use. If you find a new resource, or find that one has moved, notify the person whose resource guide you relied on to find the information initially. The Internet has grown and thrived on tremendous amounts of volunteer effort and professionals sharing their time and expertise, and that's the best way to keep it alive and vital.

PRICING

Most Internet resources are available at no per-transaction charge. Your access to the Internet may well involve a fee, however. Unless you have access to the Internet through your university or employer, you may need to use either an Internet service provider or one of the general online services (America Online, CompuServe, Microsoft Network, Prodigy). All these services allow online sign-up, provided you can supply a credit card number.

Internet service providers usually charge a monthly fee of $20 to $30, which usually includes at least 5 to 20 hours of online time. Additional time may be charged at $1 an hour or so. Some ISPs also provide a Web browser or other proprietary software to access the World Wide Web.

The general online services usually help sort through the myriad resources available on the Internet by pointing out particularly useful sources; America Online is by far the best in this regard. On the other hand, the general online services have begun blocking access to some sites and newsgroups, usually the adult-content or controversial newsgroups.

If you are just beginning to search the Internet or only need to use it sporadically, access through a general online service may make the most sense. Once your monthly bills exceed $30 or $40, though, you should consider switching to an ISP that provides more cost-effective access.

Some information resources on the Internet are beginning to charge for their services. InfoSeek and NlightN are two examples of search engines that offer limited services for free and provide more sophisticated searching or a broader range of information to subscribers. Most for-fee services offer either a free trial period or free samples of their information; depending on the source, you may find that the added value offered by these services is worth the cost, which is often minimal anyway.

EVALUATION OF THE INTERNET

It's important to remember that the Internet is still a relatively new online information resource. The World Wide Web has only been in existence for a few years. Experts are only now realizing that the Internet is a great publishing tool. It's a place of experimentation and growth—who would have known three years ago that there would soon be 10 million sites on the Internet? You need to approach the Internet with a different frame of mind than when you conduct a search in a professional online service. Use the Internet to tap into the knowledge of experts throughout the world. Use it to share your own expertise with others. And watch as it grows and develops over the next few years; the finding tools and resources will also continue to grow and develop.

What do I like most about the Internet?

- I like the ability to communicate with people throughout the world who share a common interest. Whether it's business librarianship, microbiology or Esperanto, there's probably a newsgroup devoted to it, and that means I can tap into the expertise of its participants should I need to.

- I like the Internet culture, which encourages collaboration and volunteerism. It's this cooperative culture that gives us the subject resource guides and other well-designed finding tools. The people you find on the Internet are likely to be helpful and generous with their time. I find it particularly useful that there are FYIs and RFCs available to help me figure out what the Internet's about.

- I like the fact that the Internet is growing exponentially. It's becoming more and more likely that I'll be able to find a Web home page on a company, to download a data file of information from a government agency, and to deliver the results of research directly to someone's email account.

- I like the fact that the Internet is, in John Makulowich's words, self-refreshing. There are newsgroups and mailing lists to keep people updated on new Internet resources. Internet search tools include references to each other so that if you don't find what you need through one search engine, you can try another.

What do I like least about the Internet?

- The Internet is subject to fads. Right now, the World Wide Web is perceived as the One True Source for finding information on the Internet, overshadowing such useful sources as gopher or FTP. It's easy for new Net surfers to forget that there is more to the Internet than is available on the Web.

- I find the high noise-to-signal ratio in many newsgroups frustrating. Related to this, I find discouraging the increased use of "spamming"—indiscriminate posting of advertisements to hundreds of unrelated newsgroups. When a newsgroup attracts too much spamming, the most valuable participants are likely to either abandon the newsgroup or move their conversations to private mailing lists beyond the scope of both spam artists and those of us who would benefit from their public discussions.

- Similarly, search tools tend to retrieve documents that have little relevance to the information you need. This may be remedied somewhat by the more sophisticated relevancy-ranking within search engines, but may always be a problem when searching a universe of material that has not been, and cannot be, organized or cataloged by anyone.

- As an online researcher, I find distressing the lack of standardization, the unreliability of information, and the disappearance of useful information as an Internet subscriber drops her account or changes her email address. Even the best Internet search engines regularly retrieve pointers to files that no longer exist, directories that have been renamed or deleted, or sites that are no longer available. These are times when I appreciate the peer-evaluation, indexing, and organization of information available in a professional online service.

GENERAL INFORMATION

Choosing the Right Database

With the rapid growth of information systems and the availability of databases on professional and general online services (and sometimes on the Internet as well), how do you decide which online system you should choose as your primary or home system? This depends partly on each online service's characteristics:

- Does it have the sources you are most likely to need?
- Can you understand, control, and anticipate the costs?
- Can you get the training, support, and documentation you need to be a cost-effective online searcher?
- Does the system and its search software make sense to you?

Most online researchers maintain subscriptions to at least one of the professional online services, since the professional services usually contain information sources on a variety of subjects and disciplines. Many researchers keep accounts on several online services, both professional and general, since they know that the most cost-effective or efficient way to find information may not be through their primary online service. Sometimes a source will be available on several online services but only one service offers the power searching tool you need to ferret out the information.

In addition to the online services covered in this book, there are hundreds of specialized ones that focus on a particular product or industry. If you frequently need highly-focused information in a single discipline, you should investigate the specialized online resources available. The CorpTech Database focuses on high-technology and emerging industries, for example. Profound offers access to market research reports, and the Computer Installation Data File covers the installed base of computer hardware and software. If you find that you aren't locating the information you need, do some research (online!) for descriptions or reviews of specialized online services that focus on your specific research needs. An excellent directory of online databases is the two-volume *Gale Directory of Databases*, produced yearly by Gale Research Inc., Detroit, Michigan and available at the reference desk of most larger libraries.

In any given situation, you may find that the time it takes to learn a new online system or to remind yourself of the commands and file structure of a system you use infrequently isn't worth the money you save from using this system rather than your primary online service. On the other hand, if you find that you have the time to try out an alternative and note your search strategy for later use, you may discover that you can become literate in several online services without too much pain.

Here are some of the broad categories of interest and my recommendations on the best online sources for information on each.

CHAT LINES

Chat lines are found only in the general online services, not in any of the professional services. Your choice of which service to use depends on what kind of chat you want. America Online and Prodigy both promote their chat lines, and both have a wide variety of subjects. America Online tends to attract a wider audience and seems to have a higher proportion of adults participating in the chat lines, although this is difficult to ascertain given the anonymous nature of chat lines generally. The Internet offers IRC (Internet Relay Chat), but the user interface is much more difficult than the chat services available on AOL or Prodigy. Microsoft Network also offers chat areas but does not promote the feature. CompuServe promotes its "online conferences" more heavily than its chat lines; in fact, it only offers three channels for its "CB simulator" chat service. Unfortunately, CompuServe's online conferences are not held frequently; if you want live chat, you're best off with AOL or Prodigy.

COMPANY BACKGROUND

(See also "COMPANY FINANCIAL INFORMATION" which follows.)

You can do some basic research for articles on companies through CompuServe's Business Database, Magazine Database, IQUEST, and (during off-peak hours only) Knowledge Index. You can also surf the Internet to find companies' home pages—often companies include press releases, product information, and some background information about the company on their home pages. However, if you really want to get a complete and relatively unbiased picture of what a company is doing, and you want to get it fairly quickly, you need to use one of the professional online services. The databases that best cover a broad range of companies (both geographically and in a variety of industries) are ABI/INFORM, PTS PROMT, and Trade & Industry Database; these are available in various forms on DataStar, DataTimes, DIALOG, Dow Jones News/Retrieval, and LEXIS-NEXIS. The advantage of the professional online services is that they allow you to search the sources covered by several of these databases simultaneously, which cuts down on both the time required and the likelihood of your selecting the same article twice in two different databases. (Be sure to take advantage of the "remove duplicates" feature of DIALOG and DataStar.)

Depending on the depth of research needed, the next step for gathering background on a company could be:

- Press releases (PR Newswire, Business Wire, and PTS New Product Announcements), generally available on all the professional online services.
- Investment house reports (Investext) and market research reports produced by market analysts and consulting companies and covering a specific company or market; available on DataStar, DIALOG, LEXIS-NEXIS, and (for Investext only) Dow Jones News/Retrieval.

COMPANY FINANCIAL INFORMATION

If the company is publicly-held and its stock is traded in the U.S., you should start with the company's annual report and 10K (the annual financial statement that must be filed with the U.S. Securities and Exchange Commission). The least expensive way to retrieve 10Ks is through the SEC's EDGAR program, which provides the electronic version of most 10Ks, 10Qs (quarterly financial report), and several other financial filings via the Internet, at http://www.sec.gov/edgar/edgarhp.htm. You need to do some editing of the EDGAR documents to remove the special HTML codes that format the document for WWW displays. If you want a clean copy of EDGAR documents without the embedded codes, you can download the files from America Online at a minimal cost. You cannot search the EDGAR database as thoroughly as you can either through the SEC's site or one of the commercial versions of EDGAR (Standard & Poor's, Disclosure, Global Securities Inc., and so on).

Dow Jones News/Retrieval provides a well-organized overview of financial information in its //QUICK report, which is available for both public and private U.S. companies. Standard & Poor's, Moody's, and Media General databases all offer financial information on major U.S. companies via DIALOG, LEXIS-NEXIS, and to a lesser extent, Dow Jones News/Retrieval, NewsNet, and DataTimes.

For multinational or non-U.S. companies, the most complete collection of company databases is on DataStar, the only online system covered in this book that originated outside the U.S. In addition, the WorldScope database, available on LEXIS-NEXIS, DataTimes, and Dow Jones News/Retrieval, is a good source for financial profiles of international companies. You should also keep an eye on Microsoft Network; it is developing a number of features and services specifically targeted to non-U.S. subscribers and may eventually be a good source for non-U.S. news services.

COMPUTERS

This is one area that is well-covered by virtually all the online services, to no one's surprise. America Online, CompuServe, and Prodigy all have areas in which vendors provide online help, software patches and solutions to common problems, and in which computer experts can be found to help you troubleshoot hardware or software problems. Although many hardware and software companies also maintain their own bulletin boards of product information, these usually require a long-distance telephone call. Some product information is available on Microsoft Network and on the Internet home pages of some computer companies, but I have not yet found the level of support that I find on the forums of AOL, CIS, and Prodigy. If you want information on Microsoft software, MSN is the logical place to start.

For information *about* the computer industry, the Computer Database (available on CompuServe, DIALOG, LEXIS-NEXIS, and DataStar) is a good resource.

CURRENT NEWS

Both America Online and CompuServe provide good newswire services for late-breaking news. If you need to log on frequently to check for news, NewsNet's real-time news feeds are particularly easy to use. Dow Jones' //CLIP electronic clipping service is easy to set up and monitors the newswires and saves stories that match your profile.

EDUCATION/HUMANITIES/SOCIAL SCIENCES

The related fields of education, humanities, and social sciences do not have as many online full-text sources as do other disciplines, which is somewhat ironic given that ERIC (Educational Resources Information Center) was one of the very first bibliographic databases to be publicly available online. DIALOG and LEXIS-NEXIS provide the best coverage of social science and education resources, and the Internet can be a source for dissertations, white papers, and information about computer-aided education. America Online is home to some groups that focus on particular social segments or issues, e.g., AARP, Gay and Lesbian groups, teachers, and so on.

HEALTH AND WELLNESS

(See also "MEDICINE/PHARMACEUTICALS" which follows)

The best sources for information on health-related issues are the discussion forums on America Online, CompuServe, Microsoft Network, Prodigy, and the Internet. Depending on the topic, you may find that one source or another offers the most extensive and reliable information. For example, CompuServe has a particularly good forum on Attention-Deficit Disorder and MSN has a forum dedicated to breast cancer. Support groups are most prevalent on the Internet in Usenet newsgroups; look through those with names starting with "alt.support." Be careful to check the sources of your information—anyone with an account on a general online service or access to the Internet can pose as an expert, and you would be ill-served if you based a medical decision on the word of a stranger about whom you know nothing. On the other hand, these discussion forums are excellent vehicles for exchanging tips on how to live with a disease, or finding support for care-givers, or for pointers to additional information on a health-related problem.

HOBBIES

This is another area in which the Internet and general online services shine. I have found discussion forums on paper-making, breeding German Shepherd Dogs, and competitive archery. In fact, one private discussion group I participate in is a source for Grateful Dead-related knitting patterns. One advantage that the hobby discussion groups on general online services have over the Internet is the ability to maintain easily-accessible archive files of useful information—needlework patterns, a list of sources, or a particularly interesting discussion thread. There also tends to be more continuity in these discussion groups, perhaps because these groups are moderated by Sysops whose job it is to maintain lively discussions and useful files and because the subscriber population is less transient than on Internet groups. The Usenet newsgroups on the Internet reach a wider group of people and often maintain FAQs (Frequently Asked Questions), which provide some background information on the group's focus, but you often don't have the same level of cohesion that you find in the general online services' discussion groups.

INDUSTRY OVERVIEWS

If you want an insider's view of an industry, start with industry newsletters. The most comprehensive sources for these are the NewsNet online service, followed by the

Newsletter Database, available on most of the professional online services. You can usually confine your search to a broad industry group, which enables you to use specialized buzzwords and terms of the trade.

In addition, investment reports and market research reports (see "COMPANY BACKGROUND") cover specific industries and often provide an excellent perspective on where an industry is heading. The large magazine databases (ABI/INFORM, PTS PROMT, and Trade & Industry Database) include trade publications (e.g., *Modern Tire Dealer, Food Processing, Security Management*) as well as more general business publications such as *Fortune* or *Forbes*; these trade publications often have articles providing an end-of-the-year wrap-up, overview, or forecast. One effective way to search quickly for industry overview articles is by the truncated forms of the words *overview, trend, forecast*, or *cover story* in the title field, and then to AND that with the industry term in the title and indexing fields.

Another good source for U.S. and international industry information is the Stat-USA collection of databases on the Internet, maintained by the U.S. Department of Commerce at http://www.stat-usa.gov/. Stat-USA includes the National Trade Data Bank (export and trade-related information, including information on foreign markets); the National Economic, Social and Environmental Data Bank (U.S. social economic trends, education, health-related, and environmental issues); the Economic Bulletin Board (current press releases regarding economic trends as well as more in-depth economic statistics); Global Business Opportunities Service (clearinghouse of government procurement and business opportunities); and the Bureau of Economic Analysis' economic indicators, plus recent issues of the *Survey of Current Business* and related economic information. Full access costs $150 a year; abbreviated versions of these files are available at gopher://una.hh.lib.umich.edu:70/11/ebb/.

INTELLECTUAL PROPERTY

Intellectual property research is a field in which a little knowledge is indeed a dangerous thing. If a business or legal decision is being made on the basis of your research, it is critical that you use a database that offers the appropriate coverage and depth and that you understand how to conduct as comprehensive a search as possible. If your search misses an existing patent, your company can be prosecuted for patent infringement. If a trademark is already in use and you fail to find it, you lose your use of the trademark. Enormous corporate expenditures can be at stake here—this is one area where "good enough" usually *isn't*.

It is critical that the researcher understands exactly what is—and is not—covered in each database. Does this file include patents for all countries or just the U.S.? How far back does the file go? Can I search for and display a specific trademarked image? Is this image trademarked only in the U.S. or in other countries as well?

Of the online services reviewed in this book, the most comprehensive files for intellectual property information—patents, trademarks, and copyright—are on DIALOG. Databases include Derwent World Patents Index, U.S. Patents Fulltext, and TRADE-MARKSCAN (separate TRADEMARKSCAN databases are available for a number of countries' trademark files as well as those for both U.S. federal and state trademark files). Full-text patent files from the U.S. Patent Office are available on both DIALOG and LEXIS-NEXIS. For copyright information, the Library of Congress is the best place to start—telnet://locis.loc.gov or http://thomas.loc.gov/. The Library of Congress maintains records of books, magazines, films, music, software, and other copyrightable material registered with the Copyright Office since 1978.

INVESTMENTS

This is a business-related area in which one general online service shines. Prodigy offers quite a variety of tools for the individual investor, including current quotes for stocks and mutual funds, access to the past two weeks of the Dow Jones News/Retrieval wire services and other news stories, several analysts' columns and commentary on the market, and an extensive variety of stock market analysis tools and tracking programs. Keep in mind, though, that most of these resources are premium services for which additional fees apply.

Of the professional online services, Dow Jones News/Retrieval has the widest variety of investment information sources, which is what you would expect from the publishers of the *Wall Street Journal*. The menu-driven features make this service particularly easy to use for investors who are not frequent online searchers.

LEGAL INFORMATION

The hands-down favorite for legal information is LEXIS-NEXIS, which began as a legal information resource and expanded into more general research sources later. The primary competitor to LEXIS-NEXIS in terms of legal information is WESTLAW—another online service that began by providing online access to legal opinions and has since expanded to offering gateway access to DIALOG and other information sources. There are some legal sources on the Internet, primarily U.S. Supreme Court cases and links to local or state government files, but these are scattered and by no means comprehensive. Keep in mind, too, that many lower court decisions and other legal information such as local statutes and other public records are simply not available electronically but must be obtained directly from the jurisdiction involved.

MEDICINE/PHARMACEUTICALS

The most significant online databases for medical and pharmaceutical information are MEDLINE and EMBASE. MEDLINE, produced by the National Library of Medicine, is accessible directly from NLM or on DataStar, DIALOG, and LEXIS-NEXIS. EMBASE is available on DataStar and DIALOG. MEDLINE offers better coverage of clinical medicine and has a very useful hierarchical index of subject terms. EMBASE's strength is its coverage of pharmaceutical treatments and trials. There is about a 35 percent overlap in journals covered by MEDLINE and EMBASE; it often makes sense to search the two files simultaneously and use DIALOG's or DataStar's "remove duplicates" feature. The other major medical database is BIOSIS Previews, available on DataStar and DIALOG. Use BIOSIS for biological science research. MEDLINE, EMBASE, and BIOSIS are also available on CompuServe via the IQUEST service.

A number of hospitals maintain home pages on the Internet and some are quite useful. In addition, the medical-related Usenet newsgroups are frequently used by medical researchers to notify peers of new treatment protocols and results of studies. There are also electronically-published medical journals on the Internet that are much more timely than printed journals due to the greatly reduced production time-cycle.

PEOPLE

Online information services are often good ways to locate people or to gather information about individuals. If you are trying to identify a recognized expert in a field, one straightforward way is to search the trade and industry magazines covering that field, find several that either focus specifically on the topic for which you need an expert, or that present an overview of the industry and discussion of trends, and see who is quoted regularly. If the field is one in which experts are expected to publish to establish their credibility (particularly the hard and social sciences), look to see who has written frequently on the topic. These approaches can be used in any of the professional online services. Keep in mind that most newsletters do not list bylines or authors but the editor of a newsletter may well be an expert on the industry.

In addition, once you have identified some possible experts, you can use one of the "citation" databases to see how frequently these experts' writings have been cited in others' writings. These databases (SciSearch and Social SciSearch, available on DIALOG and DataStar) index each article cited in a footnote. You can search, for example, on any article written by a specific author to see how frequently that person's writing has been cited by others—a good indication that he or she enjoys a good reputation among peers. This technique only works in industries that expect their experts to write footnoted articles. This would not work well, for example, to identify the best Lotus Notes programmer or an expert on cellular phone designs.

For identifying an expert in a field in which published writing is not critical, the best resource is usually word of mouth. The Internet is a reasonable starting place for identifying someone who enjoys a good reputation among peers; find a Usenet newsgroup focusing on the topic for which you need an expert and ask for referrals.

There are other ways of locating people on the Internet. Although there isn't a single global directory of Internet email addresses, there are several tools for finding an Internet email address. For a very useful compilation of search tools for finding people on the Internet, use the People Finder in the All-in-One search page—http://www.albany.net/allinone/all1user.html.

POLITICS

For discussions of politics, the liveliest source is the Internet. During a Presidential election year, for example, all the major candidates establish home pages that provide position papers, recent speeches, and schedules of where the candidates are visiting next. You can find political discussions on Usenet newsgroups ranging from fans of Rush Limbaugh to latter-day anarchists. These discussions tend to shed more heat than light, but perhaps that's what the participants enjoy.

If you want to track political news, your best bet, surprisingly, is Dow Jones News/Retrieval. DJN/R has the three major daily papers—*The Wall Street Journal, New York Times*, and *Washington Post*—although its *Times* archive is limited. In addition, Dow Jones offers same-day access to about 60 newspapers, particularly useful if you need to find the reactions to a speech or results of a local election. To track local and state politics, search the **DT** (DataTimes) source code in Dow Jones' Text library for local newspaper coverage of the issues. For more in-depth coverage of political issues and their impact on a specific industry, search the newsletters in the "Industry & Trade Publications" section for relevant magazines and newsletters. Search sources such as *Federal News Service* or *CNN Convention Coverage* for political news, and industry newsletters such as *Washington Telecom News* for industry-specific coverage.

REFERENCE

Virtually all the general online services provide access to an encyclopedia, thesaurus, and dictionary—something none of the professional online services can claim. If you need other reference sources, such as a book of popular quotations, the periodic table of elements, or weather service forecasts, your best bet is the Internet. One particularly helpful collection of online reference desks and sources is the Solinet Gopher, available at gopher://gopher.solinet.net/ or http://www.solinet.net/. This comprises a collection of electronic reference sources through which you can find anything from Amtrak train schedules to ZIP codes and area codes. If you find a reference tool that you use frequently, remember to mark it in your bookmark or hotlist for easier retrieval.

SCIENCE/TECHNOLOGY

Of the online services covered in this book, DIALOG offers the best coverage of science with DataStar coming in a close second. Most of the sci-tech databases are not yet available in full-text format online; the challenges to ASCII delivery of scientific articles are the loss of graphics and difficulty in formatting equations. The most commonly-used science/technology databases include INSPEC (a comprehensive index of computer, electrical and electronic engineering literature), SciSearch (a unique database that allows you to see all the times a given scientific paper was cited in later works or to see a list of all the cites within a given article) and Conference Papers Index (particularly useful because papers presented at professional conferences often provide the first printed announcement of a scientific breakthrough or a new perspective on a scientific problem).

Engineering Index produces Compendex, another high-quality index of engineering articles and conference proceedings. In addition to the Compendex databases on DataStar and DIALOG, Ei makes Compendex available on the Internet through the Ei Village and Ei Connexion—http://www.ei.org/eihomepage/village/intro.html. Ei Village is a remarkable Web site—a well-organized resource with comprehensive links to engineering sites throughout the Net, news sources, and government databases as well as to Ei's own database, available on a flat-fee basis on Ei Connexion.

The National Technical Information Service, an arm of the U.S. Department of Commerce, maintains a collection of federal government information sources on a gateway service called FedWorld. You can find summaries (and sometimes the full text) of agency reports, files, and spreadsheets through the bulletin boards accessible on FedWorld—http://www.fedworld.gov/. NTIS' own database of government-sponsored research and federal agency research is also a great resource for sci-tech researchers. This for-fee database is available on DataStar and DIALOG and is a useful tool for locating reports and studies.

Internet listservs and Usenet newsgroups often focus on new technologies, enabling you to tap into the expertise of practitioners in the field. As with medical literature, quite a few electronic journals focusing on science and technology are appearing on the Net.

SPORTS

This is another area in which the general online services excel. America Online and Prodigy have particularly good selections of bulletin boards, chat areas, and file libraries for all type of sports; you can find a fantasy baseball league, World Wrestling Federation news, National Football League statistics, and news on the International Olympics.

Getting the Most from Your Search Dollar

O nline searching can be either a cost-effective, efficient way to find information or an extraordinarily expensive exercise in futility. You need to know what you are looking for, where to look for it, how to phrase your search, and when to stop and rethink your strategy if your search is not turning up what you expect.

Advice on what search techniques work best varies depending on the subject being researched, your search budget, your experience on a particular online system, and the depth of research needed. My first advice is to know what you want to find before you start searching. In other words, be sure you are reasonably clear on the point of the search. Are you looking for a list of the top ten banks in the United States? Is that the top ten ranked by assets, number of branches, or number of customers? Are you looking for information on interstate banking? Do you want a few good articles, everything written on the subject, or just the most recent articles from *American Banker*? Defining the depth and extent of the research determines how the online search is constructed.

This chapter contains hints on how to structure your search strategy, how to narrow an overly broad search, and broaden an overly narrow one, and how to maximize the value of your time online.

DO'S AND DON'TS OF ONLINE SEARCHING

DO your homework before going online. Particularly if you are searching on a system that charges per minute or per search, be sure you are prepared before you log on. Look up the field names ahead of time. "Let's see, is that wheat()gluten/ti or is it head(wheat gluten) or is it maybe wheat adj gluten.hl.?" Map out your search strategy with synonyms for your key concepts. Look up the display formats so you know how to view a list of titles, the key search terms in context, and the full text of the retrieved records.

DO buy the documentation for any online system you use regularly. If updates are available, subscribe to them. A $90 thesaurus of a database's subject terms pays for itself after just a few searches if it enables you to quickly find the specific code for frozen orange juice when you need to search that industry.

DO read all announcements and descriptions of system enhancements, database additions, and software upgrades sent by the online service. If free time is offered when a new file is introduced, use the time to practice searching and to explore it.

DO think creatively. If you want information on drug abuse programs, remember that the material might be indexed as "drug prevention," "drug use," "drug involvement," "substance abuse," "illegal drugs," and so on.

DON'T use NOT without careful thought. NOT is a powerful search tool and may eliminate any records that contain the specified word(s) or phrase(s). Say you want to search for information on health risks of smoking tobacco but are not interested in risks of chewing tobacco. You could compose a search for cigarette(s) or smoking NOT chewing tobacco, but this would exclude potentially relevant articles that mentioned chewing tobacco as well.

DON'T spend more time on a search than it deserves. If all you need is a few overview articles on a topic, stop when you get what looks reasonably close. Log off and review the retrieved information and decide if you really need more information. Although it is tempting to keep going back to get the perfect article that neatly summarizes every issue in question, the additional cost may not be justified.

DO check prices before you log on. Is this a system that charges you for every character that comes across the screen? If so, remember not to print items that appear to be of only marginal interest. Is this a system that has high connect-time charges, but relatively low per-document charges? If so, have the relevant documents delivered to you offline (via electronic mail or fax) so you don't pay for the connect charges while the documents are scrolling off the screen. Is this a system that charges for KWIC (Keyword-in-Context) displays? If so, use other display options such as title and indexing terms to review a large search set for relevancy. Do two databases offer the same coverage of the sources you need? If so, compare prices to determine which one would be the least expensive to search while still offering you the search tools you need. Shop around—if you need an article from last week's *Business Week*, it's cheaper to download it from America Online than to search DIALOG or LEXIS-NEXIS.

DO call customer service if you aren't sure how to compose a search or are going to search a system you don't know well. Although improvisation works well in the music world, it can be an expensive exercise when searching online.

DON'T get complacent in your searching. It's tempting to start with the same three or four databases for every search simply because they're the ones you know best. Often an overlooked specialty database may offer the best information.

DO "save" your search if the online service offers this feature. Save yourself the time it takes to retype the search strategy when you change files. Log off after an initial search, review the results so far, then log back on and re-execute the search in another file. This feature may not be useful, however, if you are searching dissimilar files (moving from a file that comprises bibliographic citations only to a full-text file, for example).

DO use any relevant customized subsets of files created by the online service. You can search a subfile of articles on the O.J. Simpson trial using NEXIS' Hot Files. You can use NewsNet's MOBILCOM grouping of newsletters that cover the mobile communications industry. If you need a recent wire story, you can scan just the past few months' news sources on Dow Jones' //WIRES. A focused search in a specialized subset of files is much more efficient than a similar search in a file that includes a wide range of sources.

DON'T combine bibliographic and directory files in the same search. It may seem more efficient to run a single search in files that contain the full text of articles as well as company information in directory format. However, the search techniques for searching articles (adjacency, indexing terms, title words) are very different from those techniques used in searching directory-type files (company name, SIC code, sales figures). Display options vary as well and may force you to pay for a more expensive format than you need. (This last tip comes from painful experience. I combined an in-depth company directory database with some bibliographic files for a single search. I displayed the results in "full" format without realizing that the full format in the directory database cost $40 per record. Not only did this teach me not to combine file types, but it also convinced me of the value of DIALOG's SET NOTICE command.)

SEVEN DEADLY SINS OF ONLINE SEARCHING

Reva Basch listed the original Seven Deadly Sins of Online Searching. ("The Seven Deadly Sins Of Full-text Searching." *DATABASE* 12, No. 4 [August 1989]: pp. 15-23.) At the risk of committing the sin of Pride (or perhaps it's Sloth?), I'll modify her seven deadly sins into my own list of ways to fall from online grace. These sins probably don't carry the same dire consequences of the original seven sins of pride, covetousness, lust, anger, gluttony, envy, and sloth, but they could cost you time and money. The trouble begins when you log on to an online service without thinking—of what you want to find, how you intend to go about looking for it, and why you are searching online in the first place.

The Seven Deadly Sins of Online Searching:
1. Pride—assuming you needn't read the manual
2. Haste—rushing into a search before thinking through your search goals
3. Avarice—trying to do a comprehensive search when all you need is an overview
4. Apathy—not thinking creatively about what sources would best cover the subject
5. Sloth—using the same old databases for every search
6. Narrow-mindedness—trying only one formulation of the search
7. Ignorance—not knowing the online system's tricks and tools

Now to examine the deadly sins one by one:

Sin 1. Pride—assuming you needn't read the manual

Yes, it's tedious to look up through the file description every time you run a search. But what happens if you don't? You search for *Business Week* articles in a file that does not include that magazine. You search for an article published in 1985 in a file that only goes back to 1988. You want the full text of articles and you search a file that only contains article summaries. You want the search results in a format you can import into a spreadsheet, and the database does not support customized output. Just as the carpenter's maxim is "measure twice, cut once," the online searcher's maxim should be "check twice, search once."

Sin 2. Haste—rushing into a search before thinking through your search goals

Why are you doing this search? Are you building a list of citations for a report? In that case, you needn't limit your search to full-text sources but can include files that contain only bibliographic citations. If you are doing a search on redesigning an advertising campaign, are you looking for case studies on successful redesigns, or mentions of advertising agencies that have helped rework the familiar slogans, or articles making the case that changing a well-known advertising campaign is a bad idea? Knowing the tenor of the material you are seeking makes it much easier to scan your retrieved records and recognize the material that will be most helpful.

Sin 3. Avarice—trying to do a comprehensive search when all you need is an overview

This is closely related to the sin of Haste. Decide whether your search strategy needs to focus on precision (retrieving a small set of highly-relevant records) or recall (retrieving a comprehensive set of records on your subject, some of which may be only marginally relevant). You may need only a few good articles on the home banking industry, but you keep searching and searching for the three quintessential articles. Your search costs skyrocket and the final expense is far higher than the actual value of the material retrieved. There are a number of tricks to finding "a few good articles" listed in the "TROUBLESHOOTING" section later in this chapter.

Sin 4. Apathy—not thinking creatively about what sources would best cover the subject

Give a few minutes of thought to who would care about the subject you are searching. If you want background information on a Silicon Valley electronics firm, you should start your search with the newspapers in the San Francisco Bay area. If you want industry opinions of the U.S. Department of Defense's latest budget, you should look for newsletters focusing on the defense and aerospace industries. If you want demographics of college students in Arizona, you should identify an online version of college and university directories. Deciding what group of people would be collecting the information you want helps you define your question and guides you to the most likely resources.

Sin 5. Sloth—using the same old databases for every search

It's human nature to take the path of least resistance. I always shop at the same stores; I've been using the same communications software for the past five years; I tend to start with the same six or eight files for most market research projects. It's critical, though, to keep your mind open to search alternatives. One researcher even has a checklist she consults before she starts any search. She has to answer the following questions before going online: "Did I check the online system's index of databases to identify the most appropriate files?" "Did I compare alternate online systems for the same database?" "Is the information available more cost-effectively on the Internet?" "Which database charges the least for this specific search?"

Sin 6. Narrow-mindedness—trying only one formulation of the search

One of the most common mistakes of beginning searchers is to formulate the One True Search, and to accept blindly the results of that one search as all there is on the subject. Rather than formulating your initial search as (A or B) and (C or D) not E, try casting a wide net and then narrowing it down as necessary. Search for A or B and scan some titles to see if you are retrieving what you expect. Perhaps you see an additional synonym for the search terms A and B. Add the new synonym and see what effect that has on your retrieval. Then modify the search with the addition of C or D and review the results. As noted in the "DO'S AND DON'TS OF ONLINE SEARCHING," be very wary of using "NOT" in a search, as it does eliminate any record in which that term appears.

Sin 7. Ignorance—not knowing the online system's tricks and tools

Before logging on to an online system you aren't completely familiar with, be sure you know the essentials. What does the system use as its break key? How do you display your search results in a low- or no-cost format? How do you truncate search words, or does the system do this automatically? How do you search for one term within ten words of another term? Are the system's charges based on minutes online, number of searches run, number of records displayed, number of characters displayed, or some combination of these factors? How do you get online help in the middle of a search? How do you save your search until you get help?

TROUBLESHOOTING

Most problems with online searching come down to either not finding any information when you expected to retrieve a large number of records or turning up hundreds of items when you were looking for just a few.

Expanding a Search

The first thing to do if you retrieve suspiciously few records is to check your spelling. Did you spell "satellite" properly? How many "d's" are in "Baldrige Award?" Be careful of the differences between British and American spelling. A search for aluminum in the *Financial Times of London* should include aluminium as well. Similarly, keep in mind that the British and American words for many everyday objects differ; truck=lorry, diaper=nappy, gasoline=petrol. Be sure to include both terms for more comprehensive retrieval, particularly in databases produced outside the U.S.

Another simple mistake is mistyping the filename and searching in the wrong file. Did you type AD (Advertising databases) in NewsNet instead of AE (Aerospace)? No wonder you didn't find any articles in your search for black boxes and commuter airlines.

A related problem is searching a bibliographic citation file rather than a full-text one. If you are searching a file in which each record has only 10 or 15 searchable words (say, title and subject terms), start by using as many alternate search terms, OR'd together, as possible. Even bibliographic files may not be equivalent in searchability. The World Patents Index database has titles that often run two or three lines long. The JAPIO patent database, on the other hand, uses two- or three-word titles. Obviously, a title search in the former may retrieve far more records than the same search in the latter.

Another possible cause for low retrieval is that you are using the wrong database for the question. If you don't know which databases would be most appropriate, use the finding tools available on the online system you are using. DIALOG, for example, has DIALINDEX—a collection of indexes to most of its databases. DataStar has a similar file called CROS. Either may point you to the databases in which your search terms occur most frequently.

LEXIS-NEXIS produces specialized databases such as the TODAY file of the current day's news and specialized "Hot Files" for whatever is hot news. The Hot Files have included collections of information on subjects such as the Whitewater hearings, debate over healthcare, and NAFTA. If the subject of your research corresponds to one of the NEXIS hot files, start there and expand if you need additional material. If the online system does not provide a finding tool, call the customer service desk and ask for help in selecting the most appropriate files.

If you have trouble deciding how to formulate a search, try what's called the "cultured pearl" approach. This technique was articulated by Barbara Quint ("Inside A Searcher's Mind: The Seven Stages Of An Online Search—Part 2." *ONLINE* 15, No.4 [July 1991]: pp. 28-35); it's a way to approach a difficult, vague, or unfamiliar search topic. Say you want to search the medical literature for the effect of birth control pills on bone density. Start with a search that retrieves a few highly relevant records. For example, the first search could be for the phrases birth control pill AND bone density. You may retrieve only a few records. Display the title and subject or indexing terms for those records. You may discover that the proper subject term in this database for birth control pills is oral contraceptive agents and that the term for bone density is bone-density. You might also find related terms such as bone metabolism and oral contraception. A second search, using these additional terms, should retrieve a larger number of relevant records.

If the online system you are using has Natural Language search software, try using it in addition to your Boolean search. A search using NEXIS' FREESTYLE often retrieves a different collection of records than a Boolean search with the same terms. A combination of the two approaches should provide you with a good selection of relevant material.

Limiting a Search

What do you do if you are plagued with the opposite problem—finding far more records than you can use? One brute-force solution is to limit your search terms to the title or indexing fields. If you are looking for a few articles reviewing computer games for children, searching for the terms computer games and children in the title or subject fields may not turn up a large set, but the articles you retrieve are likely to be on target.

Another way of narrowing your retrieval set is to use proximity operators. A search for articles on healthcare for the homeless, for example, may turn up hundreds of records that mention both healthcare and the homeless, but not in conjunction with each other. To focus the search, include the requirement that the term healthcare must occur within, say, 20 words of homeless.

If your aim is simply to get an overview of a topic, you can limit your search to cover stories (the phrase "cover story" is frequently added to the title, particularly in news and business files), or restrict your search to articles of more than 2,000 words. Searching for cover stories is not as simple as it sounds, though. For a good description of what to watch out for, see Ojala, Marydee. "Covering The Story: Searching For Cover Stories." *DATABASE* 17, No. 1 (February 1994): pp. 83-85.

Another trick is to restrict your search to records that contain case studies or examples that are likely to appear in overview articles. For example, a search for case studies of how a company can revamp its trademark could be narrowed by looking for articles that mention Aunt Jemima or Betty Crocker, two images whose makeovers were widely discussed in the marketing press.

One final suggestion if you are having difficulty formulating your search—imagine what the headline would be for the ideal article. This is a common trick of reference librarians when their patrons are having difficulty describing their research project, and it works for any online searcher.

This chapter is a source list of where to get additional information about the online resources described in this book. It is not intended to be an exhaustive bibliography about or for online searchers; that task could be a book in itself. Rather, this is a list of the primary points of contact, a selection of the principle books on a topic, and a guide to where to find online experts in their own habitat—online.

ONLINE VENDORS

America Online
America Online Inc.
8619 Westwood Center Drive
Vienna, VA 22182
800/827-6364; 703/448-8700
Customer service hours:
Monday through Friday 9:00am - 2:00am Eastern time
Saturday and Sunday noon - 1:00am Eastern time
Technical representatives are available from 6:00am to 4:00am Eastern time; 7 days a week.
Email contacts:
through AOL: keyword: **Help**, click on [Email to the staff]
live online help: keyword: **TechLive** (staffed 24 hours a day; 7 days a week)
through Internet: fulfill2@aol.com
home page: http://www.aol.com/

CompuServe Information Services
CompuServe Information Services
5000 Arlington Centre Boulevard
P.O. Box 20212
Columbus, OH 43220
800/848-8990; 614/457-8650
Customer service hours:
Monday through Friday 8:00am - midnight Eastern time
Saturday, Sunday and holidays noon - 10:00pm Eastern time
Email contacts:
through CompuServe: 70006,101 or **GO FEEDBACK**
through Internet: 70006.101@compuserve.com
home page: http://www.compuserve.com/

DataStar Information Retrieval Service
Knight-Ridder Information, Inc.
2440 El Camino Real
Mountain View, CA 94040
800/334-2564; 415/254-8800
Customer service hours:
Monday through Friday 8:00am - 8:00pm Eastern time
Email contacts:
Internet: customer@corp.dialog.com
home page: http://www.dialog.com

DataTimes
DataTimes Corp.
14000 Quail Springs Parkway; Suite 450
Oklahoma City, OK 73134
800/642-2525; 405/751-6400
Customer service hours:
Monday through Friday 8:00am - 10:00pm Eastern time
Email contacts:
through EyeQ software: click on the [Customer Service] icon
through Internet: datatime@datatimes.com
home page: http://www.enews.com/clusters/datatimes/

DIALOG
Knight-Ridder Information, Inc.
2440 El Camino Real
Mountain View, CA 94040
800/334-2564; 415/254-8800
Customer service hours:
Monday through Friday 8:00am - 8:00pm Eastern time
Email contacts:
through Internet: customer@corp.dialog.com
home page: http://www.dialog.com/dialog/dialog1.html

Dow Jones News/Retrieval
Dow Jones & Company, Inc.
P.O. Box 300
Princeton, NJ 08543-0300
609/452-1511
Customer service hours:
Monday through Friday 8:00am - midnight Eastern time
Saturday 9:00am—6:00pm Eastern time
Email contacts:

through Internet: djnr.support@cor.dowjones.com
home page: http://bis.dowjones.com/djnr.html

LEXIS-NEXIS

Reed Elsevier Inc.
P.O. Box 933
Dayton, OH 45401
800/346-9759; 513/859-5398
800/227-4908 for new accounts
Customer service hours:
24 hours/day; 7 days a week except Sunday between 2:00am and 10:00am Eastern time
Email contacts:
home page: http://www.lexis-nexis.com/

Microsoft Network

Microsoft Corp.
One Microsoft Way
Redmond, WA 98052-6399
800/386-5550
Customer service hours:
Monday through Friday 7:00am - 2:00am Eastern time
Saturday and Sunday noon - 10:00pm Eastern time
Email contacts:
through MSN: Click on [Member Lobby] from the MSN Central screen. Click on [MSN Support]. Click on [MSN Help Desk]. Click on [For More Information], then click on [Ask Member Support]. You are guided through the creation of an email message to Customer Support.
home page: http://www.msn.com/

NewsNet

NewsNet Inc.
945 Haverford Road
Bryn Mawr, PA 19010
800/345-1301; 610/527-8030
800/952-0122 for new accounts
Customer service hours:
Monday through Friday 8:30am - 6:00pm Eastern time
Email contacts:
through NewsNet: mail newsnet at the main menu
through Internet: custserv@newsnet.com
home page: http://www.newsnet.com/

Prodigy

Prodigy Services Co.

445 Hamilton Avenue
White Plains, NY 10601
800/776-3449; 914/448-8000
Customer service hours:
24 hours/day; 7 days a week
Email contacts:
through Prodigy: [Jump] Member Help for help files and email to Customer Service.
Or [Jump] Live Help for member services chat area
home page: http://www.prodigy.com/

INTERNET ACCESS

Following is a list of selected Internet service providers (ISPs) that provide access throughout the U.S. America Online, CompuServe, Microsoft Network, and Prodigy also provide Internet access for their subscribers.

internetMCI
800/955-6505
6325244@mcimail.com
http://www.internetmci.com/

NETCOM On-Line Communication Services, Inc.
800/353-6600; 408/983-5950
info@netcom.com
http://www.netcom.com/

PSI (Performance Systems International)
800/827-7482
info@psi.com
http://www.psi.com/

UUNet
UUNET Technologies
800/265-2213
info@uunet.uu.net
http://www.uu.net/

In addition to the preceding Internet service providers, there are many other ISPs that offer access to the Internet. Some provide nationwide or international coverage; others provide service to just a few geographical areas. For a current list of Internet service providers available in your geographic area, see:

• The List at http://thelist.com/ (provided by MecklerMedia); or

• The *EFF Guide to the Internet*, formerly known as *The Big Dummy's Guide to the Internet*.

on America Online: keyword **EFF**
on CompuServe: **go EFFSIG**
on the Internet:
    http://www.eff.org/papers/eegtti

To take advantage of the graphics and easy navigation of the World Wide Web, you need to have Internet browser software. Many of the larger Internet service providers provide browser software to subscribers and, as mentioned earlier, all the general online services provide access to the Internet with their proprietary software. Other ISPs offer the SLIP/PPP connection you need but do not provide the software to enable you to take advantage of the point-and-click navigation available on the WWW. Following is a list of selected Internet browser software; shareware or freeware versions can often be downloaded from these or "mirror" web sites.

NCSA Mosaic
National Center for Supercomputing Applications
217/244-0072
orders@ncsa.uiuc.edu
http://www.ncsa.uiuc.edu/SDG/Software/Mosaic/NCSAMosaicHome.html

Netcruiser
NETCOM On-Line Communication Services, Inc
800/353-6600; 408/983-5950
info@netcom.com
http://www.netcom.com/

Netscape Navigator
Netscape Communications Corp.
800/528-6292; 415/528-2555
info@netscape.com
http://www.netscape.com/

PSInet Pipeline
Pipeline Inc.
800/453-7473
http://www.usa.pipeline.com/

SPRY Internet In A Box
SPRY Inc.
800/557-9614
iboxinfo213@spry.com

INTERNET RESOURCES FOR ONLINE SEARCHERS

Keeping up on new developments on the Internet is difficult even for dedicated Net surfers. The rest of us can easily get overwhelmed or feel that we're being left behind. There are a number of Internet services that provide regular updates of new sites and resources available on the Net. Two that I find particularly helpful are Net Happenings and the Scout Report.

• Net Happenings is compiled by Gleason Sackman of InterNIC and distributed as a mailing list and through a Usenet newsgroup. Sackman receives hundreds of email messages from people and organizations, notifying him of new home pages, gopher sites, listservs, and other resources. He compiles the best of the lot, codes each notice with an indication of whether it is a WWW site, EMAG (electronic magazine), and so on, and distributes the list. He does not include his own description of the site; this enables Net Happenings to cover a large number of new sites, but you lose the value of a reviewer's perspective. It's eye-opening to scan the day's list; invariably, there is at least one site I'm glad I saw listed. You can subscribe to Net Happenings by sending email to listserv@lists.internic.net with the body of the message: *subscribe net-happenings yourfirstname yourlastname*, or by reading it via the Usenet newsgroup comp.internet.net-happenings, or at http://www.mid.net/NET/.

• Scout Report is a weekly update prepared by Susan Calcari at InterNIC. It focuses on Internet sources of particular interest to researchers and educators. This report is compiled and evaluated by a person, so it is much more selective than the Net Happenings report. It's a bit harder to skim than Net Happenings, but it comes out only once a week so is less overwhelming. You can subscribe to the Scout Report by sending email to listserv@lists.internic.net with the body of the message: *subscribe scout-report yourfirstname yourlastname* or by reading it at http://rs.internic.net/scout_report-index.html or gopher://rs.internic.net/.

A good collection of finding tools, directories and lists is maintained by Tradewave Corp. at http://galaxy.einet.net/search-other.html. It includes links to Net Happenings and Scout Report, the major Internet search engines, and other resources for finding information on the Net.

Listservs are a great way to keep in touch with people who share a common interest—phonecard collecting, folk music, or Native American literature. Stephanie da Silva compiles the Publicly Accessible Mailing Lists file, an extensive list of mailing lists, updated monthly and sorted by general topic. The file is available at http://www.neosoft.com/internet/paml or ftp://rtfm.mit.edu/pub/usenet-by-group/news.lists/.

Online Inc., publisher of books and magazines about the online world, maintains a gopher site at gopher://online.lib.uic.edu/. This gopher includes selected articles from Online's magazines, including a collection of recent columns and feature articles about the Internet. Online Inc. also maintains a Web site at http://www.onlineinc.com.

A number of listservs for librarians and information professionals focus on specific areas of interest such as business research, legal research and law firms, or public access library computer systems. These listservs usually have discussion threads covering online, print, and Internet resources in their field of expertise. Remember to practice good netiquette—if you are not a regular member of the listserv, try other sources or check for a FAQ (Frequently-Asked Questions file) before you post a query to one of these listservs. The primary purpose of these listservs is to enable an exchange of information among peers, not to serve as the avenue of first resort for researchers.

Examples of some information professionals' listservs are:

BUSLIB-L—business librarians' discussion list. Unmoderated list with a wide range of industries represented, and many expert researchers.

> Send email to listserv@idbsu.idbsu.edu
>
> with the body of the message: *subscribe buslib-l yourfirstname yourlastname*

LIBREF-L—reference librarians' discussion list. Moderated list focusing on reference librarianship, using the Internet for research and reference work, and so on.

> Send email to listserv@kentvm.kent.edu
>
> with the body of the message: *subscribe libref-l yourfirstname yourlastname*

There are also private or member-only listservs and conferences that focus on the interests of information professionals. AIIP, the Association of Independent Information Professionals, has a private section in CompuServe's Working From Home forum, accessible to AIIP members only. (More information on AIIP follows under "INFORMATION BROKERS.") The Investigative and Information Professionals Network (IPN) is a network of competitive intelligence analysts, private investigators, public records researchers, and other information professionals. IPN maintains a private listserv for its members. For more information on IPN, see http://www.ipn.net/ or http://www.best.com/~jcook or email jcook@netcom.com.

Links to the Internet resources described in this book are also available at the author's home page at http://www.access.digex.net/~mbates/.

SELECTED BOOKS AND MAGAZINES ABOUT ONLINE SEARCHING

Books

American Library Association Guide to Information Access. New York, NY: Random House; 1994. 533 pp.

This handbook describes online and print sources for a number of basic research categories, as well as pointers to associations, government agencies, and other sources of expert advice. If you are finding that an online search is not yielding the quantity or depth of information you need, consult this guide for pointers to some alternatives to online searching.

Basch, Reva. *Secrets of the Super Searchers.* Wilton, CT: Pemberton Press (an imprint of Online Inc.); 1993. 235 pp.

This is one of those books you read again and again, dog-earing it and writing notes in the margin each time. Reva Basch, a super searcher in her own right, interviewed 23 power searchers and presented their tips, techniques, secrets, and cautions. It is of value to both beginning online searchers and those who have been in the business for years.

Fulltext Sources Online. Needham Heights, MA: BiblioData; biannual publication.

This is one indispensable tool for online searchers. It lists virtually all magazines and periodicals that are available in full-text format on any of the professional online services, along with an indication of whether indexing is cover-to-cover or selective, the lag-time between hardcopy publication and online availability, and the earliest available issue.

Gale Directory of Databases. Detroit, MI: Gale Research Inc.; biannual publication.

This is a two-volume directory of online databases (volume 1) and CD-ROM, diskette, magnetic tape, and batch-access products (volume 2). This directory is particularly useful if you need to find a specialized database not available through the professional online services or to compare access options from one service to another.

O'Leary, Mick. *THE ONLINE 100: ONLINE Magazine's Field Guide to the 100 Most Important Online Databases*. Wilton, CT: Pemberton Press; 1995. 233 pp.

Mick O'Leary provides his take on the 100 most important databases for researchers, broken out in categories such as business, life sciences, intellectual property, and general reference. Each entry includes a description of the database, search tips, notes on when not to use the database, and a listing of how to get access to the database. This book helps you select the best sources for your information needs, a daunting task these days.

Magazines

DATABASE. Wilton, CT: Online Inc.; bimonthly.

DATABASE covers online and CD-ROM databases as well as resources on the Internet. The emphasis is on search techniques, comparisons among databases, and file quality. It also covers software for locally-produced databases.

The Information Advisor. New York, NY: FIND/SVP, Inc.; monthly.

This newsletter focuses primarily on online information sources but includes print resources as well. It often has charts comparing sources—Internet search tools, online sources for SEC documents, wire services, and so on.

ONLINE. Wilton, CT: Online Inc.; bimonthly.

ONLINE, also published by Online Inc., covers a broad range of online issues including search techniques across online services, analyses of new technologies, Internet searching and management of Web pages, and computer hardware and software as they are used for online searching.

ONLINE USER. Wilton, CT: Online Inc.; bimonthly.

Online Inc.'s newest magazine, *ONLINE USER* focuses on practical information for "knowledge workers"—professionals who use online information sources but are not primarily researchers. The emphasis is on pragmatic, how-to articles rather than on information industry news or trends.

Searcher. Medford, NJ: Information Today, Inc.; nine times a year.

Searcher calls itself "the magazine for database professionals" and is edited by (and carries the voice of) Barbara Quint, sometimes called the Ralph Nader of the online world. This lively magazine covers general, professional and specialized online systems, the Internet, information entrepreneurs, and computer hardware and software.

Articles

It would be futile to attempt to provide a bibliography of articles about online searching. Following are a few that are particularly well-written, that articulate basic online searching principles, and that I have found to be particularly helpful.

Basch, Reva. "The Seven Deadly Sins Of Full-text Searching." *DATABASE* 12, No. 4 (August 1989): pp. 15-23.

Basch lists the original seven deadly sins of searching full-text databases and suggests ways to avoid or work around each one.

Basch, Reva. "What's Online: A Trekker's Guide to the Online Universe." *ONLINE USER* 1, No. 1 (October/November 1995): pp. 16-21.

This is an introductory article to the world of online information, particularly helpful in providing an overview of the basic issues of online searching, options for getting connected, a comparison of the Internet to other online services, and a discussion of how to decide on which online services to use.

Hawkins, Donald T. and Robert Wagers. "Online Bibliographic Search Strategy Development." *ONLINE* 6, No. 3 (May 1982): pp. 12-19.

This article, though somewhat dated, set forth many of the basic principles of online searching such as the "cultured pearl" technique, use of indexing codes and thesauri, and the use and abuse of acronyms.

Ojala, Marydee. "Covering The Story: Searching For Cover Stories." *DATABASE* 17, No. 1 (February 1994): pp. 83-85.

If you are trying to find a few definitive articles about a subject, looking for cover stories is often a quick way to locate an overview article. This column is about how best to search for cover stories in a number of full-text databases.

Quint, Barbara. "Inside A Searcher's Mind: The Seven States Of An Online Search." (Two parts) *ONLINE* 15, No. 3 and 4 (May and July 1991).

Barbara Quint, the self-described "grasshopper" searcher (as opposed to the plodding ant in Aesop's fable), outlines the seven steps involved in online searching, along with tips for interviewing the person for whom you are doing the research and different ways to approach an online search.

TOOLS FOR SPECIFIC ONLINE SERVICES

Only a few of the following books and magazines listed focus specifically on using a professional online service. For the most part, these services provide adequate (and often excellent) documentation, making third-party books unnecessary. On the other hand, the general online services provide very little in the way of system documentation and, it seems, rely on third parties to provide the printed documentation essential for effective research.

America Online

Bjørner, Susanne. "Mercury Center: fit for supersearchers?" *SEARCHER* 2, No. 7 (July/August 1994): pp. 36-39.

You could spend months on America Online and never discover the Mercury Center, one of the few in-depth newspaper databases on AOL. This article describes the information available and compares it to the traditional professional online services.

Lichty, Tom. *The Official America Online Tour Guide*. Chapel Hill, NC: Ventana Press; 1995. 550 pp.

This book goes into great detail on how to get the most out of America Online. Along with many examples and screen shots, it explains technical aspects of AOL such as how to save stock portfolios in Excel format, how to download graphics files, and the mechanics of live chat rooms.

CompuServe

Orenstein, Glenn S. and Ruth M. *CompuServe Companion: Finding Newspapers and Magazines Online*. Needham Heights, MA: BiblioData; 1994. 198 pp.

This book, similar in focus and format to *Fulltext Sources Online*, is a guide to identifying full-text periodicals on CompuServe, the only general online service with a sufficient selection of full-text databases to be truly useful for researchers. This book also analyzes the relative cost of a search in different CompuServe databases. The pricing structure has changed since this book was published, but the relative costs remain the same. If you intend to use CompuServe for research, this book is essential.

Internet

Compiling a current list of the best Internet books is like trying to shoot a moving target. Books covering one aspect of the Internet or another appear on an almost daily basis. The books listed here are ones I have found helpful and that are of the most use to online searchers. In addition, I encourage readers to consult Hope N. Tillman's excellent bibliography of Internet books and magazines available at gopher://gopher.babson.edu:70/11/.intbib/ or at gopher://gopher.babson.edu, and follow the path:

Internet Information
    Internet Bibliography
        Internet Books

Books about the Internet

Basch, Reva. *Secrets of the Super Net Searchers*. Wilton, CT: Pemberton Press (an imprint of Online Inc.); 1996.

As a follow-up to her *Secrets of the Super Searchers*, Reva Basch interviewed about three dozen Internet searchers, surfers, and pioneers to learn how they mine the Internet for information. Expected publication date is Fall 1996.

Gaffin, Adam. *Everybody's Guide to the Internet*. Cambridge, MA: MIT Press; 1994. 211 pp.

This book was based on the Electronic Frontier Foundation's *The Big Dummy's Guide to the Internet*. An electronic version of the book is available on the following EFF sites:

on America Online: keyword **EFF**

on CompuServe: **go EFFSIG**

on the Internet:

http://www.cff.org/papers/eegtti

Hahn, Harley and Rick Stout. *The Internet Complete Reference*. Berkeley, CA: Osborne McGraw-Hill; 1994. 818 pp.

A well-written and useful Internet book. Due to its 1994 publication date, it is a bit weak on WWW coverage. On the other hand, the descriptions of how to find someone on the Internet and in Usenet newsgroups are very good.

Hahn, Harley. *Internet Yellow Pages*. Second ed. Berkeley, CA: Osborne McGraw-Hill; 1995. 812 pp.

Generally, Internet white or yellow pages are out-of-date before the ink dries on the pages. However, Harley Hahn's list of resources is so wide-ranging that this volume is worth purchasing. If the URL is no longer valid, use the Internet's finding tools to locate the current site.

The Internet Unleashed. Indianapolis, IN: Sams Publishing; 1994. 1,387 pp.

Like *Tricks of the Internet Gurus*, this book is a collaboration of 40 experts who discuss their Internet tips, techniques, and hard-won insight.

Krol, Ed and Paula Ferguson. *The Whole Internet for Windows 95 User's Guide & Catalog*. Sebastopol, CA: O'Reilly & Associates, Inc.; 1995. 625 pp.

This is one of the best-written and most readable books on the Internet. Krol writes clearly, describes Internet protocols well, and never uses technical terms without explaining them. This edition covers the Microsoft Internet Explorer as well as other Internet tools.

Stoll, Clifford. *Silicon Snake Oil: Second Thoughts on the Information Highway*. New York, NY: Doubleday; 1995. 247 pp.

Stoll is the author of *The Cuckoo's Egg*, an engaging story of how he tracked down a spy network that broke into a university computer system. In this book, he presents a contrarian's view of life on the Internet; it's a discussion of the electronic world, not an instructional book like the rest of the titles in this section. Some find his arguments questionable; coming from a long-time Internet denizen and confirmed non-Luddite, they at least deserve consideration.

Tillman, Hope N. *Internet Tools of the Profession: A Guide for Special Librarians*. Washington, DC: Special Libraries Association; 1995. 200 pp.

Hope Tillman has written extensively on Internet resources from a librarian's perspective. This book offers guides to Internet resources along with descriptions of Internet finding tools and effective search strategies.

Tricks of the Internet Gurus. Indianapolis, IN: Sams Publishing; 1994. 809 pp.

Twenty-one Internet experts contributed to this book, each writing a chapter on an area of expertise. This book is particularly useful for Internet searchers who are familiar with the basics but need an in-depth tutorial on a specific aspect of the Internet, such as faxing from the Internet or setting up a listserv. It even has a chapter on "What to Do When Things Don't Work."

Magazines about the Internet

Internet World. Westport, CT: Meckler Corporation; monthly

This glossy magazine is of more interest to beginning and intermediate Internet users than to "power users" but usually has something of interest to anyone. Well-written and always fun to read.

NetGuide: The Guide to Online Services and the Net. Manhasset, NY: CMP Media; monthly.

A fairly new glossy magazine with a variety of feature articles, a monthly "cyberguide" and regular columns.

The CyberSkeptic's Guide to Internet Research. Needham Heights, MA: BiblioData; monthly.

Another relatively new newsletter with useful tips and techniques for finding information on the Net. The newsletter also includes reviews of Internet finding tools and information resources on the Net.

In addition, a number of newsletters focus on a specific industry's use of the Internet such as *The Internet Connection: Your Guide to Government Resources*, *Internet Bulletin for CPAs*, and *Internet Security Monthly*.

Although it is pointless to list even a few of the articles that have appeared about the Internet lately, two ongoing Internet columns are particularly helpful to online searchers.

Greg Notess writes the ON THE NETS column in both *DATABASE* and *ONLINE* magazines. He covers new finding tools, new resources, and Internet basics and writes clearly for novice and experts alike.

John Makulowich has a regular NET SITINGS column in *ONLINE* magazine. He is a worldwide Internet trainer as well as a writer, and brings his enthusiasm to each column.

His home page contains links to all the Internet sites listed in his columns—http://www.cais.com/makulow/netsite.html.

LEXIS-NEXIS

Basch, Reva. "The 'New' NEXIS." *ONLINE* 18, No. 5 (September/October 1994): pp. 54-60.

This article reviews the redesign of the libraries and files within LEXIS-NEXIS and offers some guidelines on how to navigate through the new structure.

McQuillan, Colin M. "FOCUS Revisited." *ONLINE* 19, No. 1 (January/February 1995): pp. 32-35.

Tenopir, Carol and Pamela Cahn. "TARGET & FREESTYLE: DIALOG And Mead Join The Relevance Ranks." *ONLINE* 18, No. 3 (May 1994): pp. 31-47.

These two articles evaluate LEXIS-NEXIS search tools and provide some very helpful advice on how to use them most efficiently.

Prodigy

Hergert, Douglas. *How to Use Prodigy*. Emeryville, CA: Ziff-Davis Press; 1994. 135 pp.

An illustrated guide to Prodigy. This book consists primarily of screen shots and other visual images of the Prodigy system, along with tips and techniques for navigating the system.

INFORMATION BROKERS

In addition to building your own skills in online searching, you can take advantage of the specialized research skills of independent information professionals, also known as information brokers (IBs). If your information needs go beyond your area of expertise, if you need an extra person to help out in a crunch, or if you want research done by someone outside your organization, you may need an information broker. IBs are research professionals who either have specialized information-gathering skills or have access to a group of subcontractors who themselves are expert researchers. IBs supplement an organization's research staff, provide *ad hoc* research assistance, and assist in organizing, maintaining, and updating information within an organization.

The leading association of information brokers is the Association of Independent Information Professionals (AIIP). This association, founded in 1987 with 27 members, now has over 700 members throughout the world. You can get more information about AIIP and benefits of membership by going to its home page (http://www.aiip.org/) or by contacting them at:

Association of Independent Information Professionals
245 Fifth Avenue; Suite 2103
New York, NY 10016
212/779-1855
Fax 212/481-3071
Email: 73263.34@compuserve.com

AIIP sells its membership directory to the public. Another, more extensive directory of information brokers is:

Burwell Enterprises. *1995-1996 Burwell World Directory of Information Brokers*. Houston, TX: Burwell Enterprises; 1995. 800 pp. (Updated yearly)

For additional information on the information brokering profession, I recommend Sue Rugge's seminar on information brokering, available through the Information Professionals Institute in Oakland, California. Sue Rugge, rightly called the founder of the information brokering industry, has been in the information profession for 25 years. In addition to her seminar on information brokering, she has written a handbook that realistically outlines the opportunities, challenges, and pitfalls of starting an information brokering business.

Rugge, Sue and Alfred Glossbrenner. *The Information Broker's Handbook*. Second ed. New York, NY: McGraw-Hill (Windcrest); 1995. 453 pp. (Includes disk)

This excellent book covers the business end of running an independent information business—sales and marketing, accounting, and managing your business—as well as basics on how to do online and manual searching.

There are other seminars and training programs available to people entering the information brokering profession. Many such programs advertise in *ONLINE* and *DATABASE* magazines and are listed in AIIP's *Membership Directory*.

DataStar

ABC EUROPE: European Export In	EURE
ABI/INFORM '71-V96:I05	INFO
ACCESS CZECH REP BUSINESS BULL	CZBN
ACCOUNTS	ACCT
ADIS R&D INSIGHT	ADRD
ADVERTISE BUSINESS OPPORTUNITE	ADVE
AERZTEZEITUNG '84-WK05/'96	AEZT
AFP NEWSIRES AMERICAS '93-	AUSA
AFP NEWSIRES GENERAL '91-	AGEN
AFP NEWSIRES IN SPANISH '92-	AFSP
AFP NEWSWIRES DOCUMENTARY '93-	ADOC
AFP NEWSWIRES ECONOMIC '92-	AECO
AFP NEWSWIRES EUROPE '92-	AEUR
AFP NEWSWIRES INTL '94-	AFIN
AFP NEWSWIRES SPORT '91-	ASPO
AIDSLINE NLM 1980 - DEC. 1995	ACQS
ALLIED & ALTERNATIVE MEDICINE'	AMED
AMERICAN BANKER - TODAY	BAND
AMERICAN BANKER '81-	BANK
ANALYTICAL ABSTRACT '78 - V58/	ANAB
APPLIED SOCIAL SCIENCES '87-	ASSI
ARTS + HUMANITIES SEARCH '80-	AHCI
AUTOMOTIVE ENGINEERING (DKF) 7	DKFL
AUTOMOTIVE INDUSTRY TRIAL FILE	TRAI
AUTOMOTIVE INFORMATION & NEWS'	AINS
BALTIC NEWS SERVICE '92-	BNSA
BALTIC NEWS SERVICE TODAY	BNSD
BBC MONITORING SUMMARY SEP '93	BBCM
BDI German Industry	BDIE
BDI GERMAN INDUS TRIAL FILE	TRBD
BIBLIODATA: FULLTEXT SOURCES	FULL
BIOBUSINESS '84-V96:I08/96	BBUS
BIOBUSINESS TRIAL FILE	TRBB
BIOCOMMERCE ABSTRACTS & DIR. '	CELL
BIOETHICSLINE 1973 - 9512	ETHI
BIOSIS PREVIEWS '85- V98/I56	BIOL
BIOSIS PREVIEWS VOCABULARY	BVOC
BIOSIS TRIAL FILE	TRBI
BIOTECHNOLOGY INFORMATION EURO	BIKE
BLICK DURCH DIE WIRTSCHAFT '94	BLCK
BLICK DURCH DIE WIRTSCHAFT TOD	BLCD
BRITISH CO. FINANCIALS TRIAL	TRIC
BUSINESS & INDUSTRY '94-	BIDB
BUSINESS MONITOR '95-	BMON
BUSINESS NEWS (FR) TRIAL FILE	TRDE
BUSINESS OPPORTUNITIES SERVICE	BUSI
BUSINESS TRIAL FILE	TRBU
CAB ABSTRACTS '73-DEC.'95	CABI
CAB HEALTH '73 - 12/95	HUMN
CAB:TOURISM & LEISURE '76-	TOUR
CAB:VETERINARY SCI.& MED. '72-	VETS
CANCERLIT NLM '83 - NOV. '95	CANC
CANCORP CANADIAN FINANCIALS	CNCO
CELEX (EU LAW) '51-29 JAN '96	CLXE
CHEM SOURCES CHEMICAL DIRECTOR	CSEM
CHEM SOURCES COMPANY DIRECTORY	CSCO
CHEMICAL ABS REG NOMENCLATURE	CNAM
CHEMICAL ABSTRACTS '80- V124/I	CHEM
CHEMICAL ABSTRACTS TRIAL FILE	TRCH
CHEMICAL BUSINESS NEWSBASE '85	CBNB
CHEMICAL ENG. & BIOTECH. '70-	CEAB
CHEMICAL INDUSTRY NOTES '83-	CIND
CHEMICAL SAFETY NEWSBASE '81-	CSNB
CHEMPLANT PLUS	PLAN
CIRE CORPORATE INTELLIGENCE '9	CIRE
COMPENDEX PLUS '76-	COMP
COMPUTER.INDUSTRY.SOFTWARE '89	CISS
CORPORATE TECHNOLOGY US	CTCO
COUNTRY REPORT SERVICE	FSRI
CREDITREFORM AUSTRIA	AVVC
CREDITREFORM: GERMAN COMPANIES	DVVC
CROSS DATABASE SEARCH	CROS
CURRENT BIOTECHNOLOGY ABS '83-	CUBI
CURRENT DRUGS FAST- LAST 6 WEE	CPBM
CURRENT DRUGS FAST-ALERT '89-	CPBA
CURRENT.CONTENTS '92-WK04/'96	CCCC
D&B ASIA-PACIFIC DUNS MARKET I	DNAP
D&B AUSTRIA	DBOS
D&B BELGIUM DBBL	
D&B CANADIAN DUNS MARKET IDENT	DNCA
D&B DENMARK	DBDK
D&B EASTERN EUROPE MARKETING F	DNEE
D&B EUROPEAN FINANCIAL RECORDS	DEFR
D&B EUROPEAN MARKETING FILE	DBZZ
D&B FRANCE	DBFR
D&B GERMANY	DBWG
D&B GREECE	DBHE
D&B IRELAND	DBEI
D&B ISRAEL MARKETING FILE	DNIS
D&B ITALY	DBIT
D&B LUXEMBOURG	DBLU
D&B NETHERLANDS	DBNL
D&B PORTUGAL	DBPO
D&B SPAIN	DBSP

D&B SWISS COMPANY FINANCIALS	SWFF	FOODLINE INTL MARKET DATA '82-	FOIM
D&B SWISS MARKETING FILE	SWCO	FOODLINE: CURRENT LEGISLATION	FOLE
D&B SWITZERLAND	DBCH	FOODLINE: FOOD SCI & TECH '72-	FOST
D&B UK	DBGB	FORENSIC SCIENCE '76-DEC '95	FORS
D&B US DUNS MARKET IDENTIFIERS	DBUS	FRANKFURTER ALLGEMEINE Z. '93-	FAZA
DANISH COMPANIES FULL FINANCIA	DKEF	FRANKFURTER ALLGEMEINE Z. TODA	FAZD
DATA-STAR BASE FILE	BASE	FREEDONIA MARKET RESEARCH	TFGI
DATA-STAR NEWS FILE	NEWS	FRENCH COMPANIES FULL FINANC (	FREF
DATAMONITOR MARKET RESEARCH	DMON	FRENCH COMPANIES.FULL FINANC (	FRFF
DB ITALIAN COMPANY PROFILES	ITFF	FROST & SULLIVAN MARKET RES '9	FSMR
DB MARKET STRUC.& TRENDS IN IT	MAST	FT ACQUISITIONS WEEKLY NOV '94	FTAW
DE FINANC. EKONOMISCHE TIJD '9	DFET	FT MERGERS & ACQUISITIONS '90-	FTMA
DELPHES EUROPEAN BUSINESS '80-	DELP	FT REPORTS: ENERGY & ENVIR. '9	FTNV
DERWENT BIOTECH ABSTRACTS '82-	DWBA	FT REPORTS: TECHNOLOGY '90-	FTTC
DERWENT DRUG BACKFILE '64-'82	DDBF	FT REPORTS:BUSINESS '90-	FTBR
DERWENT DRUG FILE '83-V33:ISS0	DDNS	FT REPORTS:EASTERN EUROPE '92-	FTEE
DERWENT DRUG REGISTRY	DDRR	FT REPORTS:FINAN MGMT & INS '9	FTFM
DHSS-DATA: HEALTH ADMIN. '83-	DHSS	FT REPORTS:INDUSTRY '92-	FTIN
DHSS: MEDICAL TOXIC & HLTH '84	DHMT	German Business & Industry Dir	ABCE
DIOGENES FDA REGULATORY UPDATE	DIOG	German Buyers' Guide	E1X1
DIR POLISH COMPANIES	PLCO	GALE DIRECTORY OF DATABASES	GDDB
DIRECTORY PUBLISHED PROC '85-	DOPP	GENERAL PRACTITIONER '87-	GPGP
DISCLOSURE	DSCL	GERMAN & EURO MARKET STATISTIC	FAKT
DISSERTATION ABSTRACTS 1861-	DISS	GERMAN CO FINANCIAL DATA (EN)'	COIN
DKF VEHICLE TEST REPORTS '79-	TDKF	GERMAN CO. FINANCIALS.(GE) '83	FINN
DRT EUROPEAN BUSINESS REPORTS	DRTE	HANDELSZEITUNG '93-	SHZT
DRUG DATA REPORT - 1988 TO DAT	PRDR	HARVARD BUSI. REVIEW: '67-AUG	HB90
DRUG INFORMATION FULL TEXT	DIFT	HARVARD BUSINESS REVIEW SEP '9	HBRO
DRUG NEWS & PERSPECTIVES '92-	PRNP	HAZARDOUS SUBSTANCES 4TH.QTR.'	HSDB
ECONOVO GERMAN CO. BUNDESANZ '	ECNE	HEALTH NEWS DAILY '89	HNDO
ECOREGISTER: GERMAN CO REG. '8	ECCO	HEALTH PLAN & ADMIN '75 - DEC	HLPA
ELSA SWISS NEWSWIRE (FR) '84-	ATSA	HOPPENSTEDT BENELUX	BNLU
ELSA SWISS NEWSWIRE (FR) TODAY	ATSD	HOPPENSTEDT: AUSTRIA	HOAU
ELSA SWISS NEWSWIRE (GE) '83-	SDAA	HOPPENSTEDT: GERMANY	HOPE
ELSA SWISS NEWSWIRE (GE) TODAY	SDAD	HSELINE: HEALTH & SAFETY '77-	HSLI
ELSA SWISS NEWSWIRE (IT) '89-	AGZA	IAC AEROSPACE/DEF. MKTS TECH '	PTDT
ELSA SWISS NEWSWIRE - TODAY	AGZD	IAC BUSINESS A.R.T.S '76-WK06'	ACAD
ELSA SWISS SPORTWIRE (FR) '88-	SIGA	IAC COMPANY INTELLIGENCE	INCO
ELSA SWISS SPORTWIRE (FR) TODA	SIGD	IAC COMPUTER DB '83-WK06/'96	CMPT
ELSA SWISS SPORTWIRE (GE) '88-	SIZA	IAC F&S INDEX '78-	PTIN
EMBASE '88- 9605	EMED	IAC FORECASTS '78-	PTFC
EMBASE ALERT LATEST 8 WEEKS	EMBA	IAC GLOBALBASE '85-	EBUS
EMBASE TRIAL FILE	TREM	IAC GLOBALBASE TRIAL FILE	TREB
EMBASE VOCABULARY	EVOC	IAC HEALTH '76- WK06/'96	HLTH
ENVIROLINE '71-01/'96	ENVN	IAC LEGAL RESOURCE I.'80-MO02/	LAWS
ERIC: EDUCATIONAL RESOURCES '6	ERIC	IAC MAGAZINE DATAB. '59-WK06/'	MAGS
EURO-SELECT: Public Support Sc	ESEN	IAC MANAGEMENT CON. '74-M02/'9	MGMT
EUROMONITOR MARKET DIRECTION	MONI	IAC MKTG & ADVERT. REF SVC '89	PTMA
EUROMONITOR MARKET REPORTS '90	MOMR	IAC NEW PRODUCT ANNOUNCE. '84-	PTNP
EUROPEAN CHEMICAL NEWS '84-	CNEW	IAC NEWSLETTER DATABASE '88-	PTBN
EVENTLINE	EVNT	IAC PHARMABIOMED BUS.'90-	PTPB
EXTEL INTERNATIONAL CARDS NOV'	EXTL	IAC PROMT '78-	PTSP
F-D-C PHARMACEUTICAL REPORTS '	FDCR	IAC PROMT TRIAL FILE	TRPT
FINANZ UND WIRTSCHAFT ARCHIVE	FUWA	IAC TRADE & INDUSTRY '92-WK06/	INDY
FINANZ UND WIRTSCHAFT CURRENT	FUWC	IAC US NATNL NEWSPAPER INDEX '	NNIN
FINF-TEXT: GERMAN CO NEWS '85-	FITT	IAC US TIME SERIES '81-	PTTS
FIRMIMPORT/FIRMEXPORT: FRENCH	FRIE	ICC BRITISH COMPANY ANNUAL REP	ICAC
FLIGHTLINE: '88-	FLIG	ICC BRITISH COMPANY DIRECTORY.	ICDI
FOOD SCIENCE.& TECH. ABS. '69-	FSTA	ICC BRITISH FINANCIAL DATASHEE	ICFF

ICC KEY NOTE MARKET ANALYSIS	ICKN	MARKETLINE INTERNATIONAL REPOR	MKTL
ICC STOCKBROKER REPORTS TRIAL	TRBR	MARTINDALE ONLINE.	MART
ICC STOCKBROKER RESEARCH '87-	ICBR	MATERIALS BUSINESS '85-	MBUS
IDIS DRUG FILE '66-	IOWA	MEDICONF: MEDICAL CONF & EVENT	MCNF
IL SOLE 24 ORE '84-	SOLE	MEDITEC: Biomedical Engineerin	BMED
IMMUNOCLONES '86-	IMMU	MEDLINE TRIAL FILE	TRME
IMSWORLD DRUG MARKETS	IPWE	MEDLINE VOCABULARY FEB 1996	MVOC
IMSWORLD DRUG MKT MANUAL - COM	IPDI	MEDLINE 1993-FEB 96(-ED951228)	MEDL
IMSWORLD NEW PRODUCT LAUNCHES'	IPLL	METADEX: METALS SCIENCE '66-	META
IMSWORLD PATENTS INTERNATIONAL	IPIP	MONDO ECONOMICO, L'IMPRESA '89	MNDO
IMSWORLD PHARMA COMPANIES TRIA	TRIP	MONEYCLIPS(MIDDLE EAST NEWS) '	CLI
IMSWORLD PHARMA COMPANY PROFIL	IPCP	MOTOR INDUSTRY RESEARCH '80-	MIRA
IMSWORLD PRODUCT MONOGRAPHS	IPOP	MSI REPORTS '92-	MSIR
IMSWORLD PRODUCT MONOGS & PRIC	IPPP	NATL.TECH.INF.SERV. '92-	NTIS
IMSWORLD R&D FOCUS '91-4 WKS A	IPNA	NDA PIPELINE '91- JAN '95	NDAP
IMSWORLD R&D FOCUS DRUG UPDATE	IPUR	NEUE ZUERCHER ZEITUNG '93-	NZZA
IMSWORLD R&D FOCUS LATEST 4 WE	IPNR	NEUE ZUERCHER ZEITUNG TODAY	NZZD
IMSWORLD R&D FOCUS MEETINGS DI	IPMR	NEW ENGLAND JOURNAL OF MED. 85	NEJM
IMSWORLD R&D FOCUS TRIAL FILE	TRUR	NME EXPRESS: LATEST 2 YEARS	PRME
INCIDENCE & PREVALENCE (IPD) '	IAPV	NURSING & ALLIED HEALTH '83-	NAHL
INFOCHECK BRITISH COMPANIES	CHCK	OFFICIAL REGISTER CZECH & SLOV	CZCO
INFOTRADE BELGIAN COMPANIES	BECO	ONLINE ORDER - RESEARCH	KEEP
INPHARMA '83-TO 4 WEEKS AGO	IPHA	Packaging Science & Technology	PSTA
INPHARMA LATEST 4 WEEKS	IPHC	PAIS: INTL PUBLIC AFFAIRS '72-	PAIS
INPHARMA TODAY	IPHD	PHARMA & HEALTH CARE TRIAL	TRPI
INSPEC '87-V96:I05	INSP	PHARMA MARKETING SERVICE '87-	DPMS
INSPEC TRIAL FILE	TRIN	PHARMACOECONIMICS TODAY ONLY	ADPD
INTL MARKET RESEARCH INFO '64-	IMRI	PHARMACOECONIMICS 94-4 WEEKS A	ADPR
INTL. RISK & PAYMENT REVIEW	IRPR	PHARMACOECONOMICS LATEST	
INTL.PHARMACEUTICAL ABS '70-	IPAB	4 WEE	ADPC
INVESTEXT BROKER REPORTS '93-	INVE	PHARMACONTACTS	PHCO
INVESTEXT TRIAL FILE	TRST	PHARMAPROJECTS TRIAL FILE	TRPH
IRISH COMPANIES & BUSINESSES	IRFF	PHARMAPROJECTS: DRUGS IN DEVEL	PHAR
ISIS Software Database	ISIS	PHARMAPROJECTS:DISCONTIUNED DR	PHDI
ITALIAN TRADING COMPANIES (EN) ·	ITIE	PHARMAPROJECTS:LAUNCHED	
JAPAN NEWSWIRE '86-	JPNW	PRODUC	PHLP
JERUSALEM POST OCT '88-	JEPO	PHARMLINE:UK PHARMACY '78-	LINE
JORDANWATCH BRITISH COMPANIES	JORD	PHIND:PHARM & HEALTHCARE CURRE	PHIC
KEY BRITISH ENTERPRISES FINANC	DKBE	PHIND:PHARM & HEALTHCARE'80-	PHIN
KIRK-OTHMER ENCY.CHEMICAL TECH	KIRK	PIRA DATABASE '75-	PIRA
KOSMET: COSMETIC SCI. '85-	KOSM	POLLUTION ABSTRACTS. '70-	POLL
KREDITSCHUTZVERBAND AUSTRIAN C	KSVA	POLNISCHE FIRMEN	PDCO
KYODO JAPANESE NEWS SERVICE '8	KYOP	PSYCHINFO PSYCHOLOGICAL ABS '6	PSYC
LA STAMPA '82-TO YESTERDAY	STAA	QUEST ECONOMICS DATABASE '92-	QUES
LA STAMPA LATEST 7 DAYS	STAC	REACTIONS DATABASE '83-4 WKS A	REAA
LA STAMPA TODAY	STAD	REACTIONS DATABASE LATEST 4 WE	REAC
LAFFERTY PUBLICATIONS 94-	LAFF	REACTIONS DATABASE TODAY	READ
LANC: 1995 TO DATE	LANC	REUTER TEXTLINE '92-	TXLN
LE MONDE '87-	LMNA	REUTER TEXTLINE COMPANY LOOK-U	TXCO
LE MONDE TODAY	LMND	RTECS: TOXIC EFFECTS CHEMICALS	RTEC
LEBENSMITTEL-ZEITUNG '95-	LMZG	RUBBER & PLASTICS '73-	RAPR
LMS DRUG ALERTS '83- 3 MONTHS	AALR	RUSSIAN AND CIS NEWS '90-	SVNW
LMS DRUG ALERTS LATEST 3 MONTH	AALC	SAE Automotive Standards	SAST
MANAGEMENT & MARKETING '75-	MMKA	SAE Global Mobility	SAEG
MANAGEMENT INFO WIRTSCHAFT '87	MIND	SCAN-A-BID:BUSINESS OPPURTUN '	SCAN
MARKET & BUSINESS DEV. CURRENT	MBDE	SCIENCE CIT. INDEX '87- WK03/	SCIN
MARKETLETTER - TODAY	IMLD	SCISEARCH TRIAL FILE	TRSC
MARKETLETTER '85- JAN '95	IMLA	SCRL FRENCH CO PROFILES (EN)	SCEF
MARKETLETTER LATEST 4 WEEKS	IMLC	SCRL FRENCH CO PROFILES (FR)	SCFF

DataTimes

DataTimes' EyeQ software displays sources by group; you click on the group(s) you wish to search, or you can select individual sources within a group. DataTimes breaks out its sources into broad categories: Industry; Today's News; Finance; News Groups; All Text; U.S. Only; International

DIALOG

INTERNATIONAL	TRADELINE
TRADEMARKSCAN-AUSTRIA	662
TRADEMARKSCAN-BENELUX	658
TRADEMARKSCAN-CANADA	127
TRADEMARKSCAN-DENMARK	659
TRADEMARKSCAN-FRANCE	657
TRADEMARKSCAN-GERMANY	672
TRADEMARKSCAN-INTL REGISTER	671
TRADEMARKSCAN-ITALY	673
TRADEMARKSCAN-LIECHTENSTEIN	677
TRADEMARKSCAN-MONACO	663
TRADEMARKSCAN-SWITZERLAND	661
TRADEMARKSCAN-U.K.	126
TRADEMARKSCAN-U.S. FEDERAL	226
TRADEMARKSCAN-U.S. STATE	246
Transportation Research Info Serv	63
TRIS	63
TRW BUSINESS CREDIT PROFILES	547
TSCA CHEMICAL SUBSTANCE INVENTORY	52
TULSA(TM)	87,987
Turbine Intelligence	587
UK Kompass Register	591
U.K. Trade Names	591
ULRICH'S INT'L PERIODICAL DIR	480
United States Patents Quarterly	243
UNITERM Files (CLAIMS)	223-225
UNLISTED DRUGS	140
UPI NEWS-backfile	260
UPI NEWS-daily	261
USA TODAY	703
USDA/CRIS 60	
U.S. COPYRIGHTS	120
U.S. PATENTS FULLTEXT	654,653,652
US POLI SCI DOCS	93
VIRGINIAN-PILOT/LEDGER-STAR (Norfolk	741
Virology Extracts	76
Ward's Business Directory	479
Washington Drug Letter	158
Washington Health Cost Letter	158
WASHINGTON POST ONLINE (PAPERS)	146
WASHINGTON TIMES (PAPERS)	717
WATER RESOURCES ABSTRACTS	117
WATERNET	245
Who's Who in America	234
WICHITA EAGLE (PAPERS)	723
WISCONSIN STATE JOURNAL/MADISON CAPITAL TIMES (PAPERS)	742
WORLD PATENTS INDEX, DERWENT	350
WORLD PATENTS INDEX LATEST, DERWENT	351
WORLD TEXTILES	67
WORLD TRANSLATIONS INDEX	295
ZOOLOGICAL RECORD	185

Dow Jones News/Retrieval

In addition to the group codes listed below, you can search for sources by state using the two-letter postal abbreviation.

Industry codes:

Computers	Computers, Communications, Electronics
Construction	Construction & Real Estate
Energy	Energy
Environment	Environment & Waste Management
Financial	Financial Services
Food	Food, Beverages, Groceries, Restaurants
Health	Health
Industrial	Industrial Technology
Media	Media, Marketing & Entertainment
Political	Government & Politics
Retail	Retail & Consumer Goods
Transport	Transportation & Aerospace

Publication groupings:

DJFIN	Dow Jones Financial Wires
DJPUBS	Dow Jones Publications
DT	DataTimes - all
DTCUR	DataTimes - current and prior year
General	General Interest Publications
INDTRADE	Industry & Trade Publications
INTL	International Newspapers & General Publications
INTLWIRES	International Wires
Large	Large Newspapers
MAJNEWS	Major News Sources
MCCARTHY	McCarthy Information Services
Small	Small Newspapers
Transcripts	Media Transcripts
PR	Press Release Wires
TOP10	Top 10 U.S. Newspapers
TOP50	Top 50 U.S. Newspapers
TOPBUS	Top Business Publications
TOPINTL	Top International Papers

Regional groupings:

East	Northeast & Mid-Atlantic U.S. Sources
Midatlantic	Mid-Atlantic U.S. Sources
Midwest	Midwest U.S. Sources
Mountain	Mountain U.S. Sources
NEast	Northeast U.S. Sources
Pacific	Pacific U.S. Sources
SEast	Southeast U.S. Sources
SCentral	South Central U.S. Sources
South	South U.S. Sources
West	West U.S. Sources
CN	Canada
CH	China
GE	Germany
ISR	Israel
JA	Japan
MX	Mexico
SING	Singapore

UK	United Kingdom
Africa	Africa
NonUSAmerica	The Americas except U.S.
Asia	Asia
Europe	Europe
EEurope	Eastern Europe and Russia/CIS
WEurope	North & Western Europe
MidEast	Middle East
MEAfrica	Middle East & Africa
SAmerica	South & Central America

LEXIS-NEXIS

This includes the major business-related "group files" in the general purpose NEXIS libraries.

NEWS library

ALLABS	All Abstracts
ALLNWS	All News Files
ARCABS	Abs more than 2 years old
ARCNWS	Beyond 2 years
CURABS	Abs less than 2 years old
CURNWS	Last 2 years
HOTTOP	Hot Topics
INFOBK	Information Bank Abs
MAGS	Magazines
MAJPAP	Major Papers
MWEST	Midwest
NEAST	Northeast
NON-US	English Non-US
NONENG	Non-English News
NWLTRS	Newsletters
PAPERS	Newspapers
SCRIPT	Transcripts
SEAST	Southeast
TODAY	Today's News
TXTNWS	Textline News
US	US News
WEST	West
WIRES	Wires

TOPNWS Library

2WEEK	2 weeks News
APBRF	AP Briefs
APEMB	AP Bus Sum.
NYTBRF	NYT Briefs
NYTBUS	NYT Bus
PAGE1	Top Stories
REUBRF	Reuters Briefs
REUBSM	Reuters Business
REUINT	Reuters World
REUPOL	Reuters Political
TODAY	Today's News

MARKET Library

ALLEIU	Econ Int Unit
ALLNWS	Mkt & Ind News
ALLWLD	Combined News, Analysis & Law
AMPNWS	Adv/Mkt/PR News
ARCNWS	Beyond 2 years

BUSANL	Business Anlys
BUSOPP	Business Opps
COINFO	Company Info
CURNWS	Last 2 years
ETHNIC	Ethnic Pubs
FNDCAT	Find/SVP Catlog
IACNWS	Newsletter Db.
IACX	Ind. Express
IBFD	IBFD Treaties
ICCMKT	Keynote Mkt Rpt
INDNWS	Industry Pubs
INVTXT	Invtxt Ind Rpt
LAW EC	Legal Texts
MARRPT	Market Rsch Rpt
MARS	MARS Database
MKTRPT	NTDB Mkt Rpt
MKTSHR	Mkt Share Rptr
NIEUWS	Dutch Language
NONENG	All Non-English
PRESSE	French Language
PROFIL	Country Profiles
PROMT	PROMT Database
PROMTP	PROMT Plus
PRTHS	Pred Thesaurus
RELEAS	Press Releases
RPOLL	Roper Ctr. Poll
SIC	1987 SIC Manual
STAMPA	Italian Language
TRENDS	Trends Pubs
TXTLNE	Textline
TXTNWS	Textline & Key News Sources
USGTO	US Trade Outlook
WOMEN	Women Pubs
WORLD	Library
ZEITNG	German Language

BUSFIN Library

ABI	ABI/INFORM
ALLABS	English Abs
ALLEIU	Econ Int Unit
ALLNWS	BusFin News
ARCNWS	Beyond 2 years
BDS	Bankruptcy Rpts
BIS	Banking Info
BUS	Business
BUSANL	Business Anlys
BUSDTL	Bus Dateline
BUSOPP	Bus Opps
CURNWS	Last 2 years
FIN	Finance
INVTXT	Bus & Finance
NONENG	Non-English Nws

BUSREF Library

ABICAN	ABI Can Bus Dir
ABIUS	ABI US Bus Dir
AMMKTP	Guide/Amer Mkt
AMPOL	Alm Amer Politcs
AMSCI	American Science

Code	Name	Code	Name
APBIO AP	Candid Bios	UFRCST	US Forecasts
ARBBIO	BNA Arbitra Bios	UNELCT	Almanac Unelect
BIOS	Combined Bios	USGTO	US Trade Outlook
BKRDIR	Bkrptcy Attorney	USNAME	USCS Pop. Name
BUDGET	Pres. Budget	USTIME	US Time Series
BUSOPP	Business Opps	WHOART	Who's Who Art
CAPTAL	Capital Source	WHOEUR	Who's Who Euro
CBD	Commerce Bus Dly	WHOPOL	Who's Who Pol
CELBIO	Celebrity Bios	WHORUS	Who's Who Russ
CIINTL	Int'l Co Intel		
CIUS	Co Intel-U.S.		

NewsNet

ABI business lists and profiles	ABI

Advertising and Marketing

AMERICAN MARKETPLACE	AD13
FORECAST	AD28
INTERACTIVE MARKETING NEWS	AD27
INTERNATIONAL PRODUCT ALERT	AD25
PR NEWS	AD23
PRODUCT ALERT	AD24
VIDEO MARKETING NEWS	AD07

CMPIND	Cmptr Forecasts
CODIR	Combined Co Dir
CONDIR	Congress Dir
CZCO	Czech Bus Dir
DBAMER	Dbase America
DCA	Corp Affil
DIS/ST	Dis/St Profiles
ECINIT	Guide/EC Init
ELC	ELC Largest Cos
ENASSC	Encyclpdia Assc
EVTLNE	EventLine

Aerospace and Aviation

AEROSPACE DAILY	AE29
AEROSPACE ELECTRONICS BUSINESS	AE14
AEROSPACE PROPULSION	AE34
AIR CARGO REPORT	AE02
AIR SAFETY WEEK AE16	
AIR SAFETY WEEK ACCIDENT/ INCIDENT LOG	AE17
AIR SAFETY WEEK REGULATORY LOG	AE18
AIRCRAFT VALUE NEWS	AE36
AIRLINE FINANCIAL NEWS	AE24
AIRLINE MARKETING NEWS	AE39
AIRPORTS	AE21
ASIAN AVIATION NEWS	AE38
AVIATION DAILY	AE28
AVIATION EUROPE AE35	
AVIATION LITIGATION REPORTER	AE33
AVIATION WEEK & SPACE TECHNOLOGY	AE30
BUSINESS & COMMERCIAL AVIATION	AE08
CNS OUTLOOK AE10	
COMMUTER/REGIONAL AIRLINE NEWS	AE25
COMMUTER/REGIONAL AIRLINE NEWS INT'L	AE26
HELICOPTER NEWS	AE12
REGIONAL AVIATION WEEKLY	AE22
SATELLITE WEEK	AE01
SPACE BUSINESS NEWS	AE11
SPACE CALENDAR	AE04
SPACE COMMERCE WEEK	AE05
SPACE DAILY	AE07
SPACE EXPLORATION TECHNOLOGY	AE23
SPACE FAX DAILY GLOBAL EDITION	AE03
SPACE STATION NEWS	AE13
SPEEDNEWS	AE15
THE WEEKLY OF BUSINESS AVIATION	AE20
WORLD AIRLINE NEWS	AE31
WORLD AIRPORT WEEK	AE09

FEDDIR	Fed Staff Dir
FORBAD	Forbes Anl Dir
FPDIR	Fin Post Dir
FTI	Foreign Tr Index
FTO	Foreign Tr Opps
GALBIO	Gale Bios
GQUOTE	Speaker Quotes
HOOVER	Hoover Profiles
HOPAUS	Hoppnstdt Aust
HOPSTD	Hoppnstdt Rpts
HOPTRD	Hoppenstedt
IFRCST	Intl Forecasts
INTACC	Intl Acctng
JUDDIR	Jud Staff Dir
LACDB	Latin Amer Db
LAWENF	Law Enfor Dir
MEDIA	Media Reports
MEMBR	Congress Profls
MHPROF	M-H Profiles
MKTRPT	Market Reports
MKTSHR	Market Share Rpt
OLYFAC	Olympic Factbk
QUOTES	Combined Quotes
REDBK	Comb SDA&SDAA
SDA	Std Dir Adv
SDAA	Std Dir Ad Agn
SIC	1987 SIC Manual
SMPSON	Simpson's Quotes
SOVCO	BizEkon Co Dir
SPBIO	S&P Bios
SPCORP	S&P Corporate
STATS	Combined Stats
STLEG	State Legis. Dir
TBUS	Thomson Bank
TED	Tenders Elec Dly
TRDSHO	Intl Trade Shows
TSVGS	Thomson Sav

Agence France-Presse

AGENCE FRANCE-PRESSE INTERNATIONAL NEWS	AF01W

Associated Press

AP DATASTREAM BUSINESS NEWS WIRE	AP01W
AP DATASTREAM NATIONAL NEWS WIRE	AP02W
AP DATASTREAM WASHINGTON NEWS	AP03W
AP DATASTREAM INTERNATIONAL NEWS	AP04W

Automotive

ALTERNATIVE FUELS ONLINE TODAY	AU13
AUTOMOTIVE COMPONENTS ANALYST	AU14
AUTOMOTIVE ENVIRONMENT ANALYST	AU15
AUTOMOTIVE LITIGATION REPORTER	AU10
COMLINE JAPAN DAILY: TRANSPORTATION	AU05
ELECTRIC VEHICLE ONLINE TODAY	AU12
GREEN CAR JOURNAL	AU16
NGV NEWS	AU11
ADVANCED TRANSPORTATION TECHNOLOGY NEWS	TS07
BUSINESS WEEK GB55	
FINANCIAL TIMES FULL TEXT	FT02
FLEETS & FUELS	EY15
INSIDE ITS	TS01
INVESTEXT/AUTOMOTIVE	IX02
INVESTEXT/TIRE & RUBBER	IX51
JAPAN TRANSPORTATION SCAN	TS12
KNIGHT-RIDDER/TRIBUNE BUSINESS NEWS	KR02
STANDARD & POOR'S DAILY NEWS	SP01
U.S. OIL WEEK	EY55

Biotechnology

APPLIED GENETICS NEWS	BT03
BIOTECH BRIEF	BT11
BIOTECH BUSINESS	BT06
BIOTECH EQUIPMENT UPDATE	BT12
BIOTECH FINANCIAL REPORTS	BT14
BIOTECHNOLOGY BUSINESS NEWS	BT13
BIOTECHNOLOGY NEWSWATCH	BT08
COMLINE JAPAN DAILY: BIOTECHNOLOGY	BT07
HIGH TECH SEPARATIONS NEWS	BT04
LIFE SCIENCES & BIOTECHNOLOGY UPDATE	BT15
MEMBRANE & SEPARATION TECHNOLOGY NEWS	BT05

Building and Construction

ARCHITECTURAL RECORD	BC13
ENGINEERING NEWS-RECORD	BC06
THE CONSTRUCTION CLAIMS CITATOR	BC12

Business Wire

BUSINESS WIRE	BW01W

Catholic News Service

CATHOLIC NEWS SERVICE	CN01
CATHOLIC TRENDS	CN02
ORIGINS: CATHOLIC DOCUMENTARY SERVICE	CN03

Chemical

CHEMICAL ENGINEERING	CH19
COMLINE JAPAN DAILY: CHEMICALS	CH16
HAZARDOUS WASTE NEWS	CH10
HAZMAT TRANSPORT NEWS	CH14
MODERN PLASTICS	CH23
PESTICIDE & TOXIC CHEMICAL NEWS	CH18
PLATT'S INTERNATIONAL PETROCHEMICAL RPTS	CH20
STEREOCHEMICAL TECHNOLOGY NEWS	CH09
THE CHEMICAL MONITOR	CH15
TOXIC CHEMICALS LITIGATION REPORTER	CH22
TOXIC MATERIALS NEWS	CH12

Commerce Business Daily

CBD: CONTRACT AWARDS—SERVICES	CB03
CBD: CONTRACT AWARDS—SUPPLIES	CB04
CBD: FOREIGN GOVERNMENT STANDARDS	CB06
CBD: PROCUREMENTS—SERVICES	CB01
CBD: PROCUREMENTS—SUPPLIES	CB02
CBD: SPECIAL NOTICES	CB05

Defense

ADVANCED MILITARY COMPUTING	DE03
ARMED FORCES NEWSWIRE SERVICE	DE34
BMD MONITOR	DE05
C4I NEWS	DE32
DEFENSE & AEROSPACE ELECTRONICS	DE11
DEFENSE CLEANUP	DE27
DEFENSE CONVERSION	DE29
DEFENSE DAILY	DE01
DEFENSE MARKETING INTERNATIONAL	DE17
DEFENSE TECHNOLOGY BUSINESS	DE20
DEFENSE WEEK	DE16
DEFENSE/AEROSPACE BUSINESS DIGEST	DE08
FOR YOUR EYES ONLY	DE15
GLOBAL POSITIONING & NAVIGATION NEWS	DE24
GOVERNMENT CONTRACT LITIGATION REPORTER	DE26
MARINE TECHNOLOGY NEWS	DE33
MILITARY & COMMERCIAL FIBER BUSINESS	DE06
MILITARY ROBOTICS	DE14
MILITARY SPACE	DE04
NAVY NEWS & UNDERSEA TECHNOLOGY	DE18
PAC-RIM DEFENSE MARKETING	DE22
PERISCOPE—DAILY DEFENSE NEWS CAPSULES	DE21

ELECTRICAL WORLD	EY03
ELECTROMAGNETIC FIELD LIT.	
REPORTER	EY86
ENERGY CONSERVATION NEWS	EY59
ENERGY ECONOMIST	EY93
ENHANCED ENERGY RECOVERY NEWS	EY60
EUROPEAN ENERGY REPORT	EY94
EUW'S DEMAND-SIDE REPORT EY87	
FLEETS & FUELS	EY15
GAS DAILY	EY09
GAS MARKETS WEEK	EY08
GAS STORAGE REPORT	EY05
GAS TRANSACTIONS REPORT	EY17
GAS TRANSPORTATION REPORT	EY07
GAS UTILITY REPORT	EY100
GLOBAL PRIVATE POWER	EY23
HYDROWIRE	EY53
IMPROVED RECOVERY WEEK	EY11
INDEPENDENT POWER REPORT	EY67
INDUSTRIAL ENERGY BULLETIN	EY68
INSIDE ENERGY/WITH FEDERAL LANDS	EY69
INSIDE F.E.R.C.	EY70
INSIDE F.E.R.C.'S GAS MARKET REPORT	EY66
INSIDE N.R.C.	EY71
INTERNATIONAL COAL REPORT	EY96
INTERNATIONAL GAS REPORT	EY95
JAPAN ENERGY SCAN	EY58
MINE REGULATION REPORTER	EY10
NORTH SEA LETTER	EY97
NORTH SEA RIG FORECAST	EY98
NORTHEAST POWER REPORT	EY88
NUCLEAR FUEL	EY72
NUCLEONICS WEEK	EY73
OCTANE WEEK	EY18
OIL & GAS INTERESTS NEWSLETTER	EY04
OPEC WEEKLY BULLETIN	EY22
OXY-FUEL NEWS	EY19
PETROLEUM FINANCE WEEK	EY20
PLATT'S OILGRAM NEWS	EY74
PLATT'S OILGRAM PRICE REPORT	EY75
POWER	EY84
POWER IN ASIA	EY99
POWER IN EUROPE	EY06
POWER IN LATIN AMERICA	EY24
POWER MARKETS WEEK	EY101
POWER SOURCE	EY54
POWER UK	EY21
PUR UTILITY WEEKLY	EY80
SOUTHEAST POWER REPORT	EY89
THE ENERGY DAILY	EY57
THE ENERGY REPORT	EY50
U.S. OIL WEEK	EY55
UK GAS REPORT	EY13
UTILITIES INDUSTRY LITIGATION	
REPORTER	EY83
UTILITY REPORTER—FUELS ENERGY &	
POWER	EY12
WORLD RIG FORECAST	EY14
WORLDWIDE ENERGY	EY63

Entertainment and Leisure

HOME VIDEO MOVIE GUIDE	EL07
MINI MOVIE REVIEWS	EL06
THE FEARLESS TASTER	EL05
VIDEO WEEK	EL01

Environment

AIR/WATER POLLUTION RPT:	
ENVIRONMENT WEEK	EV10
ALTERNATIVE ENERGY NETWORK	
ONLINE TODAY	EV49
ASBESTOS AND LEAD ABATEMENT	
REPORT	EV27
ATMOSPHERIC MONITORING &	
ABATEMENT NEWS	EV60
BUSINESS AND THE ENVIRONMENT	EV36
CALIFORNIA PLANNING	
DEVELOPMENT REPORT	EV23
CLEAN AIR NETWORK ONLINE TODAY	EV50
E & P ENVIRONMENT	EV57
ENVIRONMENT WATCH: LATIN AMERICA	EV44
ENVIRONMENT WATCH: WESTERN	
EUROPE	EV55
ENVIRONMENT WEEK	EV25
ENVIRONMENTAL ISSUES REPORT	EV58
ENVIRONMENTAL LIABILITY REPORT	EV61
ENVIRONMENTAL PROBLEMS &	
REMEDIATION	EV12
ENVIRONMENTAL REMEDIATION	
TECHNOLOGY	EV62
EWIRE	EV45
GLOBAL ENVIRONMENTAL CHANGE	
REPORT	EV31
GLOBAL WARMING NETWORK ONLINE	
TODAY	EV47
GOLOB'S OIL POLLUTION BULLETIN	EV05
HAZARDOUS MATERIALS	
INTELLIGENCE REPORT	EV21
HAZARDOUS MATERIALS	
TRANSPORTATION	EV35
HAZARDOUS WASTE LITIGATION	
REPORTER	EV54
HAZCHEM ALERT	EV17
HAZNEWS — INT'L HAZARDOUS	
WASTE MGMT	EV51
INDUSTRIAL ENVIRONMENT	EV38
INTEGRATED WASTE MANAGEMENT	EV40
MEDICAL WASTE NEWS	EV30
NUCLEAR WASTE NEWS	EV03
OIL SPILL INTELLIGENCE REPORT	EV32
OZONE DEPLETION NETWORK ONLINE	
TODAY	EV46
RADON NEWS DIGEST	EV04
REPORT ON DEFENSE PLANT WASTES	EV28
SOLID WASTE REPORT	EV20
SUPERFUND WEEK	EV22
UTILITY ENVIRONMENT REPORT	EV42
WASTE BUSINESS	EV41

Government and Regulatory
ACCESS REPORTS/FREEDOM OF
INFORMATION   GT10
ANTITRUST FOIA LOG   GT33
CONGRESS DAILY   GT02
CONGRESS DAILY A.M.   GT03
CONGRESSIONAL ACTIVITIES   GT20
CONGRESSIONAL RESEARCH REPORT   GT46
DRUG POLICY REPORT   GT05
FEDERAL GRANTS AND CONTRACTS
WEEKLY   GT37
FEDERAL/INDUSTRY WATCHDOG   GT44
FTC FOIA LOG   GT19
FTC:WATCH   GT17
INSIDE DOT & TRANSPORTATION WEEK   GT41
LIABILITY WEEK   GT30
PRIVACY JOURNAL   GT48
SET-ASIDE ALERT   GT08
THE FTC AND ANTITRUST DIVISION
TODAY   GT18
THE INFORMATION REPORT   GT??
U.S. NEWSWIRE   GT42
WORLDWIDE GOVERNMENT REPORT   GT06

Health and Hospitals
AIDS LITIGATION REPORTER   HH47
AIDS WEEKLY PLUS   HH14
BLOOD WEEKLY   HH44
BREAST IMPLANT LITIGATION
REPORTER   HH49
CANCER BIOTECHNOLOGY WEEKLY   HH15
DRUG RESISTANCE WEEKLY   HH52
ELECTRONIC HEALTH RECORDS
REPORT   HH57
HEALTH ALLIANCE ALERT   HH23
HEALTH CARE STRATEGIC
MANAGEMENT   HH18
HEALTH DATA MANAGEMENT   HH73
HEALTH DATA NETWORK NEWS   HH30
HEALTH GRANTS AND CONTRACTS
WEEKLY   HH10
HEALTH INDUSTRY TODAY   HH51
HEALTH LAW LITIGATION REPORTER   HH56
HEALTH LEGISLATION AND
REGULATION   HH22
HEALTH NEWS DAILY   HH01
HEALTH PROFESSIONS REPORT   HH29
HEALTH RECORD   HH25
HEALTHCARE PR & MARKETING NEWS   HH42
HEALTHCARE SYSTEMS STRATEGY
REPORT   HH11
HMM HOSPITAL MATERIALS
MANAGEMENT   HH17
INFECTIOUS DISEASE WEEKLY   HH53
INTERNATIONAL HEALTHCARE NEWS   HH67
MANAGED CARE ALERT   HH28
MANAGED CARE LAW OUTLOOK   HH16
MANAGED CARE OUTLOOK   HH12
MEDICAL UTILIZATION MANAGEMENT   HH24

MEDICINE & HEALTH   HH21
PHARMACEUTICAL LITIGATION
REPORTER   HH34
SMART'S NATIONAL COMP & HEALTH
BULLETIN   HH46
TB WEEKLY   HH45
THE PPO LETTER   HH31
TOBACCO INDUSTRY LITIGATION
REPORTER   HH48
VACCINE WEEKLY   HH54
WOMEN'S HEALTH WEEKLY   HH66

Insurance
COMMERCIAL POLICY GUIDE   IN16
DISABILITY COMPLIANCE BULLETIN   IN11
EAST EUROPEAN INSURANCE REPORT   IN12
FEDERAL & STATE INSURANCE WEEK   IN04
IMMS WEEKLY MARKETEER   IN02
INSURANCE INDUSTRY LITIGATION
REPORTER   IN08
LIFE INSURANCE INTERNATIONAL   IN19
PERSONAL POLICY GUIDE   IN17
THE INSURANCE ACCOUNTANT   IN01
THE INSURANCE REGULATOR   IN03
WORKERS' COMP EXECUTIVE   IN07
WORLD CORPORATE INSURANCE
REPORT   IN13
WORLD INSURANCE REPORT   IN14

International
AFRICA NEWS ON-LINE   IT15
APS DIPLOMAT   IT18
ASIAN ECONOMIC NEWS   IT81
ASIAN INFRASTRUCTURE MONTHLY   IT77
BRAZIL SERVICE   IT09
CHRONICLE OF LATIN AM. ECONOMIC
AFFAIRS   IT43
COUNTERTERRORISM & SECURITY
MAGAZINE   IT101
COUNTERTERRORISM & SECURITY
REPORT   IT53
COUNTRY RISK GUIDE: ASIA & THE
PACIFIC   IT16
COUNTRY RISK GUIDE: EUROPE   IT12
COUNTRY RISK GUIDE: MID-EAST &
N. AFRICA   IT13
COUNTRY RISK GUIDE: SUB-SAHARAN
AFRICA   IT14
COUNTRY RISK GUIDE: THE AMERICAS   IT11
CZECH REPUBLIC BUSINESS/
INVESTMENT NEWS   IT49
EAST EUROPEAN MARKETS   IT06
EUROPEAN COMMUNITY: BUSINESS
FORECAST   T94
GERMAN BUSINESS SCOPE   IT105
INDIA BUSINESS INTELLIGENCE   IT76
INT'L BUSINESS CLIMATE INDICATORS   IT93
INTER PRESS SERVICE INTERNATIONAL
NEWS   IT85

Investment
APS REVIEW	IV27
FIRSTLIST:COS. AVAILABLE FOR ACQUISITION	IV18
INTERNATIONAL BUSINESSMAN NEWS REPORT	IV51
INTERNATIONAL STOCKS DATABASE	IV50
INVESTORS CHRONICLE	IV17
RATEGRAM ONLINE	IV61
SEC TODAY	IV16
TRENDVEST RATINGS	IV34

Investment Analy$t   STOCKS

JIJI PRESS TICKER SERVICE   JN01W

Knight-Ridder/Tribune News Service
KNIGHT-RIDDER FINANCIAL NEWS WIRE	KR01W
KNIGHT-RIDDER/TRIBUNE BUSINESS NEWS	KR02

Law
ANTITRUST LITIGATION REPORTER	LA28
BOWNE DIGEST-CORP/SEC ARTICLE ABSTRACTS	LA11
BUSINESS LAW EUROPE	LA23
CIVIL RICO LITIGATION REPORTER	LA26
CORPORATE OFFICERS LITIGATION REPORTER	LA27
EAST EUROPEAN BUSINESS LAW	LA24
EMPLOYMENT LITIGATION REPORTER	LA29
INDUSTRIAL HEALTH & HAZARDS UPDATE	LA04
INFORMATION LAW ALERT: A VOORHEES REPORT	LA19
LAW OFFICE MANAGEMENT & ADMINISTRATION	LA32
LAW OFFICE TECHNOLOGY REVIEW	LA15
LAWYER INTERNATIONAL	LA30
LAWYERS' MICRO USERS GROUP NEWSLETTER	LA05
LEGAL INFORMATION ALERT	LA18
MONEY LAUNDERING ALERT	LA31
PROFESSIONAL LIABILITY LITIGATION REPORT	LA25
THE LEGAL PUBLISHER	LA17

Management
ADA UPDATE	MT23
AFFIRMATIVE ACTION/EEO PERSONNEL UPDATE	MT24
CORPORATE SECURITY	MT14
DRUG DETECTION REPORT	MT03
DRUGS IN THE WORKPLACE	MT15
EMPLOYEE RELATIONS IN ACTION	MT16
HUMAN RESOURCES BANKING & INSURANCE	MT21
LABOR TRENDS	MT13
MANAGEMENT CONSULTANT	

INTERNATIONAL	MT22
MANAGEMENT MATTERS	MT11
MANAGEMENT POLICIES & PERSONNEL LAW	MT18
PEOPLE TRENDS	MT05
SUBSTANCE ABUSE REPORT	MT17

Manufacturing
CAD/CAM UPDATE	MG15
COMLINE JAPAN DAILY: INDUSTRY AUTOMATION	MG19
MANUFACTURING AUTOMATION	MG17
SENSOR BUSINESS DIGEST	MG16
SENSOR BUSINESS NEWS	MG23
SMT TRENDS	MG18

Materials
COMPOSITES & ADHESIVES NEWSLETTER	ML18
COMPOSITES NEWS: INFRASTRUCTURE	ML15
ELECTRONIC MATERIALS TECHNOLOGY NEWS	ML04
EQUIPMENT & MATERIALS UPDATE	ML14
HIGH TECH CERAMICS NEWS	ML05
MEDICAL MATERIALS UPDATE	ML16
MICROPOROUS MATERIALS TECHNOLOGY NEWS	ML17
OPTICAL MATERIALS & ENGINEERING NEWS	ML07
PERFORMANCE MATERIALS	ML06
PLASPEC PLASTICS NEWS	ML09
PLATT'S METALS WEEK	ML01
SURFACE MODIFICATION TECHNOLOGY NEWS	ML08
THIN FILM/DIAMOND TECHNOLOGY NEWS	ML13

Medicine
CTDNEWS	ME07
DRUG OUTCOMES & MANAGED CARE	ME19
MEDICAL DEVICES LITIGATION REPORTER	ME21
MEDICAL OUTCOMES & GUIDELINES ALERT	ME09
OTC BUSINESS NEWS	ME20
PHARMACEUTICAL BUSINESS NEWS	ME18
POSTGRADUATE MEDICINE	ME06
REPETITIVE STRESS INJURY LIT. REPORTER	ME17
THE PHYSICIAN & SPORTSMEDICINE	ME05
TRANSPLANT NEWS	ME04

Official Airline Guides OAG

Politics
ASIAN POLITICAL NEWS	PO03
EVANS-NOVAK POLITICAL REPORT	PO06
JAPAN POLICY AND POLITICS	PO04
THE HOTLINE	PO01

COMMUNICATIONS DAILY	TE01	TELCO BUSINESS REPORT	TE49
COMMUNICATIONS TODAY	TE133	TELCO COMPETITION REPORT	TE62
COMMUNICATIONS WEEK	TE23	TELE-SERVICE NEWS	TE21
COMMUNICATIONS WEEK		TELECOM & NETWORK SECURITY	
INTERNATIONAL	TE28	REVIEW	TE131
DATA COMMUNICATIONS	TE37	TELECOM DATA NETWORKS	TE94
DOT.COM	TE123	TELECOM MARKETS	TE115
EAST EUROPE & FORMER SOVIET		TELECOM PERSPECTIVES	TE117
TELECOM RPT	TE06	TELECOM STRATEGY LETTER	TE118
EDGE ON & ABOUT AT&T	TE73	TELECOMMUNICATIONS ALERT	TE75
EDI NEWS	TE80	TELECOMMUNICATIONS REPORTS	TE11
ELECTRONIC COMMERCE NEWS	TE22	TELECOMMUNICATIONS REPORTS	
ELECTRONIC MESSAGING NEWS	TE05	INTERNATIONAL	TE14
EN ROUTE TECHNOLOGY	TE33	TELECOMMUNICATIONS WEEK	TE59
EXCHANGE	TE24	TELECOMWORLDWIRE	TE109
FCC DAILY DIGEST	TE54	TELENEWS ASIA	TE105
FCC REPORT	TE52	TELEPHONE NEWS	TE04
FIBER OPTICS NEWS	TE29	THE CABLE-TELCO REPORT	TE106
HIGH-SPEED NETWORKING		THE LONG-DISTANCE LETTER	TE39
NEWSLETTER	TE100	THE SPECTRUM REPORT	TE36
IMAGING NEWS	TE46	TR DAILY	TE134
INFORMATION & INTERACTIVE SVCS.		TR WIRELESS NEWS	TE45
REPORT	TE41	VIEWTEXT	TE18
INFORMATION NETWORKS	TE81	VOICE TECHNOLOGY & SERVICES	
INFORMATION WEEK	TE34	NEWS	TE02
INSIDE TELECOM	TE107	WALL STREET NETWORK NEWS	TE85
INTERACTIVE AGE	TE129	WASHINGTON TELECOM NEWS	TE103
INTERNET BUSINESS NEWS	TE122	WASHINGTON TELECOM NEWSWIRE	TE137
INTERNET WEEK	TE136	WIRELESS BUSINESS & FINANCE	TE48
ISDN NEWS	TE90	WIRELESS DATA NEWS	TE104
JAPAN TELECOMMUNICATIONS SCAN	TE31	WIRELESS MESSAGING REPORT	TE111
LAND MOBILE RADIO NEWS	TE13	WORLDWIDE TELECOM	TE19
LATIN AMERICAN TELECOM REPORT	TE57		
LOCAL COMPETITION REPORT	TE87	Transport and Shipping	
LOCAL TELECOM COMPETITION NEWS	TE102	ADVANCED TRANSPORTATION	
M2 PRESSWIRE	TE127	TECHNOLOGY NEWS	TS07
MICROCELL REPORT	TE09	HIGH SPEED TRANSPORT NEWS	TS04
MOBILE COMMUNICATIONS	TE114	INSIDE ITS	TS01
MOBILE COMMUNICATIONS REPORT	TE32	JAPAN TRANSPORTATION SCAN	TS12
MOBILE DATA REPORT	TE99	THE INTELLIGENT HIGHWAY	TS06
MOBILE PHONE NEWS	TE25	THE JOURNAL OF COMMERCE	TS03
MOBILE SATELLITE NEWS	TE20	TRAFFIC WORLD	TS02
MULTIMEDIA NETWORK			
TECHNOLOGY REPORT	TE124	TRW Business Profiles	TRW
NETGUIDE	TE130		
NETWORK BRIEFING	TE116	United Press International	
NEW ERA: JAPAN	TE70	UPI BUSINESS & FINANCIAL WIRE	UP01W
NEXTNET	TE30	UPI DOMESTIC NEWS WIRE	UP02W
ONLINE PRODUCT NEWS	TE27	UPI SPORTS WIRE	UP05W
PACIFIC RIM TELECOMMUNICATIONS	TE139		
PCIA BULLETIN	TE71	XINHUA ENGLISH LANGUAGE	
PCS WEEK	TE12	NEWS SERVICE	XN01W
REPORT ON AT&T	TE50		
SATELLITE NEWS	TE03		
SATNEWSWIRE	TE108		
STATE & LOCAL COMMUNICATIONS			
REPORT	TE141		
STATE TELEPHONE REGULATION			
REPORT	TE47		

Top Professional Databases

This chart lists the top online databases available on the professional online services. The primary access point for the database on each online service through which it is available is listed. Note that different online services may offer different versions of the file; some may be less comprehensive than others, some may have different access points such as subject descriptors or lead paragraph searching.

	DataStar	DataTimes	DIALOG Information Services	Dow Jones News/Retrieval	LEXIS-NEXIS	NewsNet
	database name:	source group:	file number:	source code:	library/file:	title code:
Business Information						
ABI/INFORM	INFO		15		BUSFIN/ABI	
BCC Market Research			764		MARKET/BCC	
Business & Industry	BIDB		9			
Business Dateline		NEWS	635	BD	NEWS/BUSDTL	
Business Wire		NEWS	610	BWR	NEWS/BWIRE	BW01W
Datamonitor Market Research	DMON		761		MARKET/DATMON	
Euromonitor Market Research	MOMR		762		MARKET/EUROMN	
Extel International News Cards			501		COMPNY/EXTEL	
FIND/SVP Market Research Reports			766		MARKET/FINDSVP	
Freedonia Market Research	TFGI		763		MARKET/FREED	
Frost & Sullivan Market Intelligence	FSMR		765		MARKET/FRSTSL	
IAC Business A.R.T.S.	ACAD		88			
IAC Globalbase	EBUS	NEWS	583			
IAC Management Contents	MGMT		75			
IAC Marketing & Advertising Reference Service	PTMA	NEWS	570		MARKET/MARS	
IAC Newsletter Database	PTBN	INDUSTRY	636	PTS	MARKET/IACNWS	[entire database]
IAC PROMT	PTSP	NEWS	16	Select "Industry & Trade Publications" from //TEXT menu	MARKET/PROMT	
IAC Trade & Industry Database	INDY	NEWS	148		NEWS/ASAPII	
ICC International Business Research	ICKN		563			
Investext	INVE	FINANCE	545	//INVEST	INVEST/	IX01-IX62
Moody's Corporate News			556, 557			
PR Newswire		NEWS	613	PR	NEWS/PRNEWS	PR01W
Standard & Poor's Daily News			132		COMPNY/SPNEWS	SP01
Standard & Poor's Industry Surveys		NEWS				
Textline Global News	TXLN		799, 771, 772		NEWS/TXTNWS	
Tradeline			597 or TRADELINE	//TRADELINE		
TradeStat	TRADESTAT					
Companies						
Corporate Affiliations			513		COMPNY/DCA	
D&B Business Information Report / Payment Analysis Report						DNB
D&B Duns Financial Records Plus			519	//DB		
D&B Duns Market Identifiers	DBUS, DNAP, DNCA, DNNE, DEFR, DBOS, DBBL, DBDK, DBFR, DBWG, DBHE, DBEI, DBIT, DBLU, DBNL, BLPO, DBSP, DBCH, DBGB, DNIS, SWCO		516, 518, 520, 521, 522	//DMI		

	DataStar	DataTimes	DIALOG Information Services	Dow Jones News/Retrieval	LEXIS-NEXIS	NewsNet
	database name:	source group:	file number:	source code:	library file:	title code:
Disclosure	DSCL	FINANCE	100	//DSCLO	COMPNY/DISCLO	
Extel International Financial Cards	EXTL		500		COMPNY/EXTEL	
Media General Plus			546	//MG		
Moody's Corporate Profiles			555			
SEC Online			541, 542, 543, 544	//SEC	COMPNY/SECOL	
Standard & Poor's Corporate Descriptions		FINANCE	133		COMPNY/SPDESC	
TRW Business Profiles						TRW
Current Events / General News						
AP News		NEWS	258	ASP	NEWS/AP	AP01W, AP02W, AP03W, AP04W
CNN Transcripts					NEWS/CNN	
Dow Jones News Service				DJNS		
Financial Times Fulltext		NEWS	622	FTI	NEWS/FINTME	FT02
IAC Magazine Database	MAGS		47		NEWS/ASAPII	
Knight-Ridder/Tribune Business News			609			KR02
Major newspapers		NEWS: Newspapers, Large	PAPERSMJ	TOP10	NEWS/MAJPAP	
Newspaper Abstracts Daily			483			
New York Times			471, 472	NYT	NEWS/NYT	
PERIODICAL ABSTRACTS PLUSTEXT			484			
Reuters		NEWS	611		NEWS/REUWLD, NEWS/REUNA, NEWS/REUFIN	RN01W, RN02W
UPI News			261, 260		NEWS/UPI	UP01W, UP02W, UP03W, UP04W
Wall Street Journal				J		
Health / Medicine						
BIOSIS Previews	BIOL		5, 55			
CAB Abstracts	CABI		50			
EMBASE	EMED		72, 73		GENMED/EMBASE	
IAC Health & Wellness Database [Health Periodicals Database]	HLTH		149		NEWS/ASAPII	
IMSworld R&D Focus	IPNR, IPNA, IPUR, IPMR		445, 955			
MEDLINE	MEDL		155, 152, 153, 154		MEDLINE/	
Pascal			144			
Pharmaceutical and Healthcare Industry News Database	PHIC, PHIN		130			

	DataStar	DataTimes	DIALOG Information Services	Dow Jones News/Retrieval	LEXIS-NEXIS	NewsNet
	database name:	source group:	file number:	source code:	library file:	title code:
Humanities / Social Science						
Arts & Humanities Search	AHCI		439			
EconLit			139			
ERIC	ERIC		1			
PsycINFO	PSYC		11			
Social Scisearch			7			
Sociological Abstracts	SOCA		37			
Intellectual Property						
CLAIMS/Citation			222, 220, 221			
CLAIMS/U.S. Patents Abstracts			340, 23, 24, 25, 125			
Derwent World Patents Index			351, 350			
INPADOC/Family and Legal Status			345			
TRADEMARKSCAN			226, 246, 126, 127, 657, 658, 659, 671, 672, 673			
U.S. Patents Fulltext			654, 652, 653		PATENTS/ALL	
Politics / Government						
BNA Daily News from Washington			655		BNA/BNAWI	
CIS			101			
Congressional Record					LEGIS/RECORD	
EIU: The Economist Intelligence Unit			627		WOLD/COURPT	
Federal News Service		NEWS	660	CHTS, DAYB, WSHN	NEWS/FEDNEW	FN01W, FN02W
Federal Register			669		GENFED/FEDREG	
PAIS International	PAIS		49			
Reference						
Books in Print			470			
CENDATA			580			
Dissertation Abstracts Online	DISS		35			
Encyclopedia of Associations			114		BUSREF/ENASSC	
Eventline	EVNT		165		BUSREF/EVTLNE	
Fulltext Sources Online	FULL					
OAG Electronic Edition Travel Service			595 or OAG	//OAG		OAG
Science / Technology						
CA SEARCH: Chemical Abstracts	CHEM		399, 308, 309, 310, 311, 312, 313			
Conference Papers Index			77			
Datapro Product Specifications			752			
Ei Compendex*Plus	COMP		8			
IAC Computer Database	CMPT		275			
INSPEC	INSP		2, 3, 4			
NTIS	NTIS		6			
SciSearch	SCIN		434, 34			

Comparing online information resources on consumer services is difficult, as databases are often not comparable from one online service to another. This list does not include discussion forums, as their utility depends so much on the participants and on your specific needs. Online forums or sites that only offer information **about** a database are not included.

Following are the key resources, listed either by their name (e.g., Disclosure) or by generic description (business news).

	America Online	CompuServe	Microsoft Network	Prodigy
	Keyword:	Go:	Go To:	Jump:
Multi-Industry / Research Databases				
CENDATA		Cendata		
Computer Database		COMPDB		
Dow Jones News				Company News
Homework Helper				Homework Helper
IQuest		IQuest		
Knowledge Index		KI		
Magazine Database		MAGDB		
MEDLINE	MEDLINE	Paperchase		
Newspaper archives	Mercury Center	Newsarchive		
Business/ Investment				
Business Database		BUSDB		
Business Dateline		BUSDATE		
business news	Business News	APOnline	MSN News	Business News
company news	Company News	APOnline		Company News
Hoover's Handbook	Hoover	Hoover	Hoover	Hoover
Disclosure	Disclosure	Disclosure	Disclosure	
Duns Market Identifiers		DMI-1		D&B
Investext		Invtext		
Morningstar ratings	Morningstar			
stock quotes	Stocks	CQuote		Quote Check
Value Line		PUBONL		
Current News				
today's news	Today's News	APOnline	MSNnews, NBC News	AP Online
Business Week	Business Week			
Fortune		Fortune		
New York Times	@times			
Reference Sources				
almanac		GenAlmanac		
dictionary	MW Dictionary	Dictionary		
encyclopedia	Compton's Encyclopedia	Encyclopedia, Hutchinson	EncartaForum	Refrnce
EAAsy Sabre	EAAsy Sabre	Sabre		Easy Sabre
OAG		OAG		
thesaurus	Thesaurus			

Index

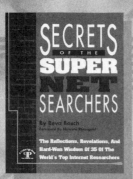